FORGETTING

FORGETTING
MYTHS, PERILS AND COMPENSATIONS

DOUWE DRAAISMA
Translated by Liz Waters

YALE UNIVERSITY PRESS
NEW HAVEN AND LONDON

Published with the support of the Dutch Foundation for Literature.

Originally published in Dutch by Historische Uitgeverij as *Vergeetboek* © 2010 Douwe Draaisma

For information about this and other Yale University Press publications, please contact:
U.S. Office: sales.press@yale.edu   www.yalebooks.com
Europe Office: sales@yaleup.co.uk   www.yalebooks.co.uk

Typeset in Arno Pro by IDSUK (DataConnection) Ltd
Printed in Great Britain by TJ International Ltd, Padstow, Cornwall

Library of Congress Cataloging-in-Publication Data

Draaisma, D.
    Forgetting : myths, perils and compensations / Douwe Draaisma.
       pages cm
    Includes bibliographical references and index.
    ISBN 978-0-300-20728-6 (hardback)
 1. Memory. 2. Recollection (Psychology). 3. Cognitive psychology. I. Title.
BF371.D68124 2015
153.1'25—dc23

                                                              2014045931

A catalogue record for this book is available from the British Library.

10 9 8 7 6 5 4 3 2 1

Contents

The archives of the Dutch province of Drenthe.

Forgetting: An Introduction

If only this could be your memory. A spacious room. The light falls in through high windows. Everything is clean and orderly. Your memories stand in rows along the walls, meticulously updated, noted down and indexed. Just walk over to them and pull out a book or a folder. Untie the ribbons, leaf through a few pages and you will soon have your hands on what you were after. Go to the table and spread your discovery out over the polished tabletop. Take a seat. You have plenty of time. It is quiet in here; no one will disturb you. When you have finished reading, you can fold all the papers together again, tie the ribbons and put the folder back. You look around the room for a moment and run your eye across the volumes, which brighten solemnly in response, and then pull the door shut behind you, calm in the knowledge that everything will remain undisturbed until your next visit. Because you can be certain no one comes in here except you.

It may not be everyone's deepest desire to have a memory like a room in the archives of the Dutch province of Drenthe, but imagine: all your memories with the dust kept off, folded away on acid-free paper, with perfect air conditioning, an index that makes it easy to find everything and above all the assurance that even items not consulted in 50 or 60 years will emerge in perfect condition. Which of us does not cherish the ideal of a memory in which all our experiences are kept safe?

When contemplating memory, we think in metaphors. There is no other way. Plato imagined memory as a wax tablet on which our experiences are inscribed, a view reflected in the word 'impression'. Later philosophers retained this writing metaphor, although with each innovation it was expressed in a new and different way: the wax tablet was succeeded by papyrus and parchment, and memories were written down in a codex or in books. Other metaphors made the memory a storeroom, either for information, like a library or archive, or for goods, like a wine cellar or warehouse. In the nineteenth century, neurologists began to look at memory with the latest techniques for preserving information in mind. Soon after 1839, the 'photographic memory' made its entrance, then the phonograph (1877) and film (1895) left their stamp on the theories of their day. Psychologists have continued in the same vein; the memory was later compared to a hologram and eventually a computer. Whatever may have changed between the wax tablet and the hard disc, our ideas about memory still stick firmly to the paths laid down by metaphors.[1]

What all these metaphors have in common is that they focus on conservation, storage and recording. In essence, metaphors of memory are museological constructs, encouraging us to imagine memory as the ability to preserve something, preferably everything, wholly intact. That this seems utterly logical is precisely the problem. Because in truth memory is dominated by forgetting.

Immediately after the outside world reaches us, forgetting takes charge. The five sensory registers, where sensory stimuli are initially processed, are equipped for an extremely short stay. Anything not quickly taken onwards from there will vanish. Of the five registers, the one dealing with visual stimuli has been researched in the greatest detail. In 1960, American psychologist George Sperling discovered that what is now known as the iconic memory can hold on to stimuli for no more than a fraction of a second.[2] He presented his test participants with 12 letters, arranged in three rows of four and exposed for just 50 milliseconds. Then he immediately asked them to reproduce the first, second or third row. They did not know beforehand which row Sperling would choose. On average they could recollect three of the four letters. It seems that in the instant after it was presented, the image, known as the icon, was still available almost in its entirety, but only if Sperling indicated within a quarter of a second which row he was after. If he waited just a little longer, 300 milliseconds rather than 250, the icon was blotted out. If when the first row had been reproduced he asked for a second or third, then the information was no longer available. In the few seconds it took to reproduce one row, the others disappeared.

This rapid erasure occurs in the other sensory registers as well, although the memory for sounds (known as the echo box) holds on to stimuli a little longer, for between two and four seconds. The retention of stimuli is necessary to enable sensory information to be processed without disturbance. It is only because the icon remains in place for a moment that our perception is uninterrupted when we blink. This brief retention allows us to experience 24 separate images per second projected onto a cinema screen as a single fluid movement, a movie. But erasure is just as essential. If the information was held just a little longer it would start to interfere with the stimuli that came next. The absence of forgetting would not create an improved memory but instead a growing confusion.

Are our senses trying to tell us something? This rapid erasure is the opposite of the ideal suggested by our metaphors of an archive or a computer. Forgetting is not a shortcoming of sensory memories but integral to the way they work. Is this the function of forgetting in other forms of memory as well? Does it always in fact have a function? And what is the best way of formulating the question: 'What causes us to forget?' or 'What purpose does forgetting serve?' Are we at the mercy of our neurological and physiological wiring or do we have some kind of say? However helpful metaphors of memory may be, they lead us away from associations with forgetting, which is perhaps one of the reasons why theories about forgetting rarely get beyond assumptions of the kind that are no more plausible than their opposites.

This lack of finesse pertains even at the level of language. The language games that have developed around memory are inventive and vivid. The language of forgetting is poor by comparison. For a start, the verb 'to forget' has no accompanying noun. What you remember is called a memory, but what you forget is called a ――? There is a gap in the language, and as a consequence no place for adjectives either. A memory can be vague or clear, pleasant or painful, but the thing you forget is only an absence, a nothingness, without attributes or qualities.

Even as a verb, 'to forget' has no real autonomy. As in 'forgo' or 'forbid' the prefix 'for' in 'forget' makes the word mean the opposite of 'get'.[3] Forgetting is a derivative concept, a negation: it is what you end up with when you think about remembering and then consider its opposite.

No less troubling is the contrast between the metaphors we use for the kind of memory that conserves our experiences and our metaphors for forgetting. Those in the former category have a certain allure. Writing is perhaps the most important invention of our entire cultural history, and archives and libraries are institutions that command respect. We compare memory to abbeys, theatres and palaces. Psychology has always chosen the most advanced and prestigious technologies for its metaphors of memory. Anyone who compares metaphors for forgetting with those for remembering – the sieve with the photograph, the colander with the computer – will have a poignant but realistic picture of the developmental gap between the two language games. Forgetting is forced to make do with an awkward reversal of memory metaphors. If we have forgotten something, then the wax tablet was too dry to receive an imprint, the ink has faded, the text was scraped from the parchment, someone pressed 'delete', or the information is no longer on the hard disc. Forgetting has never been much more than erasure, deletion or disappearance.

This reversal of metaphors for memory reinforces our intuition that remembering and forgetting are opposites and therefore mutually exclusive. What people remember has apparently not been forgotten and what they have forgotten they must be unable to remember. Forgetting is the minus sign applied to remembering. But this is an instance of being bewitched by our own metaphors. In reality, forgetting exists within remembering like yeast in dough. Our memories of 'first times' of various sorts remind us of all the forgotten times that followed. The handful of dreams we recall point to the hundreds of dreams remembered on waking that quickly evaporated. Even people with good memories for faces have bad memories for the history of faces. Which of us can honestly claim to recall, without recourse to photographs, what the people close to us looked like 10 years ago? In our lazy dichotomy of remembering and forgetting, where do we place the memory of an event that we realise we remember differently now from the way we once did? The relationship between memory and forgetting is more like the shared outline in a gestalt drawing: we can see this figure or that in it at will.

In writing this book, I spent three years consistently trying to detect the element of forgetting contained in memories. It seems the most diffi-cult questions we can ask about memory concern forgetting. Why do we have techniques for remembering but not for forgetting? If we did have them, would it be wise to use them? What is the fate – or the abode – of repressed memories? Do repressed memories actually exist? Why does a portrait tend to erase our memory of a face? Why do we have such a poor memory for dreams? Why might a colleague remember your idea but forget it was yours? What is so seductive about the notion that our brains create permanent traces of everything we experience, in other words the hypothesis of total recall? Why does a man with Korsakoff's syndrome retain part of his old professional know-how but forget what he said five minutes ago? What has gone wrong in the brain of someone who cannot remember faces?

In 2007 psychologist Endel Tulving decided to keep a tally of all the different kinds of memory mentioned in the literature.[4] He arrived at a figure of 256. No one is certain whether there are quite so many kinds of forgetting, but it is undoubtedly a number sufficient to deter us from trying to chart them all; rather, it is a number that invites us to be selective.

My first consideration in making a selection was that I would have to include the kind of forgetting that occurs in autobiographical memory, which attempts to record the events of our lives and attracts our attention, indeed worries us, when it fails to do so. This gave me my opening chapter for the book, since we will forget a great deal in our lives but never so obviously as in the first two or three years after we are born. Our earliest memories accentuate the forgetting that surrounds them, and by examining them closely we discover within them the processes of forgetting that later make us forget far more. What we can learn from our earliest recollections is that the emergence of language and self-consciousness helps the memory to develop, while at the same time closing off access to earlier events. A door opens in front of you only after the door behind you has shut.

Dreams pull the door closed behind them almost immediately. We have a notoriously poor memory for dreams. But as with those fragile first memories, the forgetting of dreams can clarify something about how memory works. When we wake up we remember – if we are lucky – the final scene of the dream, and we often begin the difficult task of searching back against the direction of time for what came before the final scene and what happened before that. Why do our memories have so much trouble with this reversed chronology? What can we learn about dreams by looking at the causes of their transience?

A second consideration in making my selection was the desire to show that pathological forms of forgetting can furnish unexpected insights into memory processes. In 1953, Henry Molaison, then aged 27, underwent a radical brain operation intended to bring his epileptic fits under control. The outcome was disastrous. A sizable portion of the hippocampus was removed from both sides of his brain and as a result Henry lost the ability to form memories. He spent the rest of his life locked in a present that was less than half a minute long. His brain damage made him the perfect participant in brain experiments. His career as 'Henry M.' lasted more than half a century and made him the most famous experimental subject in the literature of post-war neuropsychology. He died in December 2008, and in this book I try to honour more than simply the test participant in him.

In that same literature of neuropsychology, 'soldier S.' is no more than a footnote. In March 1944 he suffered a serious injury to his occipital lobe as the result of an exploding shell on the German front line. It caused an extremely specific memory disorder: S. could no longer remember faces, nor could he spot familiar faces. When he came upon his mother in the street he walked straight past her. He could not even recognise his own face in the mirror. The case of soldier S. led to the identification in 1947 of a disorder known as 'prosopagnosia' or 'face blindness'. Over the past few years it has become clear that a congenital form of this syndrome exists, and that it is far more common than was previously thought.

The brain damage that causes the syndrome named after Sergei Korsakoff produces the most drastic form of forgetting known to us, since it reaches through time in both directions. Large areas of the past are erased and the future is affected as well, since new experiences are not laid down in the memory. It makes the patient an invalid, although such patients are often remarkably relaxed and accepting of their handicap, being unable to recall many reasons to complain. For a long time it was thought that the semantic memory, the memory for facts and meanings, was spared in Korsakoff's patients, but experiments involving one Professor Z. – not a researcher but a patient – have refuted that notion. Several years before the syndrome struck, Z. wrote his autobiography, so it was possible to carry out tests using material that had without doubt once been lodged in his memory. The tests showed that even his semantic memory had gaps in it and that those lacunae were larger when the questions he was asked related to a more recent past. His case demonstrates the insidious progress of Korsakoff's syndrome: a slope, followed by an abyss.

Henry M., soldier S. and professor Z. suffered varieties of forgetting that we will not experience if we remain healthy, but even aside from cases of pathological memory loss, forgetting furnishes us with knowledge about memory processes. Over the past 20 years, attempts have been made to understand through experimentation a phenomenon known as 'cryptomnesia', whereby you arrive at an apparently original idea that you later turn out to have heard from someone else or to have read somewhere. It can occasionally be the cause of what has perhaps rather generously been called 'unconscious plagiarism'. In the laboratory, cryptomnesia can be replicated through subtle manipulation of the processes of forgetting. The trick is to mix just enough forgetting with remembering at just the right moment, such that the memory concerned does not disappear but is no longer recognised as a memory.

A third consideration was that an attempt needed to be made to uncover the roots of current ideas about forgetting, which go back a long way. In the defence by many people of the theory that our memories retain permanent traces of everything we experience, we see residues of neurological experiments carried out in the 1930s. Today's notion of 'repression' has associations redolent with ideas formulated by Freud from 1895 onwards. We still talk about 'burying' traumas and believe they can reside in the unconscious, from where they cause mischief. In recent debates, such as those about 'recovered memories', metaphors are used that were introduced by psychoanalysis and have played upon our intuitions about forgetting for more than a century. It is possible to go back even further. The notion that one part of the mind has no idea what is going on in another part was put into words long before Freud by a London family doctor nobody has heard of today. His name was Arthur Wigan. In 1844 he claimed that the right and left halves of the brain each have their own consciousness and memory. His theory convinced no one in its day and there are still good reasons for dismissing it, but much of what Wigan – who saw himself as 'the Galileo of neurology' – was able to explain with his two brains, Freud would derive half a century later from the relationship between the conscious and unconscious parts of our minds.

My most important aim of all in making my selection, however, was this: to show that the study of forgetting confirms what we hope or fear about our memories, namely that they have a disturbing ability to change. Sometimes it does not take a great deal to make this happen. You hear something about someone that throws new light on your memory of them. Or it becomes clear that for some time you have been deceived in some way. You can then only watch as one memory after another is forced to adjust to the new version of your past. You want to protect precious memories from this effect. Best of all would be to store them away with a security code, as 'read only' files. But sometimes life adds memories that change something about the memories that were already there. Hungarian writer Péter Esterházy was harshly confronted with this in January 2000, when files released from the archives of the security services made clear to him that ever since childhood he had lived in a reality different from that he assumed he was in. In a book to which he gave the title *Revised Edition*, Esterházy describes how he was forced to give his beloved childhood memories a new and sometimes intensely embarrassing interpretation. This too is a form of forgetting – no longer having access to what memories used to mean for you.

Perhaps no technology has been deployed with such enthusiasm against forgetting as photography, yet none contains so many paradoxes in its relationship with memory. We like to photograph unforgettable moments, which suggests we are aware that even the unforgettable can be forgotten. Our hope is that photographs will underpin our memories, but sooner or later we notice that they are in fact starting to replace our memories, an effect that is particularly marked in the case of portraits. When a loved one dies, a photograph slides in front of our memories of them. Why do our brains not retain both the photograph and the memories? Photography has been called 'a mirror with a memory', but how much faith can we have in a memory prosthesis that makes us forget so much?

The determination not to forget becomes an intense desire where memories of deceased loved ones are concerned. We would like to cherish them in such a way as to preclude forgetting. That is the promise contained in letters of condolence. It is also an incantation, a promise to ourselves about our own memories. Conversely, a person forced to depart this life hopes to live on in the memories of loved ones. Disappearing from those memories has been called a 'second death'. A collection of valedictory letters written in France in the time of the Terror (1793–94), by people who knew they would die the next day, demonstrates how human beings try to find comfort in the thought that those they love will never forget them.

The intractability of memory expresses itself in forgetting in two directions. There is no such thing as a forgetting technique. The Greeks bequeathed to us an *ars memoriae*, but no *ars oblivionis*, nothing we could use deliberately to forget something. Unfortunately we also lack the opposite facility: a safeguard against forgetting. What we forget or do not forget is up to our memories, not us. A technique for forgetting exists only in the form of thought experiments. In the film *Eternal Sunshine of the Spotless Mind* (2004), the main character turns to the advanced computers of a company called Lacuna to erase her memories of an unhappy love affair. The same thought experiment was carried out years earlier in a 1976 story by Marten Toonder called 'The Little Book of Forgetting', in which the author presents a succinct, wise philosophy of forgetting. The fact that in the story the technique is invented by a 'master of the dark arts' is an invitation to the reader to think hard about whether it would actually be sensible to have unhappy memories removed.

In this book we hear mainly from neurologists, psychiatrists, psychologists and other scientists of memory, but even if they could provide us with answers on the how and why of forgetting, there would still be an awkward distance between our theoretical knowledge of memory and what we ourselves experience. It is in that no man's land between science and introspection that questions arise that force us to think about our own remembering and forgetting. Between the ages of 55 and 60, Swiss writer Max Frisch occasionally included in his diary lists of penetrating questions.[5] They helped to inspire the difficult questions about forgetting with which this book ends. Frisch did not answer any of the questions himself, setting an example that I have been more than happy to follow.

First Memories: Islands in the Stream of Forgetting

Years ago I watched the Tunisian film *Halfaouine*, originally released in 1990. I could not recount much of the story now, but I do remember a few fragments about a little boy called Noura. He is 12, still young enough to be allowed into the women's bath house with his mother. Every week he enters a wonderful steaming world, in which women surge into view out of the clouds of vapour, kneel down beside him, soap him, soap themselves, rinse and then slowly rub their arms, legs and breasts with oil. Noura feasts his eyes. He is beginning to reach the age of curiosity about women's bodies. His gaze is becoming a stare, although he puts on his most innocent face. Naturally he cannot get away with that for long. One of the women spots something in his look. Next time he needs a bath he has to go with the men.

The boundary between still young enough and too old is hazy, but it is certainly a boundary and once across it there is no way back. Just as Noura at the age of six had no idea how he would look at women when he was 12, so the Noura ejected from the women's bath house can no longer remember what it was like to be surrounded by warm, naked bodies without even noticing, seeing nothing when there was so much to see. His awakening sexuality has created two Nouras who are mutually impenetrable.

But is that impenetrability truly mutual? Surely your memory allows you to summon up your former self and experience the world as you once did? Some writers of autobiographies almost convince us it does. In their opening chapters they evoke a child who sees the world through a child's eyes, thinks like a child and behaves like a child. Where could that child have come from if not from memory?

The question is naive. Children are not to be found in the memory; it is at best the place where they are engendered afresh. And even if memories are needed in order to get a child down on paper, they are not simply retrieved – they are dug up, often with great difficulty. They then need to be subjected to literary adaptation, since a collection of memories from childhood is not the same thing as the story of a childhood. Descriptions of childhood that are convincing, that seem authentic, that cause the reader's own childhood memories to resonate, are the product of literary craftsmanship and in that sense far removed from a child's experience. We are all at a distance from our own memories, but the writer of an autobiography is removed from them by that same distance squared, so to speak, because of the need to put those memories into words and arrange them into a narrative.

For the type of memory at issue here, psychologists invented a term in the 1980s: autobiographical memory. It has metaphorical associations that fit with ideas about autobiographies that emerged far earlier in literary theory. Philippe Lejeune wrote in 1975, 'Everyone carries with him a rough-draft account of his own life that is continually being revised.'[1] A quarter of a century of psychological research later, the conclusion reached is roughly the same. Our memories are more reconstructions than recapitulations of our experiences, and those reconstructions are influenced not only by who we once were but by who we have become, not just by the past but by the time in which memories are called to mind. And yes, that notebook is continually being adjusted, in the passive tense. We do not rewrite our memories ourselves, it is done for us, and if confronted with all those adaptations, when reading old diaries or letters, for example, we are astonished at what has been deleted or recast in the intervening years.

Or indeed added. In his autobiography *The Tongue Set Free* Elias Canetti writes about his earliest memory:

I come out of a door on the arm of a maid, the floor in front of me is red, and to the left a staircase goes down, equally red. Across from us, at the same height, a door opens, and a smiling man steps forth, walking towards me in a friendly way. He steps right up close to me, halts, and says: 'Show me your tongue.' I stick out my tongue, he reaches into his pocket, pulls out a jackknife, opens it, and brings the blade all the way to my tongue. He says: 'Now we'll cut off his tongue.' I don't dare pull back my tongue, he comes closer and closer, the blade will touch me any second. In the last moment, he pulls back the knife, saying: 'Not today, tomorrow.' He snaps the knife shut again and puts it back in his pocket.[2]

Every morning that scene is repeated and every morning he is more fearful than the last, but he keeps all this to himself and only 10 years later does he ask his mother about it.

She could tell by the ubiquitous red that it was the guesthouse in Carlsbad, where she had spent the summer of 1907 with my father and me. To take care of the two-year-old baby, she had brought along a nanny from Bulgaria, a girl who wasn't even fifteen. Every morning at the crack of dawn, the girl went out holding the child on her arm; she spoke only Bulgarian, but got along fine in the lively town, and was always back punctually with the child. Once, she was seen on the street with an unknown young man, she couldn't say anything about him, a chance acquaintance. A few weeks later, it turned out that the young man lived in the room right across from us, on the other side of the corridor. At night, the girl sometimes went to his room quickly. My parents felt responsible for her and sent her back to Bulgaria immediately.[3]

Elias Canetti, born on 25 July 1905, turned two that summer. The red, the girl, the man and the knife are components of a very early first memory, since on average our earliest recollections date from somewhere between our third and fourth birthdays.[4] In fact first memories of an event like this, featuring a progression through time, usually come from later still. But even if we take this passage to be as unadulterated an account as possible of what Canetti came upon as a first note in his memory, it contains elements that cannot have been experienced as he describes them by an infant who had just turned two and was largely devoid of language. The three sentences spoken to him by the man must have been converted into language later. Every attempt to call experiences of childhood to mind relies upon instruments unavailable at the time. The fact that Canetti relates this memory in the first person and gives his explanation in the third person ('the two-year-old baby', 'the child'), suggests that a memory can be described independently of any explanation, as an original, pure experience. This is a bifurcation of perspective that does not exist in reality.

The Scheepmaker collection

The first notes in autobiographical memory are preceded and followed by empty pages. Although they mark the start of our existence as beings with memories, they also highlight the extent of the forgetfulness surrounding them. The first memory of Dutch author J. Bernlef is of looking through bars and shouting loudly 'Uilie, Uilie!'. His parents later explained to him that he must have been sitting in his playpen calling the German nursemaid, whose name was Uli. His next memory dates from a full three years later. The English author Frederick Forsyth was 18 months old when his parents left him in his pram for a moment, with the dog to guard him. Afraid of the dog, he climbed out, fell, and felt the animal licking his face. After that came a gap of a year and a half. The childhood memory resembles an engine that sputters briefly and then stalls.

These earliest memories of Bernlef and Forsyth can be found in a little book published in 1988 called *De eerste herinnering* (The First Memory).[5] Over a period of six years, journalist Nico Scheepmaker asked everyone he came upon, whether privately or through his work, for their earliest memory. The result was a collection of 350 first memories. Scheepmaker had no scientific pretensions in compiling his collection. There are certain disadvantages to that – he did not always ask how old people were at the time, for example, so we can determine their approximate age in only 263 of the total – but certain advantages as well. He had not immersed himself in theories about childhood memory and he noted down the stories told to him without any commentary or adaptation. Over the past century, psychologists have put together several collections of earliest memories for research purposes, but they almost always rely on questionnaires given to students. The memories in the Scheepmaker collection are from people with extremely diverse jobs, backgrounds and ages. Its greatest asset as a collection, however, is its size. Ask 10 people for their earliest memory and you will hear 10 stories; ask 350 and you will start to see patterns.

Forgetting is an integral part of every first memory, which often turns out not to be the earliest after all. Scheepmaker thought that his own memory of the still warm white bread he fetched from the bakery on holiday was his earliest memory, until his mother told him the family returned from that holiday early because of the death of his grandfather and he realised he also had memories of Grandpa. Publisher Geert van Oorschot sent Scheepmaker a letter describing a first memory that was even older than his previous first memory. Often people had three or four early memories that belonged together, from before moving house, for example, or featuring someone who died a short time later. The chronology was impossible to recall.

Sometimes people had even forgotten precisely where their first memories originated. Were they recounting something they had actually experienced, or was it a dream, or a story told in the family? The photograph that becomes a memory is notorious. A black-and-white snap is fleetingly glimpsed, and a few years later the memory has brought that frozen moment to life and turned it into a colourful recollection, rather in the way that some films begin with a still image in sepia that suddenly starts to move. Journalist Henk Hofland was for years convinced that his first memory was a dream. In the drainage channel behind their house in Rotterdam, the Dutch ocean liner the *Statendam* with its three funnels came steaming past. Eventually he described that dream to his father and was told it was not a dream at all. 'The *Statendam* did actually steam along there. Our neighbour was a model builder and he once made a replica of the *Statendam* and put it in the water at the back of our house. You didn't dream that, you saw it!'[6] Some people really do have a dream as their first memory. In the case of lexicographer Piet Hagers it was a classic waking-up dream. He dreamed he was falling off the swing and woke on the floor next to his bed. Artist Peter Vos had a dream as his earliest memory as well. 'I dreamed about one of those Mondrian trees with branches that got all tangled up, which was very frightening.'[7]

In the Scheepmaker collection the child is on average three and a half at the time of the first memory, but there are outliers in both directions. Poet Neeltje Maria Min's first memory dates back to the liberation of the

Netherlands from German occupation. Her mother held her as they looked out of the window at people celebrating. She was nine months old. Poet Kees Stip told Scheepmaker that in 1913, during celebrations to commemorate the centenary of Dutch independence from Napoleonic France, he was only three months old when he saw from his cradle, which had salmon-coloured curtains, a triumphal arch in the neighbour's hedge. These are details that immediately raise the question of how reliable very early first memories are, a matter to which we will return. Scheepmaker's book records five early memories from before the age of one. By contrast, nine of the earliest memories are from after the child's seventh birthday. Even with half an hour to think about it, Björn Borg could not recollect anything that happened before he stood on the steps of his school in Stockholm as a seven-year-old. Bertrand Flury, a cognac merchant, was walking with his grandfather at the age of seven when he was unexpectedly smacked for carelessly using the familiar form of address, 'tu', instead of the polite 'vous'. Others could remember nothing beyond what they were given for their seventh or even eighth birthdays.

People who say that their earliest memory is from such a late stage are usually rather embarrassed and concerned about it, wondering whether they are normal. They introduce their memory by saying, 'It may sound crazy, but …'. All we can say is that they are a statistical aberration but not alone; every study turns up such late first memories in people who are otherwise completely normal. Embarrassment about a late first memory is misplaced, as is the remarkable pride seen at the other end of the normal distribution, in people convinced they were only seven, four or two months old at the time. In the Scheepmaker collection they are represented by conductor Claudio Abbado ('I still remember the chaconne by Bach that my father played when I was two months old') and by Dutch writer Jan Wolkers, who said he recalled the floral-patterned fabric of the hood of the pram he lay in as a six-month-old baby.[8] Anyone who starts talking about first memories with a fair-sized group of people will notice that a kind of competition emerges to see whose is earliest. Those who drop out of the running, with their memories of events from when they were three or four, listen with growing disbelief to stories about the things people remember from before their second or first birthdays, until even they are trumped by someone who can recall their own birth. Fortunately no sensible person expects a psychologist to settle the issue. The competition usually ends, incidentally, in discreet hilarity when a lady of a certain age with long grey hair parted in the middle starts talking about what she recalls of a previous life.

More interesting is the connection between age and the type of first memory. In his introduction Scheepmaker mentions journalist Dieter Zimmer, who distinguished between three types of memory recalled by the 70 people he asked: images, scenes and episodes. The category 'image' denotes precisely that: a single image, a fragment, sometimes merely a fleeting sensory impression. A 'scene' involves rather more: the location, the surroundings, the other people present; this is a memory of a situation, although still short and fragmentary. With an 'episode' there is some kind of development, an incident, an event, and in some cases the child actually does something. The boundaries between the three are of course fluid, though it is easy to point to typical examples. In the Scheepmaker collection the image of a handful of chestnuts on a sheet of newspaper recalled by writer Harry Mulisch belongs in the first category, as does the earliest memory of poet Simon Vinkenoog: 'I lay on my back and watched the sun play on the ceiling.'[9] Examples of scenes include that sudden slap for saying 'tu', being lifted onto someone's shoulders to watch a procession, or visiting the circus and suddenly seeing an elephant's foot close to you. An example of an episode is Greek tourist board director Sakis Ioannides's frightening memory of being bullied by his sisters:

> I was lying in bed when they hit me on the head and pretended to be sawing my skull open. They pulled the straw out of my head (as they described it), saying that without that straw I'd no longer be able to stand upright. Then they started to bounce around on the bed so that I did indeed keep falling down and at the same time I was looking under the pillows to find out where the straw had got to. When I was finally crying loudly enough, they stuffed the straw back into my head and stopped bouncing, so I was able to stay on my feet again.[10]

In research that predates Scheepmaker's book – including Zimmer's study – early first memories often turn out to be images, while late memories are usually episodes. Scene-like first memories fall somewhere in between. Scheepmaker writes that he did not see those links in his own collection, and he points to the fragment of an image recalled by Borg from when he was seven. But if you arrange the 263 dated memories according to the three categories and then look at ages, you see precisely that sequence. Images, which account for 17 per cent of all the datable first memories, are linked to an average age of two years and ten months, scenes (53 per cent) to an average of three years and two months, and episodes (30 per cent) to four years and three months. So the difference between images and scenes is only four months, but between scenes and episodes almost 13. The first memories from before the age of one are mostly images and they include no episodes. Of the nine first memories from after the child turned seven, Borg's is the only one that can really be described as an image; the others are predominantly episodes. This connection between the child's age and the type of memory must be even more pronounced than it appears from these statistics, since with memories that could be categorised as images, the age of the child was more often missing than with scenes and episodes, probably because when looking back to later childhood there are more milestones to go by, such as starting kindergarten or primary school.

Practically all Scheepmaker's 350 first memories are described as visual images. They include only 16 memories that have no visual elements, divided evenly among the other senses. The number is too few to serve as a basis for statistically reliable conclusions, but in this collection, taste sensations usually produced unpleasant memories – of a mouthful of sand, a horrible banana or the taste of coal – whereas smells were associated with feelings of intimacy. As a baby, author Monika van Paemel was laid in a basket of puppies. 'I can still sense the smell of the nest and feel the panting of those little puppy bodies.'[11] German writer Michael Ende remembered the odour of the neighbour's dog. 'Then I was under the table with the dachshund and we were fighting over a bone; I can recall the smell of that dachshund to this day. But the smell is mixed with the scent of bread rolls that our neighbours were warming on the fire. It's a smell that comes from when I was just two.'[12] The neighbours moved away when he was two and a half. Sounds, in those rare cases in which they penetrate the memory, can leave a powerful impression as well. Artist Jeroen Henneman remembers the children next door tying a dog to a tree in their garden. The neighbours also kept bees and the dog was attacked by a swarm. Henneman didn't see anything, since there was a hedge in the way, but he did hear the yowling of the dying dog. Journalist Marijn de Koning remembers the terrifying sound of the V-1s. But sounds can also evoke a sense of familiarity and safety, as with the footfall on the stairs that could only be Mother. Touch sensations are preserved for a life-time in the first memory of actress Liz Snoyink: a citrus press fell over and orange juice spilled onto her hands. Guitarist Julien Coco came from a family of 10 children: 'My mother was a big, sturdy Surinamer who was always in a hurry, with all those children, and in her haste she once thrust her nipple smack into my eye when she was trying to breastfeed me. Since then the sight of a woman's bare breast has always made me recoil . . .'.[13]

First memories that have to do with touch, taste, smell or sound date back on average to the age of two and a half, almost a year earlier than the average first memory. They have the unstructured, fragmentary character of other first memories laid down at that age; they fall into the category of images or scenes, and there are no episodes among them. Those early, non-visual memories are interesting for another reason. They cannot have been confused with photographs, and because memories of smells or tastes exist largely independently of language, their origins cannot lie in stories doing the rounds in the family. The smell of a recently unfolded tarpaulin, the feeling of juice being spilt over your hands and the taste of a mouthful of sand are impossible to describe. Michael Ende took this as evidence for the authenticity of his memory of the smell of the dachshund and the bread rolls.

After just three or four pages of Scheepmaker's book you start to notice the astonishing number of accidents great and small. Footballer Frank Rijkaard fell into the next door neighbour's tub of hot laundry water when he was three and was admitted to hospital. Taking a tumble and having to get your teeth fixed, walking backwards into a hot iron and burning your calf, being pursued by a German shepherd dog, falling over-board, toppling out of a window, almost drowning, getting a shard of glass embedded in a leg – dozens of such accidents are recorded as first memories.

Danger, too, real or imagined, can easily find its way into the memory. Runaway prams and pushchairs alone, with the terrified child still in them, account for at least 10 first memories in the book. Many others have to do with suddenly being alone: lost, stuck inside a cupboard, left in the attic with the trapdoor shut. Truman Capote recalled the maid taking him to the zoo in St Louis, then leaving him on the path and running away when someone shouted that two lions had escaped. Less spectacular, but a classic of Dutch first memories, is having your tonsils out.

The overrepresentation of fear-filled first memories, noticed as early as 1929 by Moscow educationalist Pavel Petrovich Blonsky, is reflected in an analysis of the emotions that accompany the memories in the Scheepmaker collection.[14] In the case of 126 memories – one in three – an indication was given of the accompanying emotion. On average those first memories came from slightly later in childhood, at an age of three years and eight months. Image memories were distinctly underrepresented in this category, their place taken by episode memories. The distribution of positive and negative emotions was completely out of balance. In only 17 per cent of first memories did the child feel happy, proud or safe; in 83 per cent the memory was associated with a negative feeling, and in two out of three cases that feeling was fear: memories of a cap that blew off, a bottle of cough syrup spilled in a bed, watching a rabbit being skinned, unexpectedly being lifted onto a Belgian horse, fireworks, shooting in the distance, a nightmare, the first day at nursery school. The Scheepmaker collection includes a handful of frightening first memories of faces suddenly looming up over the pram – clearly something we should be cautious about. The two biggest categories after fear and shock are distress and anger.

Those emotions are sometimes attached to the first memory by the response of parents. For Neeltje Maria Min, being held by her mother as they watched people celebrating her country's liberation in 1945 was a fearful memory because she could feel that her mother did not entirely trust the situation, eventually taking a step back from the window. Children do not remember their own fear when fire breaks out, instead they recall their parents' panic. They have no recollection of grief when a brother died, but the weeping of adults has stayed with them. Actor Walter Crommelin failed to recognise his father, who had returned from the East Indies after two years away, and would have preferred to carry on playing. Later he remembered how upset his mother was by that. Children judge the world through their parents' eyes.

Roughly 50 first memories in the Scheepmaker collection have to do with the Second World War. You could almost describe the Dutch experience of that war in first memories alone. A man remembers going off to search for his father, who was billeted at a fort during mobilisation. Then there is the bombing of Schiphol airport, and of Middelburg, and later of Bezuidenhout and the Philips factories, then the raids on homes near the

Ypenburg airstrip, sheltering under a table during an air raid, a beating meted out to a Jewish road-mender, and the sight of Jews secretly sleeping in an attic or looking up anxiously from a cellar. A two-year-old Jewish girl guilelessly told passers-by her name and had to be moved without delay to a different hiding place. Another little girl felt astonished at hearing her mother lie when German soldiers asked whether her husband was home. Later comes a little boy stealing bread from near the V-2 launch pads, then the strips of silver paper dropped by allied aircraft to interfere with German radar, British bombers flying over and food drops, followed by the liberation (five of the first memories concern the arrival of Canadian troops), parents fumbling to hang out a Dutch flag, Germans marching away and finally, after the war, toy cars found in the ruins of bombed houses.

Scheepmaker does not mention how old his respondents were, so there is no way of knowing whether first memories featuring the war really are overrepresented in his collection, but given that those who mention it must have been born between 1937 and 1943, the figure of 50 memories for this window of six or seven years does seem high. Anyone focusing on the experiences laid down in those memories will find support for a relatively recent theory about the cause of all the forgetting that wipes away first memories.

Latecomers

The greatest puzzle of first memories is that so much comes before them. Life has been going on for quite some time before we start permanently recording events and impressions. 'We are latecomers in our own history,' wrote philosopher Cornelis Verhoeven.[15] The paradox is that a young child's memory seems to be working perfectly well at the time. Two-year-olds know whose company they enjoy, or don't, so they welcome one person's visit and crawl away as soon as they spot someone else. They must surely recall previous experiences. Yet within a couple of years all those memories have disappeared without trace.

Elsewhere I have written at length about theories as to why autobiographical memories start so late and so falteringly, but it is worth recapitulating here and adding the results of new studies.[16] Some researchers find an explanation for all that forgetting in the speed of neurological ripening. The weight of the brain at birth is about 350 grams. Adult brains weigh between 1,200 and 1,400 grams. Most of this growth, almost an explosion, happens in the first year, when the brain's weight increases from 350 to 1,000 grams. The hippocampus, essential to the forming of memories, is underdeveloped in the early years of life and may well be incapable of sending records, as it were, to the neocortex, which is itself still under construction. The brain is delivered at birth in a rudimentary state, with most of the wiring yet to be done. No one could expect lasting memories to be formed in it. So the fact that young children 'forget' almost everything is often attributed to a failure of storage.

This theory of cerebral maturation would explain why autobiographical memory develops only at an age when the growth of the brain starts to stabilise a little, but it does not account for those huge differences (huge in relation to the duration of childhood, at any rate) in how far back we can remember. The ripening of the hippocampus and the brain in general happens within far narrower margins of individual variation than the age at which the first memory is laid down. Wiring that is missing or still being installed cannot entirely explain the phenomenon.

A more psychologically oriented theory seeks an explanation for forgetting in the absence of self-consciousness. Young children do not yet have an ego, a self that can integrate experiences into an account of an individual's history.[17] As long as there is no ego, no autobiography can be compiled. There are only fragmentary events, not yet held together by an individual who experiences them all as components of a personal past. What we call forgetting is in fact the loss of memories that have never been recalled. Only a child who is starting to realise 'I'm experiencing this' will be able to lay down lasting memories.

Self-consciousness usually develops gradually, but some children experience it as a sudden insight, which in a few cases is actually the first memory. Writer Hans Magnus Enzensberger told Scheepmaker that when he was two he stood on his bed looking at the electric vans used by the parcel post and their hum gave him 'the feeling of knowing that I was myself'.[18] Developmental psychologist Dolph Kohnstamm has collected several hundred 'I am I' memories of this kind and devoted a well-written book to them.[19] He became fascinated by the subject after reading what Carl Jung wrote at the age of 84 about the 'awakening' of his own self-consciousness when he was 11: 'Suddenly for a single moment I had the overwhelming experience of having just emerged from a dense cloud. I knew all at once: now I am *myself!* It was as if a wall of mist were at my back, and behind that wall there was not yet an "I". But at this moment *I came upon myself.*[20] Such memories often have a clarity that resembles a camera flash. The child recalls where it was, who was there and what it was doing at that moment. This is a realisation that evokes emotions in the child, sometimes because it realises with a shock that it is unique, not interchangeable with anyone else, different from its brothers and sisters, the only 'I'. Sometimes the child is aware above all that it is alone, closed off, a prisoner of its body, insignificant in the vastness of the world. Reactions can range from intense happiness to mild panic.

Most of the 'I am I' memories in Kohnstamm's collection date from the age of about seven or eight, or even older, rarely arising at a younger age. So they are of a later date than first memories, but they do pinpoint the years when autobiographical memory starts to function fully. Although other memories precede them, that earlier period is sometimes described as 'fog' or as a darkness against which the 'I am I' memory stands out like a 'brief crack of light', as Vladimir Nabokov describes it. Beatrijs Ritsema was staying with her grandmother when she was

> suddenly caught off guard by the thought 'I am I'. What was so remarkable was that I immediately realised it was the first time in my life I'd thought that. As if all the time before then I hadn't really existed. It was a moment of great clarity. I no longer coincided with myself but was looking at myself from above, as it were. Just the fact that I could think 'I' about myself was new and strange.[21]

The arrival of a conscious self seems to close off something else.

The development of self-consciousness, whether sudden or gradual, is not the only change in this phase of life. As they develop a vocabulary and linguistic skills, children start to process and store away their memories in the form of language. Their recollections gradually become stories and the revival of them relies from then on mainly on verbal associations.[22] It is surely no coincidence that most people can trace the first memories they are able to recount to somewhere between their third and fourth birthdays, a time that coincides with the rapid development of linguistic skills. After that we quickly lose sight of memories that are not stored in language; they come to lie beyond the reach of verbal associations.

This is the kind of forgetting that has nothing to do with deletions from the memory, an immature hippocampus or unstable neuronal traces. It is not the recollection itself that vanishes but access to it. A door has clicked shut and none of the keys available to us will unlock it – an explanation that fits neatly with the types of first memory we find at different ages. The memory that is no more than an image comes from the earliest age, when a child has little, if any, grasp of language. Scenes and episodes appear only when a child can look back on experiences by using language to think about, tell itself, or tell others about what it has experienced.

Are children not capable of converting those early, non-linguistic memories into language at a later stage and holding them in their memories that way? This is after all what the opening page of *The Tongue Set Free* suggests: young Elias must have put his frightening experiences as a two-year-old into words later, when he was able to tell his mother. The penknife, the blade, all those words that were unavailable to him in the arms of the nanny helped him to turn a series of images into an episode. In the Scheepmaker collection we see examples of the same thing. Take writer Adriaan Venema's story:

What I can still remember is sitting very high up on someone's shoulders and holding on with my little hands to something round and cold, made of steel. My mother described to me later what had happened. I'd walked out of the garden on the Groenelaan in Heiloo and crossed the main road. I was three years old. That was very dangerous, of course, even though in 1944 there won't have been anything like the amount of traffic there is now. A German soldier, wearing a helmet, picked me up and put me on his shoulders. He asked the people there whether they knew where I lived. I had almost orange hair at that time, so everyone in the neighbourhood knew me. My mother had a terrible fright when she opened the door and saw me there on the shoulders of a German soldier.[23]

The separate sensory experiences – sitting high up, feeling something round and cold – have been adapted with a little outside help into a final version, a first memory that can be described as an episode. Might that be something all children do sooner or later, with or without help, with their earliest memories? Two psychologists have used an ingenious experiment to show that this is probably not the case.[24] It turns out that children hardly ever 'rewrite' early experiences using vocabulary learned later.

The experiment involved children in three age groups, the youngest group aged two years and three months on average, the oldest three years and three months. The passive and active vocabulary of each child was determined beforehand. They were then introduced to a remarkable piece of equipment, the Magic Shrinking Machine. A handle and a crank were attached to a cabinet. When the child pulled the handle the machine began to work and a few lights flashed. The experiment supervisor took a toy out of a chest, dropped it into the machine and turned the crank, at which point a few cheery noises could be heard and shortly thereafter the child was able to take a miniature version of the same toy out of the cabinet. All the children quickly learned how to operate the machine.

The researchers visited half the children again after six months, the other half after a year. The number of things they remembered about the game with the shrinking machine – such as the order in which things were done and which toys were used – increased with age and decreased according to how much time had elapsed, exactly as you would expect. But the experiment actually focused on a quite different question: to what extent would children describe their memories of the machine in words that were not yet in their vocabulary at the time? On the second visit, the psychologists asked the children what they could recall of their experiences during the first visit. When they had finished talking about it, they were given photos of toys that had been dropped into the machine. The relevant toys were accompanied by 'distractors'. A teddy bear might be placed in between three bears the child had not seen before. Finally, the machine itself was brought out and the child was asked to describe how it worked. The identification from the photos of the toys used in the game and the demonstration of how the machine worked presented no problems at all. The children clearly remembered playing with the machine. The surprise was that none of the children, when talking about the first visit, used a word that was not in his or her vocabulary at the time but had been introduced since. Even if a child had in the meantime learned the word 'handle' or 'crank', those words were not used in describing what had happened during the game six months or a year before. The children's verbal reports, the researchers write, were 'frozen in time, reflecting their verbal skill at the time of encoding, rather than at the time of the test'.[25]

Anyone observing from close proximity the way magnificent linguistic skills develop in children at an astonishing speed feels as if they are watching a miracle. The mushrooming vocabulary, all that conjugation and inflection, trying out the effects of intonation: it all seems to come from nowhere to develop into the most important means of communication for the rest of a person's life. But that development has a downside. It seems that as children grow up their brains do not take the trouble to apply a new code to old memories and thereby keep them accessible. Like files stored in outdated programs, they disappear from view and eventually they can no longer be consulted. For early memories, the rapid development of language works like a Magic Shrinking Machine. It reduces years of a child's life to no more than a few disconnected images, fragments of experience, scenes lasting three or four seconds with nothing preceding or succeeding them.

Those who like simple explanations would do well to ignore theories about childhood amnesia. Every explanation along the lines of 'children forget simply because . . .' is misleading. A mature hippocampus is at best a necessary condition, not a sufficient condition, for a working memory. The hippocampus is fully developed when the autobiographical memory is still in its early stages. Other factors must be at work as well, which in itself introduces a problem. In this phase of a child's life, a great many things happen at once. A rudimentary self-consciousness develops, an ego that starts to regard experiences as amounting to a personal past. The time horizon expands, in both directions. A consciousness arises of all kinds of 'past', as the child comes to understand that yesterday is different from last week or last summer.[26] The development of language contributes significantly to this, since an increasingly refined network of temporal relationships requires words to mark the intersections. At the same time, language does something else: it turns personal experiences outwards. Children who can share their memories with parents, brothers, sisters and friends by using language convert those memories into something that can be exchanged, making them social experiences. Talking about what you have experienced does not just mean that you call up memories and so in a sense rehearse them; it also gives them a verbal form and makes them easier to retrieve later through verbal associations. A memory that has a place in a narrative becomes part of a network of concepts and skills and implies a consciousness of before and after, of cause and effect, of a position in time in relation to other experiences. All those relationships help reinforce the recollection.

Meanwhile, along with language and self-consciousness, something else develops that has the effect of deleting memories. Children start to order their experiences into routines, fixed sequences that psychologists call 'scripts'. There are scripts for dressing in the mornings, for getting ready for school, for playing at friends' houses or staying with Grandpa and Grandma. Such scripts will continue to develop all through life. As a result, separate experiences are sucked up into a schematic image, becoming increasingly hard to recall as independent experiences. What the child goes through from day to day changes over years of repetition into background, into a general idea about what getting dressed, or staying at Grandma's house, is like. It is precisely here that first memories reveal the mechanisms at work in the autobiographical memory that is just starting to emerge.

Take the little girl who was so surprised to hear her mother lie to a German soldier when he asked whether her husband was home. The child's astonishment could exist only against the background of a mother who never told lies. All the experiences she had of her mother, which collectively produced the image of a mother who never lied, were subsequently absorbed into that general idea and therefore disappeared. Along with the remarkable, the out-of-character, we briefly glimpse things since forgotten, namely the experiences that determined what was normal: all those times the girl's mother spoke the truth. From this perspective it is understandable that the war produced so many first memories. They can all be described as departures from the norm: a father who no longer lives at home but is billeted in a fort because of mobilisation, people in hiding who sleep in an attic, a Jewish road-mender being beaten, getting under the table when the air raid siren goes off, or strips of silver paper fluttering down from an aircraft.

Aberrations are also crucial to all those 'first times' recorded in first memories: the first day at nursery school, the first experience of electric light, the first taste of a banana. The former politician Wim Duisenberg recalled his surprise at the ice cream he was given on the boat from Lemmer to Amsterdam, the first he had ever seen on a stick. He can no longer remember the ice creams with wafers that made this one so special. Crucial to this explanation is that the child must first have developed an awareness of the normal, an extensive repertoire of scripts in which memories gradually gave way to something more accurately referred to as 'knowing': knowing what an ice cream looks like, knowing that your mother doesn't tell fibs. Only when you experience something that departs from the norm will you remember it later, perhaps forever. So in order to remember something, you first have to forget a great deal. That is simply the way memory works. It takes away the first three or four years of our lives.

'You can't have forgotten that!'

Charles Darwin's earliest memory came from before he turned four. He was sitting in the dining room on his sister Caroline's knee as she cut up an orange for him. A cow ran past the window. He was so startled that he straightened up suddenly and was accidentally cut by the knife. It left him with a small scar. Darwin was convinced the memory was real and not, as so often with memories of this kind, derived from a story related within the family. He reasoned: 'I clearly remember which way the cow ran, which would not probably have been told me.'[27] Like Darwin's, the first memories in the Scheepmaker collection are often accompanied by arguments as to why it must be a real memory: family stories don't include descriptions of smells; there is no photo of a child with sand in its mouth; the teller of the story saw or did something nobody witnessed. The urge to certify the memory as authentic probably points to the scepticism so often encountered. Taking into account the various explanations for forgetting, what can we say about the reliability of first memories?

First of all, this: research on the subject is so difficult as to be almost impossible. The fact that a person did something no one saw, which therefore cannot have been described to them later, may perhaps contribute to their subjective sense of certainty, but it also points to an absence of witnesses able to verify their story. First memories rarely feature events others felt worthy of note. No one will have kept a record of that time when the neighbour's children snatched your toys, or you first tasted a banana, or your skin got caught in your zip, or you were accidentally locked in the attic. However memorable that event was for the child, it will have been met with a shrug by its parents, and perhaps even by older siblings. In fact the response to anyone describing what they can remember from the age of four or five will often be 'but you can't have forgotten that ...'. Around the same time, the neighbour's house may have caught fire, an uncle may have fallen through the ice and almost drowned or the family may have bought its first car – all forgotten. In this sense, too, early memories tell us more about forgetting than about the emergence of an ability to remember.

Research into events that can be verified brings complications of its own. Psychologists JoNell Usher and Ulric Neisser attempted a study of this kind in 1993 with memories of events such as the birth of a brother or sister, moving house or admission to hospital.[28] Their test participants had to try to recall who looked after them while their mother gave birth, how they were told whether the baby was a boy or a girl and who went with them to the hospital. Most participants managed to answer a good number of those questions and afterwards their answers were checked by asking their mothers. The conclusion was that their memories were largely correct, but five years later Madeline Eacott and Ros Crawley thought up a variation on this experiment that undermined those earlier results to a great degree.[29] They divided the participants into two large groups. One group was used in a repeat of part of the experiment staged by Usher and Neisser, with the same list of questions about the birth of a brother or sister two or three years younger. Participants in the other group were given comparable questions, but about their own birth, such as who was looking after their older brother when they were born. Members of this group, being unable to draw upon memory, had to consult information gained later, perhaps from family stories or photo albums. The second group turned out to find questions about circumstances surrounding their own birth just as easy to answer as the first group found questions about the birth of a younger sibling. So the fact that mothers were able to confirm the accuracy of the answers given by the first group is no guarantee that they were dealing with genuine memories. It seems that at the age of three or four it is hard to remember not just information but its origins.

Most spontaneously related first memories are impossible to verify, and memories of events about which information is available are hard to separate from 'memories' of information gained from other sources. These two things combined make it hard to say anything conclusive about the reliability of first memories, or at least anything scientifically authoritative. The great merit of studies such as Eacott and Crawley's is that they explain why. An appraisal of the reliability of individual first memories has to rely on general ideas about maturation and growth. Given what we know about the development of the brain during the first year of life and the initial stages of the development of cognitive capacities, it would be impossible to recall hearing a chaconne by Bach at the age of two months. The same goes for that triumphal arch in the hedge seen by a three-month-old baby, or the floral-patterned fabric of the pram that Jan Wolkers said he remembered. After those first months of life things get trickier. Neurological and cognitive development can be comparatively early or late. So what about Monika van Paemel's memory of being laid in a basket of puppies when she was a baby? Or Neeltje Maria Min's memory of looking out of the window at people partying in the street when she was a baby of nine months in her mother's arms? Here we enter territory where a simple 'that's impossible' has to make way for something more subtle. We need to consider how likely it is that she really remembers that event and how likely it is that memories of liberation at the end of the war were talked about in the family several years later so that Neeltje, as a girl of five or six, made them her own. It is also possible that she dreamed about those stories and recalls her dream images, having forgotten they were a dream. If Henk Hofland remembered what later turned out to be a real event as having been a dream, then it is conceivable that a dream could be remembered as a real event. In the literature on early memories there are dozens of well-documented examples of this kind of transposition. But again, there is nothing conclusive about such theories. They do not cross out the memory with an authoritative stroke of the pen; they merely place a few question marks here and there.

Transitions

Writing about human memory brings into play the most flattering metaphors. It is the crown jewel of evolution, the citadel of the human spirit. But the building of this citadel does not seem to be a priority. In the first few years after we are born, the young brain has more important things to work on, such as refining the reflexes needed for eating and moving around, developing eye–hand coordination, discovering patterns in sensory information and interpreting facial expressions. All these are capacities for which a passive type of memory suffices for the time being.

The development of a memory from which past events are called up more or less at will can wait. These early years are essential for the attachment and moulding of a child, so the fact that they leave so little trace seems at first sight a contradiction, but things that are important for a child's emotional attachment to others need not remain available for the memory to pick from whenever it chooses.

In later years, too, there are many memories during childhood and few memories of it. By the time children begin to develop a memory that enables them not just to remember something but to be aware they are remembering something, they have acquired other capabilities that would have to be included under the heading of 'memory'. The slow development of autobiographical memory, which as adults we think of as the highest form, is actually an indication of its complexity. For this type of memory, many different things, both neurological and cognitive, all have to be ready, intact and working.

It is a process with stages and transitions. In our first 10 or 15 years we move rapidly between critical periods, and none is so drastic as the transition to the stage of being able to use language. From that moment on, memories steadily acquire a different character, often involving an interior monologue and linguistic exchanges with others. The effect of this transition is twofold. It opens up new opportunities for forming and storing memories while at the same time making access to earlier memories more difficult. The development of scripts, such as staying with Grandma, works both ways as well: they are able to emerge only because a collection of similar events is lodged in the memory, but those same scripts absorb memories and make them invisible. Transitions and passages like these occur throughout our lives, even if the gaps between them increase. Noura, who had to leave the women's bath house, will acquire new memories as a result of his emerging sexuality, but as a 12-year-old he is losing access to memories of the eight-year-old he used to be. In this early forgetting lie all the mechanisms that will make us forget so much in the years that follow.

However we may explain forgetting, its consequences can fill us with a deep melancholy. The beginning comes too late. You see your son, just turned two, playing with his grandpa and know that his first memory will not be laid down for at least another year and a half. What young children lack is a record button, with a red light to assure you that the child's memory is registering its experiences.

Evolution had other plans for memory. It is intended to keep us out of trouble and therefore has priorities of its own. It immortalises as our first memories not a playful grandpa but an insulted grandpa giving us a slap; not a walk among the poppies but instead a hot iron, shards of glass, angry dogs; not mothers reading bedtime stories but dark cupboards that have fallen shut; not safe and happy cycle rides but instead that one time when your foot got caught in the spokes – and all for your own good. Memory obeys not its owner but its designer.

We cannot command our own memory, let alone anyone else's, and this is especially true when it has only just started to work. Our impotence in the face of the very young memory, our own or that of our children, is perhaps expressed most poignantly of all in the first memory of painter Arja van den Berg. When she was about three her mother gave her a penetrating look and said: 'You must always remember this!'[30] And that is all she remembers.

CHAPTER TWO

Why We Forget Dreams

There's no time to lose, I heard her say
Catch your dreams before they slip away[1]

When we sleep, wrote English psychiatrist Havelock Ellis over a hundred years ago, we enter a 'dim and ancient house of shadow'. We wander through its rooms, climb staircases, linger on a landing. Towards morning we leave the house again. In the doorway we look over our shoulders briefly and with the morning light flooding in we can still catch a glimpse of the rooms where we spent the night. Then the door closes behind us and a few hours later even those fragmentary memories we had when we woke have been wiped away.[2]

That is how it feels. You wake up and still have access to bits of the dream. But as you try to bring the dream more clearly to mind, you notice that even those few fragments are already starting to fade. Sometimes there is even less. On waking you are unable to shake off the impression that you have been dreaming; the mood of the dream is still there, but you no longer know what it was about. Sometimes you are unable to remember anything at all in the morning, not a dream, not a feeling, but later in the day you experience something that causes a fragment of the apparently forgotten dream to pop into your mind. No matter what we may see as we look back through the doorway, most of our dreams slip away and the obvious question is: why? Why is it so hard to hold on to dreams? Why do we have such a poor memory for them?

In 1893, American psychologist Mary Calkins published her 'Statistics of Dreams', a numerical analysis of what she and her husband dreamed about over a period of roughly six weeks. They both kept candles, matches, pencil and paper in readiness on the bedside table. But dreams are so fleeting, Calkins wrote, that even reaching out for matches was enough to make them disappear. Still with an arm outstretched, she was forced to conclude that the dream had gone. She would sink back 'with the tantalizing consciousness of having lived through an interesting dream-experience of which one has not the faintest memory.'[3] Even the most vivid of dreams dissolved into thin air:

> To delay until morning the record of a dream, so vivid that one feels sure of remembering it, is usually a fatal error. During the progress of the observations, the account of one dream, apparently of peculiar significance, was written out in the dark by the experimenter, who then sank off to sleep with the peaceful consciousness of a scientific duty well done. In the morning the discovery was made that an unsharpened pencil had been used, and the experimenter was left with a blank sheet of paper and no remotest memory of the dream, so carefully recalled after dreaming it.[4]

That arm reaching for the matches and falling back says it all.

A few preliminary remarks. Research into dreams is a methodological nightmare, if you will forgive the irresistible metaphor. One of the problems is that the results of research into dreams vary according to the methods used. In the time when rapid eye movements were taken to be evidence of dreaming, it seemed you might as well carry out experiments using animals, as long as they exhibited rapid eye movement (REM) sleep. A series of experiments was done to test the theory that preventing an animal from dreaming would eventually have a deleterious effect on its memory. The chosen laboratory animals, rats, were placed on floating platforms. During deep sleep they lay motionless and all was well, but during REM sleep they became slightly restless and would slide off into cold water. Splash: wide awake. After a few nights without REM sleep they did indeed forget a learned task, a route through a maze, more quickly. Another experiment was designed to test the same hypothesis about REM sleep and memory, again with rats but using a different procedure. As soon as rapid eye movements occurred, the rats were carefully woken by being shaken, rather in the way that a child will wake its guinea pig. These rats had no problem at all with learning their maze task. It seemed the learning difficulties had arisen not because of the deprivation of REM sleep but as a result of the stress caused by sliding into cold water. The conditions of the experiment determined the conclusions about dreams and memory to be drawn from it.

A second complication is that we have no direct access to another person's dreams. Personal access to our own dreams itself presents all kinds of unavoidable obstacles. All we can measure about dreams is the behaviour of the dreamer, such as the eye movements made while dreaming, which provide only indirect data, as we shall see. The researcher is dependent on the dreamer's own report and no one understands better than the dreamer that the report does not correspond precisely with the dream. Dream research is the domain of oblique measurement, derivative knowledge and hunches. We should not expect any absolute conclusions or definitive answers here. The dream researcher, just like the dreamer, explores dimly lit rooms.

Then there is the incoherence of many theories on the subject. In psychology you are almost guaranteed to encounter the most diverse and sometimes contradictory theories about one and the same phenomenon. Insights change, interests shift, some questions lose the background from which they derived their significance, but even in psychology it is rare to find such a wide range of theories as there are concerning dreams. This applies to the details, but it is no less true of some of the most general insights and attitudes. We come upon the belief that dreams provide a profound understanding unachievable by any other means right alongside a conviction that they mean nothing at all. Some psychologists are convinced dreams are absolutely essential to good mental health, others that nothing will change if a person no longer dreams, perhaps as a result of certain medication. Dreams are utterly indispensable, or a chance by-product, or anything in between. Reading about dreams and memory, I often had the feeling that I too was wandering through a dim and ancient house of shadow.

The lizard dream

The most obvious explanations as to why we forget dreams were put forward in 1874 by German philosopher Ludwig Strümpell.[5] He suggested that dream images are too weak to penetrate the memory, just as in daytime many stimuli are too weak to leave any trace. Dream images are rarely experienced more than once, so repetition, which is generally a powerful strategy for remembering things, does not occur. It is perhaps no accident that those dreams we do remember tend to be recurring dreams. Most people simply care too little about their dreams; as soon as they wake, the tasks of the day demand their full attention and all memories of the dream evaporate. Strümpell observed that people who kept a dream diary for a while found that they dreamed more and became better at remembering their dreams, a phenomenon that has since been corroborated repeatedly. Lastly, dream images were thought too incoherent to be recorded with the help of orderly associations. They consist of unconnected images and our memories are better at dealing with a series of events that follow each other in a natural order. To use a metaphor that was not available in Strümpell's day, dreams are like a chaotically edited film, with fragmentary scenes, so it is hardly surprising that we fail to remember the images. To Strümpell the puzzle is not so much why we forget dreams as why we occasionally remember them.

Strümpell's explanations are old, but that does not mean they are outdated. Many modern researchers point to a lack of associative cohesion in dreams, or to poor concentration in the transitional phase between sleeping and waking. It is hard to test the validity of the argument that in a dream all kinds of things happen that are inexplicable, illogical or downright impossible and that lack of cohesion makes them hard to recall. We might just as easily arrive at the opposite conclusion. If in real life I suddenly found myself in the basement with the attractive lady next door, I would certainly remember it a week later, all the more so because our house has no basement. I know I have had dreams of that kind from time to time, but I cannot remember a single one of them. Even the sometimes decidedly peculiar content of our dreams is no guarantee that we will file them away. Moreover, the realisation that there is something odd about the events of a dream usually comes later, when you relate or contemplate the dream. You then spot one incongruity after another: people who could never have met, dead people brought back to life, people who turn up out of nowhere and with whom you start chatting without first asking where they have suddenly sprung from. In dreams you may be able to speak fluent Spanish, or you meet someone in Berlin even though you were at home a moment ago. When dreaming, nothing surprises us. So how the strange nature of many dreams affects our ability to remember them remains an open question.

What makes the forgetting of dreams so puzzling is that there seem to be so many intimate connections between dream and memory. Take 'day residues', those fragments of the day's events that return to us at night in our dreams. They surely suggest that dreams derive some of their material from our memories. There are even examples of dreams that seem to prove the dreamer has access to more memories than in waking life. This is an example of the phenomenon known as hypermnesia. It is as if the dreamer's memory holds open doors that remain closed in daytime. Freud – there he is already – writes in *The Interpretation of Dreams* about the experience of Belgian philosopher and psychologist Joseph Delboeuf.[6]

Delboeuf dreams he is walking across his snow-covered land when he finds two half-frozen lizards. He picks them up, warms them and puts them in a cleft in the wall. He plucks a few fronds from a fern and holds them out to the lizards. In his dream he knows the name of the fern: *asplenium ruta muralis*. A little later he spots another two lizards coming to eat the fronds and when he looks round he sees a whole throng of them, so many that they cover the path, all on their way to the cleft in the wall.

Delboeuf knew hardly anything about plants, but he was curious about the name he had dreamed and to his amazement it turned out to exist in reality: *asplenium ruta muraria*. In his dream he had merely bastardised *muraria* into *muralis*. It was a mystery to him how the name of a plant he had never heard of before could pop up in his dream.

Sixteen years later, while visiting a friend, he happened to look through a herbarium. There he recognised the fern frond from his dream. The Latin name was written beneath it, in his own handwriting. Only then did he recall that the friend's sister had visited him in 1860 with that very herbarium, intended as a present for her brother, and that he had offered to write in it the Latin name of each plant, with the help of a botanist. Two years before his dream, he had written it out in full: *asplenium ruta muraria*.

That is not the end of the story. One day, when he was looking through old copies of an illustrated newspaper to which he had a subscription, he suddenly saw the procession of lizards from his dream, on a cover dated 1861. So it was only after 18 years that Delboeuf was able to reconstruct the correct chronology: in 1860 he noted the Latin name in a friend's herbarium, in 1861 he saw the cover featuring the march of the lizards, in 1862 he had his lizard dream, in 1877 he saw the depiction of the march of the lizards for the second time and in 1878 he looked at the herbarium again.

Delboeuf published his account in 1885, in a monograph about dreams, recalling his dream of 1862.[7] The striking thing is that the dream included elements that at the time were in the fairly recent past, only two years or so back. Furthermore, the dictated Latin name was actually written out by him, an example of what would now be called 'dual coding', a trace both aural and visual, which meant he ought to have been able to remember it all the more easily, yet he could recall neither the name nor writing it down. The dream, by contrast, a thing usually so fleeting, was still in his memory 16 years later when he saw the herbarium. If all this happened precisely as he said it did, then it is a typical example of hypermnesia, when the dreamer remembers something that is not accessible to his waking consciousness. Delboeuf, incidentally, died in 1896, four years before the publication of *The Interpretation of Dreams*, so he never read Freud's explanation of his dream as an unconscious protest against castration. Lizards that lose their tails are able to grow them back.

Freud and other dream researchers collected many examples of hypermnesia in dreams. In his waking hours, Havelock Ellis tried in vain to come up with the name of an unpleasant Chinese scent. It suddenly came to him while he slept: 'patchouli'. When he woke in the morning the name had gone again. One of Freud's patients described during analysis a dream in which he ordered a glass of 'Kontuszówka' in a coffee house, adding that he had never heard of the drink. Impossible, said Freud, it's a Polish brandy and they've been advertising it in this city on posters for quite some time. The man refused to believe him, until a few days later he saw just such a poster at a street corner he had walked past at least twice a day for months. Freud himself was mystified by the dreamed image of a church tower he could not place – until some 10 years later, when he spotted it from the window of a train and realised he must have seen it on a previous journey along the same route. In our waking consciousness, Havelock Ellis wrote, our associations are focused, concentrated; in our dreams they are diffuse, more wide-ranging, but we lose the power to steer them: 'Our eyes close, our muscles grow slack, the reins fall from our hands, but it sometimes happens that the horse knows the road home even better than we know it ourselves.'[8]

Hypermnesic dreams are sometimes regarded as proof of the theory that nothing of what we experience ever disappears from the memory (we will return to this in the chapter 'The Myth of Total Recall'). A brief glimpse of a drawing, a Latin name in a long list, a poster, an absent glance from a train window – it is all still there; the neurological traces of these experiences are laid down for the rest of our lives, even if they are activated again only by chance.

For some of Delboeuf's contemporaries, that same hypermnesia explained a puzzle no less fleeting: the déjà-vu experience. All experiences, including dreams, even the dreams we do not remember the following day, are stored away in our brains. If we experience something in daytime that has enough associations in common with what we have dreamed, we will feel we have experienced it before. In a sense we have, since beneath our experience in the present lies the shadowy image of the dream that resembles it. Because we cannot date the dream and the associations are vague, it seems like an event of long ago, as if part of an earlier life.

Whether our memories really do contain everything we have ever experienced is impossible to know in any absolute sense. Whether in our dreams we have access to a larger, deeper, richer or even completely different collection of memories than in daytime is no less hard to determine, since that would involve comparing examples like those of Delboeuf, Havelock Ellis and Freud with what remains inaccessible in a dream yet can be remembered when we are awake. Such bookkeeping is impossible to perform. It is undoubtedly the case that in dreams things can pop up that lie off to one side of the day-to-day paths of association. Havelock Ellis's explanation is hard to fault. During a dream some associations fall away and stories lose coherence as a result, but new connections may arise, which in turn lead to places in the memory containing material that has not risen into consciousness for so long that it seems forgotten. To quote Havelock Ellis's own cryptic recapitulation: 'We remember what we have forgotten because we forget what we remembered.'9 Emigrants of a certain age who have been speaking a second language for 50 or 60 years may to their own surprise start dreaming in their mother tongue again. The dream seems to provide access to a vocabulary that the associations of daytime never touch upon.

Sometimes dreamers have the feeling of hearing or seeing something that is so perfect and so far outside normal experience that they would like nothing better than to lay down the experience in their memory immediately and forever. In 1766, the French astronomer Jérôme Lalande made a trip through Italy that took him to Padua, the university city of the Veneto region. There he decided to visit Giuseppe Tartini, a composer, music theorist and, for the past year, since injuring his hand in a fencing duel, retired virtuoso violinist. Tartini, then 74 years old, told Lalande the story of the 'Sonata del Diavolo'. At the age of 22, he had dreamed one night that he had made a pact with the devil for his soul, and that he had given his violin to the devil to see whether he could play something beautiful. Lalande's account goes on:

> How great was his surprise when he heard him play a sonata so extraordinarily beautiful and so exquisitely performed that it surpassed everything he had heard up until then. He felt ecstatic, enchanted, he was carried away, his breath caught in his throat and these great emotional shocks woke him up. He immediately reached for his violin in the hope of capturing some of the sounds he had just heard. In vain. The piece he wrote then is the most superb he ever composed and he actually called it the Devil's Sonata, but it compared so poorly with what he heard in his dream that he would have been willing to smash his violin and give up music forever if only he could have secured the means of capturing the piece he had heard.[10]

There is no reason at all to assume that Tartini invented the dream, if anything quite the opposite, since he was known as a reserved, self-effacing man. He had never previously revealed anything about the inspiration for his music. The mottos he attached to his compositions were written in a code that was not deciphered until 1932; they turned out to be derived in part from the work of Petrarch. The essence of what he experienced that night may well be true exactly as he describes it: you hear something of unearthly beauty in a dream and realise on waking that you cannot recapture it. Many of us will have had personal experience of this, if not with music then with a voice, a poem, a landscape, a painting. Or you may dream of a bodily sensation such as floating or flying that, once awake, you can no longer reproduce in its dreamed intensity. After a while, what you recall of the dream is no longer the music, the landscape, the floating, but the ecstasy you felt during the dream. It truly seems like a pact with the devil. As soon as you are in a position to record the dream, whether in your memory or on paper, it starts to disappear.

Everyone has at some point reached for a violin, as it were, after a remarkable dream and for no one has the result been any different than it was for Tartini. What we manage to conjure up as we write or talk about a dream is but a poor reflection. No matter how convincing the account may seem to the listener, the person recalling the dream is only too well aware of the inadequacy of the version conveyed. Of course even if we are fully awake when listening to music that transports us, it is not easy to remember or reproduce it accurately. Even in a waking state we often write down entire stories using a pencil that turns out not to have been sharpened. So really the question is: why does the memory have so much more difficulty with dreams than with things we experience in a waking state? We do not need to explain why we forget, but rather why dreams are particularly easy to forget.

Day residues

Aside from hypermnesia, there is another connection between dream and memory: day residues. The term is Freud's but the phenomenon is as old as dreaming. Fragments of those things that occupied us during the day reappear at night. This was discovered, and statistically documented, by researchers before Freud's time and it has been confirmed by modern dream research.

The percentages of day residues vary a good deal. Mary Calkins was able to connect practically everything that happened in her dreams to daytime experiences, whereas others have found a far smaller proportion of such residues. Dream research that made use of measurements during REM sleep found that day residues peaked in the first night and declined quickly after that; the dreamer could make a connection with events from the day before yesterday, three days ago and so on far less frequently. French dream researcher Michel Jouvet, who analysed no fewer than 2,525 of his own dream memories, arrived at roughly the same conclusion.[11] A little under 35 per cent of his dream memories during, say, a Sunday night had to do with what had happened on Sunday, the following night the figure was less than 20 per cent and soon the proportion of dream memories relating to Sunday had declined to just a few per cent. But Jouvet made a surprising discovery. After a week, on the eighth night, there was a new peak of more than 10 per cent, relating not to the Sunday just past but to that of a week before. It is a curious phenomenon. The peak defies the general law of memory, which dictates that the likelihood of being able to reproduce something we have experienced declines rapidly with time and never increases again. The explanation may be that for most people each day of the week has emotional connotations. A Wednesday feels different from a Friday and if the working week begins on a Tuesday because of a bank holiday Monday, we may get a 'Monday morning feeling' on that day instead, a misapprehension that can shift the entire week by one day so that even the Friday feels more like a Thursday. As a result it may be easier to recall on a Friday things that happened the previous Friday than events of three or four days ago. This 'last week at this time' effect may be what increases the frequency of day residues from a week ago.

An equally strange and still unexplained periodicity operates when dreams are adjusted to fit a different environment. Research into the dreams of travellers shows that for the first seven or eight nights of a journey, day residues in our dreams continue to be set against the familiar décor of home and only after that does the new environment enter the dream. When we arrive home it takes just as long for the décor of the trip to disappear from our dreams. A similar delay has been observed in the dreams of prisoners. Things they experience in the first few days of their incarceration turn up in their dreams as day residues, but transposed to the surroundings of home. The reverse happens after their release. This delayed assimilation suggests that separate memory processes are in operation in the recording and reproduction of events on the one hand and the visual-spatial setting of those events on the other.[12]

Memory traces

One thing that often strikes people who keep dream diaries is that day residues have nothing to do with what might be called the main events of life during the day, those things that worry us most or dominate our daily activities. Instead they are often insignificant images, a glimpse of things barely noticed at the time, trivial details of some kind, a snatch of a conversation. Some people have the impression that at night a film of daytime is played and day residues are nothing more than glimpses of that film.

There are two neurophysiological theories that suggest an explanation for this phenomenon.

The first is that of geneticist Francis Crick and molecular biologist Graeme Mitchison. They hypothesised that in daytime the brain absorbs a surfeit of associations, most of which are parasitic or irrelevant, and that at night it calmly works through the information of the day and disposes of most of it.[13] We have no awareness of this 'reverse learning', except that in dreams we occasionally catch a glimpse of the sorting process and from time to time we see one of the fragments passing by as it is dispensed with.

The second theory comes from neuroscientist Jonathan Winson.[14] He argues that at night the brain has an opportunity to transfer memories from a temporary storage place to a more permanent repository and that this data traffic, so to speak, can be seen in the activity of certain circuits in the brain and the production of the neurotransmitters it requires. It is thought to be a function laid down early in evolution, as its characteristics attest: dreams circumvent language. We dream in images. Dreams take place largely in the unconscious because consciousness developed at a later evolutionary stage.

Both theories are supported by EEG studies, reports on brain damage, biochemical research, simulations of neural networks, neuronal imaging and animal studies, but all that empirical firepower does nothing to alter the fact that the two theories are in conflict. Crick and Mitchison sum up their findings with the famous statement 'We dream in order to forget', whereas Winson believes we dream in order to remember more effectively. Common to both theories is the suggestion that dreaming has a function linked to the management of memories – which actually makes it all the stranger that we forget dreams more readily than other experiences.

So again: why do we have such a poor memory for dreams?

Dreams and time

The film Histoire d'un Crime (1901) by French director Ferdinand Zecca lasts less than six minutes.[15] There are five scenes. The main character commits robbery and murder, he is arrested in a bar, the police confront him with the body, he is put in a cell and finally he is executed by guillotine. The historical importance of the film lies in what happens in the fourth scene. The murderer is lying on the plank bed in his cell. Above his head we suddenly see scenes from his life, showing him as a child walking into his father's workshop, as a boy sitting down to eat with his parents and as a young man in a bar with a friend. *Histoire d'un Crime* deploys the first flashback in the history of film. Its break with linear chronology was part of a rapidly developing repertoire of temporal manipulations. When Auguste and Louis Lumière showed their first films in 1895, the audience saw records of events, such as workers coming out of a factory or a train arriving at a station. But in the first decade after the turn of the century, film was transformed into a medium that could tell a story. This required new techniques of montage. By about 1910 most of the techniques for speeding up or slowing down time or making it overlap, as well as flash-backs and flash-forwards, had been introduced and audiences had learned to look at films according to the new conventions.[16]

Film changed the experience of time, but it also offered a new collection of metaphors for thinking about dreams and time. Even back in the 1890s there were intense debates about the subjective and objective duration of dreams and the speed of dreamed events. After 1910 it seemed impossible to avoid using film metaphors in such discussions. In 1911, Havelock Ellis wrote that the rapidity of dreams was an illusion: 'At the most the dreamer has merely seen a kind of cinematographic drama which has been condensed and run together in very much the way practised by the cinematographic artist'.[17]

Some researchers have sought an explanation for the forgetting of dreams in the anomalous temporal relationships that seem to occur in them. The duration and chronology of events in dreams are subject to strange adaptations in our memories. The dreams with which we wake sometimes deviate from normal reality in two ways at the same time, by the astonishing speed at which they seem to be produced and by the reversal of chronology within them. The most famous example is the 'guillotine dream' of French doctor and historian Alfred Maury. Still living with his parents, he felt unwell one day and went to lie down. His mother was at his bedside. He fell asleep and dreamed of the Terror. The dream was vivid and detailed. He witnessed executions, met Robespierre, Marat and Fouquier-Tinville, was himself arrested, gave evidence to the Revolutionary Tribunal, received a death sentence, rode on a cart through a huge crowd to the Place de la Révolution, climbed onto the scaffold, was tied down, felt the executioner tilt the platform so that he was in the right position to be executed, heard the blade of the guillotine being raised and then coming down to slice his neck, even felt his head being severed from his torso – and at that moment woke up in mortal fear. He put his hand to his neck. A plank from the head-board of the bed had fallen across it. According to his mother it had happened just a moment earlier.[18]

Maury noted down the dream only years later and it may be that over time it gained in detail and length. It is also possible that the dream had been going on for a while and took a turn towards the blow to the neck only right at the end. But on a rather less spectacular scale, almost all of us have experienced at some time a dream that culminated in a sensation that in reality must have been the stimulus that prompted it in the first place. Havelock Ellis dreamed that he asked his wife whether she had been in a neighbouring room and she answered, 'Can't get in.'[19] He woke up and realised that his wife had in fact just said that, not to him but to a servant who had come to ask whether he could go into that room. Havelock Ellis attributed the reversal of question and answer to a deeply rooted need to see events in their natural order, an instinct so powerful that it gives precedence to logic over time. In the golden age of the sleep laboratory, sleep researchers tried to evoke such dreams experimentally. Dream researchers William Dement and Edward Wolpert woke their test participants using various different stimuli to see how those would be incorporated into the dream.[20] One participant had cold water sprinkled on his back. On waking he told a fairly complex story about how he had found himself part of a stage play. Then followed the scene that must have been triggered by the water:

> I was walking behind the leading lady, when she suddenly collapsed and water was dripping on her, I ran over to her and felt water dripping on my back and head. The roof was leaking. I was very puzzled why she fell down and decided some plaster must have fallen on her. I looked up and there was a hole in the roof. I dragged her over to the side of the stage and began pulling the curtains. Just then I woke up.[21]

The fact that the dream was remembered as preceding its own origins is a peculiar reversal of chronology, but in 1888 American biologist Julius Nelson noticed a second violation of the temporal order. A person who wakes from a dream can often recall the last few images. In order to reconstruct the story of the dream, you search back in your memory to find out what went before those last few frames 'and so on back into the night'.[22] Having woken with an image of yourself in a basement, you try to think how you ended up in there. Then you suddenly remember that you were trying to hide from men who had broken into the house. You are moving in the reverse of the normal direction of memory, because we always recall events forwards. If in ordinary life we tell others about our experiences, our memories move through them in such a way that one thing leads to another. Acts have consequences that lead to other acts. As we reproduce the story, we have the familiar chronology to hold onto. But with memories of a dream we wade against the current, passing first the effect and only then the cause, first the answer, then the question, and only at the end do we reach the earliest point in the dream. The reconstruction often judders along, since we spring back to earlier scenes that in themselves move forwards. In 1888 Julius Nelson compared this to a chain: 'The links only are recalled in the inverse order; the events inside each link are seen in their true progressive relations'.[23] Had he lived in our time he would perhaps have referred to the film *Memento* (2000), which is edited in such a way that it resembles the reconstruction of a dream. The film begins with the denouement, jumps back to the scene that preceded it and then moves further back. Within each scene time moves forward in the normal way.

It is not easy for us to reproduce events that depart from the familiar linear chronology, as demonstrated when someone tells you what happens in a film that includes flashbacks. You will almost always first be told the story chronologically and then, separately, the story of the flashbacks. As with my earlier description of *Histoire d'un Crime*, you are first told one narrative and then the other, rather than one interrupted by another. This is not merely a matter of storytelling. After you watch a film it is as if your memory secretly re-edits it, so that what you later remember are storylines, not the jumps in time that, in combination, convey those storylines. This almost irrepressible preference for a linear chronological development of memories is a handicap when it comes to recounting a dream that you need to follow against the temporal flow. You begin at the tail end and it takes a great deal of time and effort to reach the head. This could be part of the reason why it is so hard to fix dreams firmly in the memory.

REM sleep and dreams

In 1992 Michel Jouvet published a curious novel, *Le château des songes* (it appeared in English translation as *The Castle of Dreams*).[24] He was a professor of medicine at the University of Lyon at the time and known as a veteran of research into the neurophysiology of sleeping and dreaming. In 1959 he had discovered 'paradoxical sleep', the phase in which the EEG pattern is very like that of someone who is awake. The novel begins with a man who has got hold of an antique trunk in which he finds the scientific legacy of an eighteenth-century researcher, one Hugues La Scève, who recorded his own dreams over a period of more than 20 years, producing a dream collection of some 5,000 dreams. He also carried out a series of experiments and documented them in a diary. As a novel the book is perhaps less than irresistible, but it is absolutely fascinating to read about the historical thought experiments contained within it. What might a man of the eighteenth century, without any of today's technological tools, have been able to discover if only he had known what to look for?

In the eighteenth century, science was above all a matter of observation. La Scève begins his research by observing how a sleeper behaves. His first test participant is called Hans Werner, a tall, blond Swiss cavalryman serving with the palace guard. For 14 gold ducats, Werner is prepared to allow the researcher to watch him all night as he sleeps. After dinner and a scented bath, he goes to bed. It is a warm night. The cavalryman lies naked under a sheet and soon falls asleep. La Scève places candles in a circle around the bed and settles down at a small table with a notebook, quill pen and chronometer. After about an hour and a half, the sleeping soldier's breathing changes. La Scève hurries over to him and sees that Werner's eyes are half-open and moving in all directions. The arteries in his neck are swollen. His heartbeat is irregular. But the most striking change of all is outlined by the sheet: a full erection. La Scève wakes his test participant – '*Kavalier Hans Werner, wachen Sie auf!*' – and asks what he is dreaming about. Werner tells him that in his dream he was walking through a garden enjoying the scents of the flowers. He promptly goes back to sleep. Half an hour later the scene repeats itself. La Scève sees a full erection develop in less than a minute, wakes the soldier and is again told of a dream without any erotic significance. Towards morning La

Scève observes an erection for a third time, one that lasts for the full duration of a dream, some 20 minutes.

All this cries out for comparative research. With an appeal to the interests of science, La Scève manages to persuade his mistress Béatrix to spend the night with him. He waits until he can see rapid eye movements beneath her half-open eyelids. Her irregular breathing indicates that she is dreaming. He reaches between her thighs to confirm she is warm and moist. Satisfied, he notes the experimental evidence in his journal: the reactions of the woman while dreaming correspond to those of the man.

La Scève is dependent on experiments of nature and the generosity of fate, but time and again he makes good use of them. One day he is called upon to help a neighbour who has been kicked by his horse. The horseshoe has struck the left side of the skull and splinters of bone have entered the brain. The man is unconscious. La Scève removes the fragments of bone, leaving a hole the size of a ducat. Swollen red tissue can be seen through the hole, and within it the throbbing blood vessels of the cerebral cortex. He covers the wound with a thin bandage. The patient's daughter reports that at night, keeping a vigil at his bedside, she has observed the brain apparently swell up through the hole on several occasions, pushing the bandage outwards. La Scève's curiosity is aroused, so he comes to sit with the sleeping man and after an hour he sees the phenomena familiar to him from the cavalryman: agitated breathing and rapid eye movements. He surreptitiously lifts the covers. Sure enough, the man has an erection. Bending down over the hole in the skull, he can see the capillaries on the surface of the brain filling with blood and growing increasingly red. After 15 minutes the pressure decreases and the brain becomes pink again.

Observations about periodic brain activity, nocturnal erections and eye movements preceded the arrival of sleep laboratories in the 1950s. Jouvet's novel is not the only example. Rapid eye movements were observed by Aristotle. The swelling of the blood vessels in the brain was noted in 1831 by the French doctor Claude-Charles Pierquin de Gembloux, in a patient who had lost part of his skull as the result of an illness. Turin physiologist Angelo Mosso was the first to record this swelling accurately, in 1877. He traced the pulsing of an 11-year-old's brain using a pressure meter. The larger waves on his graph, Mosso thought, might be a result of 'the dreams that came to cheer up this unhappy child in his sleep, the image of his mother or of his early childhood years that rose to the surface again and illuminated the darkness of his mind, sending vibrations through his brain.'[25] In guarded terms the nocturnal erections had also found their way into the scientific literature, but the integration of all these periodic phenomena and the opportunity to measure them reliably came only with the arrival of the sleep laboratory.

In 1953, Eugene Aserinsky discovered REM sleep, those phases of sleep in which our eyes move rapidly.[26] The first period of REM sleep occurs after about an hour and a half and lasts for roughly 10 minutes. The second and third periods arrive rather more quickly and last slightly longer. The fourth period has a duration of almost half an hour and is followed by waking. Dreams seem to take place mainly during REM sleep. People woken while it is going on report dreams, whereas far fewer people woken from deep sleep do so. In REM sleep our motor system is blocked, which might explain the sensation of floating or flying that we sometimes experience in dreams, and indeed the feeling of being unable to move when faced with a mortal threat.

The discovery of REM sleep gave a huge boost to dream research. The measurement of eye movements did not reveal the dream but it did reveal dreaming. It was now possible to investigate dream behaviour under controlled conditions in laboratories, to study which physiological changes took place during dreaming by measuring heartbeat, blood pressure or brain activity, and to experiment with sleep deprivation. If REM sleep and the dreaming that takes place in it have a function, then long-term deprivation of such sleep was likely to have physical or psychological consequences.

Half a century later it is clear that the huge amount of research carried out into REM sleep in dozens of sleep laboratories all over the world has produced interesting discoveries about dreaming. We now know, for example, that the longest, most vivid and bizarre dreams take place during the fourth and final period of REM sleep, and that much of the forgetting happens very shortly after the end of a dream. If researchers waited a few minutes after the last physiological signals that dreaming was taking place before waking the test participant, the likelihood that he or she would remember the dream was considerably reduced. Some 80 per cent of REM sleep is accompanied by an erection or increased blood flow to the vagina, but not in response to erotic dreams. As we have seen in the case of Jouvet's Swiss cavalryman, erections also occur during neutral dreams or nightmares, and only one in 10 dreams at most have an erotic content. The irregular eye movements have nothing to do with the content of the dream either. For some time it was thought that they were a result of dreamers trying to follow the scenes in the dream with their eyes. This 'scanning hypothesis' has since been dismissed. The same eye movements have been observed in adults who were born blind and have no visual dreams, and in newborns who have not yet learned to track objects with their gaze.

Research in sleep laboratories has likewise put paid to some of the more simplistic assumptions. For a start, dreaming does not strictly coincide with REM sleep. We dream in other phases of sleep, only less. As a result of a neurological defect, some people do not experience REM sleep, but they do dream. The reverse is also true: some people who have suffered brain damage no longer dream, although their REM sleep is unaffected. People who never dream, at least as far as the usual REM measurements are concerned, seem to suffer no ill effects in the long term. Some antidepressants repress REM sleep, yet those affected do not have memory problems. L-dopa, which is prescribed to patients with Parkinson's disease to compensate for reduced activity of the neurotransmitter dopamine, raises the frequency of dreaming (and, unfortunately, of nightmares), whereas REM sleep is not increased. It has become clear that there is no simple one-on-one relationship between dreaming and REM sleep.

Over the past 10 or 15 years, dreams have been investigated with imaging techniques such as PET scans. As in the early days of research into REM sleep, expectations are high. In one such experiment it was discovered that during dreaming intense activity takes place in the lower regions of the brain, but none at all in the parts of the brain involved with memory. This might be a perfectly straightforward and adequate explanation for why we forget dreams: they cannot be recorded because the parts of the brain required to do so are temporarily out of action. But that is a conclusion that introduces a series of problems. How are we to explain our ability to recall dreams in some instances, or even to have recurring dreams? And what does this finding mean for Francis Crick's theory that during dreaming the memory is busy sorting and cataloguing? Or Jonathan Winson's theory, which asserts that during dreaming the memory is busy consolidating traces? With complex psychophysiological matters like dreaming, the introduction of new techniques usually leads to new hypotheses, but not to the convincing refutation or confirmation of older hypotheses. We tend to regard research using neurophysiological techniques as 'hard' and 'objective', but answers to questions about why we forget dreams remain vague and ambiguous.

Left hemisphere, right hemisphere

If anything typifies dream research over the past century and a half, from before Freud up to and including the most recent experiments in sleep laboratories, then it is the idea that dreaming involves two distinct systems. There are of course various ways of defining the divide between them, but it always comes down to the notion that there is a system that produces dreams and a system that processes or interprets them, and that a faulty transfer of information from one to the other is responsible for the forgetting of dreams. This divide transcends scientific disciplines; it is as clearly seen in neurology as in psychiatry and psychology. We might call the first system the 'producer' and the second the 'interpreter'. Here are a few examples:

Producer	Interpreter
id, unconscious	ego
right hemisphere	left hemisphere
brain stem	cortex
visual activation	verbal rendition
diffuse activation	narrative intelligence

What is common to all these dichotomies is that the dream needs not just a source or origin but something that thinks, mediates, translates, orders, interprets, narrates: in short something to give it a shape that we can deal with in our waking lives. Dreams need to be translated into conscious thoughts and during any translation process elements can be distorted or lost. One theory that has prompted a great deal of research since the 1970s is that the left and right hemispheres each have their own part to play in dreaming.[27]

It seemed initially that there was a great deal to be said for the idea that we dream with the right half of the brain while the left half creates a story that, also relying on the left hemisphere, we can talk about. This was a division of tasks that fitted perfectly with the prevailing theory about left–right differences. In practically all right-handed people, the speech centre is on the left, as it also is in a majority of left-handed people. The left half coordinates tasks that have a strict and precise serial development, which of course includes processes such as speaking and writing. The right half was thought to specialise in dealing with spatial information and to be geared to synchronous rather than serial processing, as well as detecting the symbolic significance of images and having a greater sensitivity to the emotional value of information. Since dreams have a strong visual component, there was a temptation to think that in a sleeping brain it was mainly the activity of the right cerebral hemisphere that produced our dream images.

A particularly detailed variant on this theory asserts that both left and right hemispheres produce images during sleep, but that the images produced by the left brain are immediately taken up into a logical narrative thread, whereas those of the right remain unattached to that thread and therefore create the bizarre, associative, sometimes almost hallucinatory fragments that turn up in so many dreams.

Conclusions drawn from various experiments and case studies supported this notion. After certain kinds of damage to the right brain, people lose the ability to understand metaphors. They can no longer form an image based on the verbal component of the metaphor and thereby understand its figurative meaning. There are also certain kinds of right-brain injury that cause people to lose the ability to dream. In addition, it seemed that during most of REM sleep there was more activity in the right half of the brain than in the left. The suggestion was that dreams are mainly the product of the creative right hemisphere, which is able not only to register emotions but to express them in a symbolic and primarily visual fashion. To the left hemisphere fell the thankless task of reducing all these emotionally laden images to something that could be expressed in words. No wonder so much is lost in the process, leaving us with the impression that the dream was far richer and deeper than the meagre verbal remnants our left brains have produced.

But this notion of 'the right dreams, the left speaks' has become much more diffuse as a result of recent research. The most vivid dreams occur in the final phase of REM sleep, which is actually a period in which the left brain shows more activity than the right. Then there are the studies of people who have undergone a split-brain operation. In patients with the most serious forms of epilepsy, surgeons will sometimes sever the connection between the two cerebral hemispheres. The tissue connecting them is known as the corpus callosum, and an incision made there will obstruct the transfer of signals from one side to the other. Such patients retain the ability to dream and to describe their dreams, which means that the left brain is describing what was dreamed by the left brain – what it dreamed itself, one might say. These dreams, which compared to dreams from before the operation do tend to be rather flat and boring, include images.

Studies like these have forced us to adjust our notion of the dream as a product of the right hemisphere. Dreams are now regarded as demanding the integrated activity of both halves of the brain. Verbal fragments can evoke images and vice versa. Injuries to the left brain also affect the quality of the images. The pattern of the dream is created on a loom whose shuttle is invisible because of the speed at which it moves back and forth – which dispenses with the notion that we forget our dreams because the left brain cannot deal with everything thrown at it by the right.

Gibberish

The belief that dreams are composed of random fragments that mean nothing and that the reasons for this are neurological has a long history. In the seventeenth century, René Descartes regarded the nervous system as a finely branched network of minutely thin tubes, filled with a gaseous substance that he called the *spiritus animalis*, so that as a whole they functioned as a hydraulic system. Descartes believed that dreams arise because in a sleeping brain even weak and random movements of the *spiritus animalis* can reach the mind, rather in the way that a gust of wind can easily make a ship's sails flap if the ropes are hanging loose. Dreams are therefore generally speaking meaningless, confused and fragmentary.

This theory about how dreams originate still has its adherents, although the gusts of wind and loose ropes are now described in neurophysiological terms. Allan Hobson and Robert McCarley, then attached to Harvard, suggested in 1977 that periodic and chance electrical discharges from brain cells were responsible for REM sleep and for the dreams that arise during it.[28] Stimuli from the brain stem cause activity in the prefrontal cortex, which does all it can to turn that series of chance events into a story. The brain stem is a relatively primitive part of the brain and there is no pattern to the discharges, so this might explain the bizarre character of dreams. Hence the abrupt relocation of scenes, the sudden emergence of people from nowhere, the strange associations. For Hobson the 'activation-synthesis hypothesis' was part of a larger theory about hallucinations, epileptic seizures, and the disintegration of thought and experience in schizophrenic patients – all of these being examples of chance activity in primitive parts of the brain in which other brain structures then had to discover meaning.

A related theory is that of David Foulkes, who claims that dreams arise as a result of the spontaneous firing of cells that are part of memory traces.[29] These cells fire completely at random, which again explains the lack of coherence in dreams. In his own words: 'The reason why dreamers can't understand what their dreams mean, and why we have such difficulty in reconstructing adequate accounts of what they might have meant, is that they didn't mean anything.'[30] True, we sometimes have what are known as 'lucid dreams', in which we realise we are dreaming yet carry on doing so and sometimes even have the feeling of being able to direct the course of the dream. They are the exception, however. Most dreams imprison the dreamer in his or her own story, as a passive observer. Foulkes believes the dreamer experiences the dream as real rather than as a dream because it is produced largely by the same neuronal machinery as that which processes our sensory impressions and experiences during the day. The dreamer is in the dark. Despite the sense of experiencing, seeing and hearing, the brain is in fact hard at work fabricating something understandable from material derived from the brain itself: memories, fantasies, expectations, fears. In this sense dreams have something in common with hallucinations, which also seem to come from outside but are in fact produced by the brain itself. Dreams often follow a bizarre and whimsical course, not because we have forgotten the things that connect the narrative together but because of the absence of steering by the outside world. Even the hypnagogic images that flash through your mind as you doze off and make you realise, if you are still sufficiently awake, that you are falling asleep, fit in with this theory. The series of images is rapid and haphazard because they are increasingly undirected by external stimuli.

This seems clear enough. Anyone trying to explain dreams sees order where chaos reigns and detects patterns in random events. Our brains contemplate gibberish and produce apparent clarity.

Our ability to construct a coherent story out of chance elements is confirmed by a game described by philosopher Daniel Dennett.[31] The 'dupe' is sent out of the room for a moment. When he comes back he is told that one of the others has related a dream and that by asking yes or no questions he must find out what the dream was about. Meanwhile the others have been told that there is no dream, but they are to answer yes if the last letter of the question ends with a letter from the first half of the alphabet and no to the rest. They are to deviate from that rule only if it would mean contradicting an answer to a previous question. The funny thing, Dennett says, is that the answers that provide an indication as to the story of the dream are completely random, yet a story always emerges. It may be full of strange twists and turns and absurdities, but it is never-theless a story. We can see the answers as representing the chance firing of neurons in the brain stem (Hobson) or the random activities of brain circuits (Foulkes). The story the 'dupe' ultimately tells represents the dream.

Dennett calls this game 'psychoanalysis', but that seems to me a gratu-itous insult. Even if the separate elements in a dream are based on chance discharges, the course and experience of the dream are not necessarily meaningless. In fact perhaps the opposite is the case and the way in which people try to impose order on chaos gives an insight into what they think, fear and desire. The story that emerges may be meaningful precisely because so many other patterns could be woven from the same threads.

'The thing is gone from me.'

It was during his second year on the throne that Nebuchadnezzar, king of Babylon, woke from a nightmare so horrified and fearful that he was unable to sleep for the rest of the night.[32] The next morning he asked all the soothsayers, sorcerers and sages to come to his court in the hope that one of them would explain the dream and his mind would be set at rest. The gathering of soothsayers invited the king to describe his dream, so that they could contemplate what it meant. But Nebuchadnezzar refused. He wanted them to tell him what he had dreamed, since then he would know without doubt that they were telling the truth. They had a choice. If they succeeded in describing the dream and explaining it, he would shower them with gifts. If they failed he would have them torn limb from limb and destroy their houses. The shocked soothsayers tactfully explained that no one can know another person's dreams. Nebuchadnezzar took that as an infuriating attempt to play for time and repeated his threat. When the magicians, diviners and astrologers again explained that it is impossible to know another man's dreams and that no ruler in the world, no matter how powerful, had ever asked it of his soothsayers and sages, he lost patience and issued an order that all the wise men in his kingdom must be killed. Daniel was among those who suddenly found soldiers at his door. Fortunately his God provided a solution by revealing the dream to him in a nocturnal vision. Daniel hurried to the court and offered to tell and interpret the dream. Nebuchadnezzar, he said, had dreamed about a statue of terrifying size. Its head was of pure gold, its chest and arms of silver, its belly and thighs of bronze, its legs of iron and its feet partly of iron and partly of baked clay. A stone that came loose without any apparent cause fell onto the feet of the statue, which collapsed, disintegrated and turned into a pile of dust that was blown away like chaff on a threshing floor in summer. Daniel then gave his interpretation. His God had caused Nebuchadnezzar to dream of the end times. The gold head was his own kingdom, the silver, copper and iron were the three kingdoms that would come after his. The feet of iron and clay stood for the discord that would afflict the fourth and final kingdom. On hearing this interpretation, Nebuchadnezzar knelt before Daniel in gratitude, acknowledged that his God was the God of gods and put him in charge of all the sages of Babylon.

This is the story as it is told in modern Bible translations, but in two places a crucial element has been lost, turning it into a rather different story.[33] When the soothsayers are standing before Nebuchadnezzar and asking him to tell them his dream, he does not immediately say they must describe it to him; first he says that he no longer knows what it was. The seventeenth-century King James Bible reads, 'My spirit was troubled to know the dream,'[34] which still contains the original suggestion that Nebuchadnezzar has forgotten his dream. A little later, when the soothsayers insist that nobody can know another's dream, he says 'The thing is gone from me: if ye will not make known unto me the dream, with the interpretation thereof, ye shall be cut in pieces, and your houses shall be made a dunghill'. Clearly he can no longer recall the dream. The king does not ask the sages to tell him his dream simply as a test; that is merely how he makes a virtue out of necessity. He has no choice but to ask them. However horrifying the dream was, it has gone, or at least it is tucked away somewhere such that he recognises it as soon as Daniel describes it, but could not call it to mind by his own volition.

No categorical conclusions have been reached about the kind of forgetting Nebuchadnezzar experienced, which will be familiar to us all. But our wanderings through a dim and ancient house have not been entirely unproductive. There are some aspects that concern the structure of dreams. In our waking lives, too, our memories have more trouble dealing with loose, fragmentary elements than with coherent entities, and dreams are frequently muddled. We also know that our memories find it easier to handle things that can be recalled as happening in a forward direction, whereas we are often forced to trace dreams back against the normal chronological order of events. At the edge of sleep, the memory works significantly less well. We have all had the experience of holding a short and coherent conversation with someone who was briefly awake, only to find the next day that they have completely forgotten what was said. In that sense, dreams happen at an unfortunate moment. Then there are aspects that have to do with a transformation or a translation between two cognitive systems that do not automatically connect, between images and words, for example. Visual scenes include a huge amount of information. Try looking at a photograph for four seconds and you will find it can take four minutes to put into words what you have seen. The difficulty lies not just with the translation as such. The mere fact that the translation takes time is a critical factor. While you are describing your dream, whether to yourself or to someone else, starting at the end, the beginning silently falls out over the edge of your memory. In trying to hold onto dreams, every second counts. Nebuchadnezzar must have sensed as much on that night in 603 BC, Mary Calkins experienced it in 1893 when she reached out for the matches, and it was no different for dreamers wired up to EEG machines in sleep laboratories. Dement and Wolpert found that if they allowed their test participants to do something else for a few seconds – rearranging the sheets or having a sip of water – nothing of the dream remained.[35]

CHAPTER THREE

In Memory of Henry M.

The death of Henry Gustav Molaison in the early evening of 2 December 2008 was hardly unexpected. He was 82 years old and had not been in the best of health for some time. Osteoporosis, a side-effect of the anti-epileptic medication he had been prescribed since the age of 16, meant he could no longer walk or even stand. He moved in a wheelchair along the corridors of the nursing home in Hartford, Connecticut, to which he had been admitted in the mid-1980s. Apnoea disrupted his sleep. He had a swollen spleen. He was taking more than a dozen different kinds of medication and breathing difficulties had recently been added to his long list of ailments. There were no close family members at his bedside. He had never married; there was only a distant nephew. Molaison died at 5.05 p.m. The cause of death was recorded as respiratory failure.

The staff of the nursing home worked through a number of important telephone calls in the hours before he died. One was to the other side of the continent, to Jacopo Annese, neuroanatomist and head of the Brain Observatory at the University of California, who had travelled from San Diego to meet Molaison back in 2006.[1] Now that the elderly man's death was approaching, Annese again took a flight to the east coast, arriving at the nursing home shortly after Molaison's death. A second call was to neuropsychologist Suzanne Corkin at the Massachusetts Institute of Technology 200 kilometres away. She arranged an appointment for a post-mortem MRI scan.

After the death certificate was signed, events followed each other in quick succession. Within a few hours, Molaison's body was in the scanner at MIT. Images were made of his brain in situ for the last time, then it was removed from the skull and prepared for transport to the Brain Observatory. It has since been cut into 2,401 slices, each of them photographed and digitalised, resulting in a virtual brain that can be accessed online for research purposes.[2]

Why all this trouble for an old brain, damaged by medication? Who was Henry Molaison?

H.M., the story

His full name was a closely guarded secret until his death and will probably quickly be forgotten again. But as H.M., Henry Molaison has been imprinted on the collective memory of the neurosciences for more than half a century. The 1957 article that reported on the disastrous brain operation that robbed him of his memory is to this day one of the most quoted publications in neurology.[3]

The story of H.M. has embedded itself in hundreds of neurological textbooks and introductions to neuropsychology. It is always told in the same way. The story begins in the summer of 1953, when H.M., then 27 years old, was admitted to hospital in Hartford. He was subject to severe epileptic seizures that were occurring with increasing frequency. His condition had proved unresponsive to medication. The surgeon proposed operating on him to remove part of both hemispheres of the brain, in the hope of eliminating the focus of his epilepsy.

The operation concentrated mainly on the hippocampus, a dual organ that lies in both the left and the right cerebral hemisphere, on the inner side of the temporal lobe. It is shaped rather like a seahorse – hence the name – and is extremely sensitive to electrical stimulation. After the operation the fits were indeed reduced, but the price H.M. had paid soon became clear. Part of his past had been wiped from his memory, but far worse was the fact that he was no longer able to form new memories, a type of memory loss known as 'anterograde amnesia'.

Tragic though this was for H.M., the story goes on, it represented an important step forward for neuropsychology. Alzheimer's disease and Korsakoff's syndrome also cause memory loss, but they affect the brain as a whole and do not allow us to draw any conclusions about the location of specific memory processes. Trauma caused from the outside, such as a bullet wound, cannot impact upon areas deep within the brain without damaging those closer to the surface. Because of H.M. it was now clear that the hippocampus, much of which had been removed on both sides, is essential for the storing away of new memories. It emerged that memories do not reside in the hippocampus itself, because H.M. still had access to some of his 'older' memories. The fact that he could retrieve them indicates that the reproduction of memories relies on different neuronal mechanisms from the storing of them.

For many years, H.M. was the purest case of anterograde amnesia known to the medical world. Researchers at MIT regularly brought him to their lab to take part in experiments, which provided a series of new insights into the neuronal representation of memory processes. Everyone described Henry as friendly and cooperative, and he was always more than willing to participate in experiments or to have his damaged brain scanned using yet another new imaging technique. As recently as 2004, when he was in his late seventies, he willingly allowed himself to be slid into an MRI scanner.[4] An obituary in *The Lancet* summed up 55 years of helpfulness: some hundred researchers had made use of his services as a test participant and his initials had appeared in almost 12,000 scientific articles.[5]

However much space all those articles give to the story of H.M., or however little, these are the elements that always recur: intractable epilepsy in 1953, a courageous surgeon, an experimental operation, and a patient more or less cured of his epilepsy whose cooperative attitude enabled brain science to move forward by several major strides. There is a quite different story to be told, however, about the fate of H.M.

Henry Molaison, a life cut short

The fact that Molaison suffered from anterograde amnesia does not mean that his memories of the time before the operation were unaffected. The months immediately preceding the operation had vanished entirely. Even the death of a favourite uncle in 1950 was wiped from his memory. Recollections of times further back in the past – his schooldays, holiday jobs, childhood – quickly became scraps and fragments, refusing to fit

Henry Molaison at the age of 21.

themselves together into stories. Or perhaps it would be more accurate to say they were just that – endlessly repeated anecdotes, episodes dished up again and again. After the operation, old memories continued to present themselves, but Molaison would be completely unaware of having shared them with someone 15 minutes earlier, or even just a few moments before. They became a repertoire that contracted as the years went by. Interaction with Molaison demanded a great deal of patience.

By the early 1990s, when science journalist Philip Hilts tried to collect biographical information for a book about Molaison, his grandparents, parents, aunts and uncles were no longer living. Hilts had to make do with stories by people who knew him, notes from the case history and the by then extremely vague memories retained by Molaison himself, who was in his mid-sixties.[6] There were few photographs, no family documents, nothing that could have helped to prompt memories. Hilts managed to determine that Henry was born on 26 February 1926 and grew up in Hartford and nearby villages. He had spent much of his childhood outdoors, fishing, swimming in the local reservoir and above all hunting. Henry retained a lifelong passion for firearms. As for his other hobbies, all we know is that he liked doing crossword puzzles and enjoyed listening to marches by John Philip Sousa. His father was an electrician, and as a boy Henry had decided he wanted to be one too, but on his 15th birthday, sitting in the passenger seat of the Chevrolet next to his father on the way back from an outing, he had an epileptic fit, the first of a series that steadily increased in severity and frequency. It changed more than just Henry's own future. His father, at first worried, later disappointed and finally embittered that such a thing should happen to his only son, began to withdraw from family life and took to drink. Henry had to abandon his plan to become an electrician, since his affliction made it dangerous for him to work on ladders. He finished high school, but he was not allowed to mount the podium to be handed his diploma because the staff feared he might have a fit. After school he took the simplest of jobs, in a carpet warehouse and on the assembly line of the Underwood typewriter factory.

By the summer of 1953 his epilepsy had worsened to the point that he was having about 10 'petit mal' seizures a day and a serious fit every week. Not even the maximum dose of anti-epileptic drugs could prevent the attacks. Henry and his mother went to the Hartford Hospital to find out whether there was anything the specialists could do to bring him relief. Two surgeons ran a joint practice at the hospital. One of them was Ben Whitcomb, who specialised in the surgical treatment of epilepsy, but Henry was seen by the other surgeon, William Scoville. He could not have crossed Bill Scoville's path at a worse moment.

Lobotomy

In his conversation with Henry and his mother (Henry's father did not accompany them), Scoville proposed an 'experimental' operation. What he had in mind was a variation on a technique that had won its inventor, Portuguese brain surgeon Egas Moniz, a Nobel Prize for medicine in 1949. Moniz called his operation 'prefrontal leucotomy', from 'leuco' meaning white and 'tomy', cutting. Deliberate damage was done to the white matter in the frontal lobes on both sides, tissue that consists largely of nerve fibres and lies beneath the grey surface of the brain, the cerebral cortex. The history of the operation has been documented many times. The details still come as a shock.[7]

The first operation was performed in 1935 on a woman of 63 who was suffering from depression and paranoid delusions. Under local anaesthetic, holes were drilled in her skull above the frontal lobes on both sides. Moniz's assistant – Moniz was 60 and suffering from gout, so he had to leave the actual surgery to others – stuck a needle in through each hole and injected pure alcohol into the white matter. Then the woman was taken back to the psychiatric ward. The idea for the operation had occurred to Moniz a few months earlier during a congress in London, when neurologists Carlyle Jacobsen and John F. Fulton of Yale University presented their findings on the partial removal of the frontal lobes of two female chimpanzees. It had resulted in serious learning disorders. By way of an aside, Jacobson mentioned that behavioural changes had been noted in one of the animals as well. Before the operation it had regular outbursts of anger and was fearful, refusing to enter the room where experiments took place. After the operation it underwent tests willingly, almost cheerfully. When the presentation was over, Moniz stood up and asked whether surgery at that location might not be a way of helping people who were experiencing states of anxiety.[8] Back in Lisbon he set up a programme in which the frontal lobes were not removed but damaged to the extent that they lost part of their control over the rest of the brain. The tissue-destroying alcohol injections soon made way for an instrument known as a leucotome, with which connections deeper in the brain could be efficiently severed without too much damage being done to the cerebral cortex.

The theory used to justify the operation can be explained very simply. Moniz believed that the pathological thought processes responsible for psychiatric problems had become locked in the white matter and these 'fixations' were impossible to rectify either by therapy or by medication. Whatever the nature of the pathology – addiction, depression, paranoid delusions, hallucinations, obsessions – only a radical interruption of the neuronal circuits could bring real relief. The effects of the surgery were not tested on animals. Both sides of the brain were damaged in a single operation. A systematic assessment of the longer term consequences did not take place, although there could be no doubt that there were consequences, since after surgery the patients appeared apathetic, slow and disorientated. Moniz claimed that such effects might perhaps be seen shortly after the operation, but that everything would soon come right again. He did not wait for evidence. Within two months, after 20 operations, he had written his first articles. A year and a half later he had published a dozen articles in six countries. It made him the central figure in a programme that attempted to solve psychiatric problems by surgical means, which Moniz dubbed 'psychosurgery'.

In many countries brain surgeons added leucotomy to their repertoire. The rapid dissemination of a crude intervention with little in the way of a convincing theoretical justification undoubtedly had to do with dissatisfaction about the existing therapeutic options. Psychoanalysis had little effect on the most serious disorders, and in a time before psychopharmacology, little could be done with agitated, aggressive or suicidal patients other than to lock them up, tie them down, sedate them, or put them into a coma by administering an overdose of insulin. Leucotomy was a practical and cheap technique that could be learned quickly. In America especially, an intensive psychosurgical campaign started up, led by Walter Freeman, a neurologist practising in Washington.[9] He had attended the same congress in London as that which inspired Moniz and in the spring of 1936 he read one of Moniz's early articles describing the results. He immediately ordered two leucotomes. After the summer vacation, he carried out his first operation on a depressed and agitated patient. Working on both halves of her brain, he cut no fewer than six cores. Following the operation, Freeman asked the woman a few questions:

'Are you happy?'
'Yes.'
'Do you remember being upset when you came here?'
'Yes, I was quite upset, wasn't I?'
'What was it all about?'
'I don't know. I seem to have forgotten. It doesn't seem important now.'[10]

Freeman renamed the operation 'lobotomy', since he believed actual nerve cells in the frontal lobes were severed, not merely the nerve tracts in the white matter. Like Moniz, who had meanwhile sent a signed copy of his monograph about leucotomy to Washington, Freeman operated as quickly as possible on a large number of patients, in order to have sufficient cases to present in articles and at congresses. He used a local anaesthetic, so that his patients remained conscious during the operation. They were asked to sing songs or to count backwards from 100 in steps of seven. His best results were achieved when he went on cutting connections until the patient's sense of anxiety suddenly made way for a sleepy indifference. After that final cut, the openings were stitched shut.

On Christmas Eve 1936, Freeman performed his 15th operation, although after the surgery was finished he had to go in search of his patient. Back on the ward, the man, an alcoholic, had got dressed, put a hat on his bandaged head and left the hospital for a drinking session in a local bar.

This incident makes clear that, again like Moniz, Freeman took a broad view when it came to deciding who would benefit from lobotomy. It was intended as a treatment for those suffering from 'melancholia', anxiety disorders, schizophrenia or obsessive-compulsive disorders, but according to Freeman the indications should also include alcoholism, gambling addiction and homosexuality.

Over the years a number of variations on lobotomy developed within the flourishing specialism of psychosurgery. Freeman himself ultimately opted for 'orbital undercutting', a procedure in which he drove a narrow double-edged knife into the skull through the eye sockets from holes just above the eyes to immediately under the frontal lobes and then moved it back and forth like a windscreen wiper. Carried out on both sides, this operation – which its opponents dubbed ice pick surgery – had the same effect as the more invasive operation with the drill and leucotome, but with the advantage that it could be carried out in polyclinics. Freeman performed demonstration surgery all over America using this particular technique.

More laborious but also more precise was a version described in print in 1949, whereby holes were drilled in the skull above the eye sockets through which the surgeon inserted a pincer-like instrument that was used to make space between the convolutions of the frontal lobes. Then deeper lying brain matter could be sucked out using a silver straw. The developer of this technique was an enthusiastic follower of Freeman called Bill Scoville, based at Hartford Hospital.[11]

Two handshakes

William Beecher Scoville would have liked to have been a car mechanic, but his father insisted he study medicine.[12] All his life he retained a passion for fast sports cars, especially red Jaguars. As a surgeon he had the greatest affinity with the technical side of his job, developing a number of instruments and introducing a new surgical technique for fractures of the spine. His colleague Ben Whitcomb described him as averse to rules and regulations. In the late 1940s, Scoville became enamoured of psychosurgery. In just a few years he carried out hundreds of operations on patients diagnosed as schizophrenic, neurotic, manic depressive and psychotic. When Henry Molaison walked into Scoville's consulting room in the

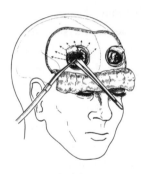

The variation on the lobotomy developed in 1949 by William Scoville, in which a straw was inserted between the convolutions of the frontal lobe and brain matter sucked out through it. In the operation on H.M. in 1953 he used broadly the same technique to remove parts of the temporal lobe further back in the brain.

summer of 1953 and politely introduced himself, he was only two handshakes away from Egas Moniz.

But then, what did he have to fear? He was there because of his epileptic seizures, and lobotomy was intended as a treatment for psychiatric conditions, not for neurological disorders. The answer is that lobotomy was by then being used outside psychiatry, for example for the treatment of chronic pain. Even more dangerous was the prevailing mentality in the field of psycho-surgery. Some psychiatrists were quite matter-of-factly putting their patients forward as candidates for 'experimental' operations. These were carried out on both sides of the brain and on relatively large numbers of people. There was no waiting for documentation of the long-term effects of the new operations. Surgery using the leucotome or the knife was carried out 'blind', since it was difficult to determine the precise location of the damage done. There were no theories about the functions of specific parts of the brain. The frontal lobes were terra incognita and the surgeons entering them felt rather like explorers embarking on voyages of discovery. Not all brain surgeons were as reckless as Freeman and his followers – lobotomy always encountered a great deal of opposition among neurologists – but no mechanism existed for banning a specific type of surgery. There was no supervision and no obligation to allow colleagues to check the methods or results. The fact that the other partner in Bill Scoville's practice, Ben Whitcomb, a specialist on epilepsy, advised against the operation that Henry was to undergo made no difference at all. Even if Scoville had not been averse to regulations, he could have carried on operating anyhow, since there *were* no regulations.

The fact that Henry was seen by Scoville rather than Whitcomb was not the end of his misfortune. By the early 1950s, tens of thousands of

William Beecher Scoville (1906–84).

lobotomies had been carried out in America and family doctors and patients' relatives had been confronted with drastic and permanent side-effects. The operation resulted in apathy and a lack of initiative. The physical effects were serious too, sometimes fatal: epilepsy, bleeding, infections. This had led Scoville to switch his attention to the area of the brain that lay behind the frontal lobes, namely the temporal lobes. He suspected that damage to or removal of the limbic system that resided there would have a beneficial effect on patients whose problems were psychiatric or neurological. In an article he sent to the *Journal of Neurosurgery* in mid-October 1953, Scoville wrote that he had achieved good results with resection and the severing of connections in this part of the brain, which sometimes involved removing a large proportion of the limbic system on both sides. Unfortunately, in two of his patients the operation had resulted in 'a very grave recent memory loss'.[13] One of those two patients was the 47-year-old D.C., a former doctor who had been admitted with paranoid schizophrenia. The other was H.M.

Henry had undergone the operation six weeks earlier under local anaesthetic. The procedure was very like the technique Scoville had developed in 1949 as a variant of the lobotomy. First the skin across Henry's forehead was cut, loosened and flapped down, half covering his eyes. Scoville then took a hand-cranked drill ('which can be purchased for $1.00 from machine tools or auto supply stores,' as it says in the operation notes) and drilled two holes above the eye sockets, each more than three centimetres in diameter.[14] Through those holes he inserted metal spatulas that he used as levers to lift the frontal lobes, causing dents that were still visible on scans half a century later. The way was now clear for the actual surgery.

Scoville inserted his silver straw below the spatulas. He went on pushing until he reached the inner side of the temporal lobe and then began sucking out tissue across some eight centimetres. Most of the limbic system disappeared through the straw, including the entire amygdala and a large part of the hippocampus. There was now a large hole on either side of Henry's brain. Scoville marked the cavities with metal clips, easily visible on the X-rays used to document the operation.

Later articles make clear that Scoville carried out the same operation many times after that, almost always bilaterally. We should not gloss over this rough – and plainly wrong – surgery.[15] And the fact that Scoville operated on both halves of the brain brought him particular criticism from doctors with more experience in the surgical treatment of epilepsy. He ought to have worked more conservatively, they said, on one side only, especially since the operation was still, in the words of Scoville himself, 'frankly experimental'. The fact that no other cases of anterograde amnesia were diagnosed probably has to do with the fact that most of the patients were so deeply disturbed that memory loss would not be noticeable. But Henry was of above average intelligence and had no psychiatric disorder.

At this stage, incidentally, it seems Scoville was not greatly troubled by Henry's catastrophic memory loss. He may have expected it to resolve itself as the years went by. He makes only fleeting mention of it in an article recording that he has operated on 230 mainly schizophrenic patients, making diverse interventions in the temporal lobe. In half of those cases improvements were seen. In depressive and neurotic patients he achieved good results with 'undercutting'. He ends by describing some encouraging prospects for psychosurgery, writing that research into the limbic system might eventually allow selective electroshock treatment to be applied to the hypothalamus, so that psychoanalysis could finally be expelled from the realm of science. For that matter, perhaps the surgical excision of areas of the brain might 'raise the threshold for all convulsions, and thus dispense with pharmaceutical anticonvulsants'.[16]

The opposite occurred. Within a few years the improved effectiveness of antiepileptic medication drove surgical interventions to the margins. The year 1953 was actually the worst possible moment at which to visit Scoville's consulting room. A few years earlier Henry would probably have undergone 'only' the standard lobotomy. A few years later and he would have been given drugs. In either case his memory would have been spared.

Forever 30

What does a life look like when it is over but not yet ended?

First of all, Henry went home. There the full extent of his handicap became clear. He no longer recognised people apart from close family members. He could perform simple tasks as long as he was not inter-rupted. If he was called indoors for a moment while mowing the lawn, the rest of the grass would be left uncut. He forgot where to find things, even if they were always kept in the same place. He realised something was seri-ously wrong. Like many others with this form of memory loss, he compared his situation to the first few moments after waking from a deep sleep. With an intact brain we experience no more than two or three seconds of disorientation before beginning to recall a reassuring network of memories and plans. For Henry there was only a permanent confusion, the intimidating start of a blank day and behind him an emptiness that caused vague unease. Had he just done something inappropriate? Had he perhaps said 'Shut up!' or used a swear word?

In 1956 the Molaison family moved to a house further up the same street. From then on, Henry could no longer be allowed out on his own, since he kept returning to the old house and could not remember his new address. With such a disorder it was impossible for him to make friends. The doctor had already told him, when he was merely suffering from epilepsy, that it would be better not to start a family, and after the opera-tion Henry seemed to have lost all interest in anything of that sort. At home he let everyone in, even complete strangers, since he was too polite to give any indication that he did not recognise them. His bedroom grad-ually turned into a time capsule, with objects, newspapers and posters from his youth in the 1940s.

When Henry was discharged from hospital, Scoville noted his status as 'improved', but that must have been a reference to his epilepsy alone. When the memory loss failed to ease after a few months, Scoville rang neurosurgeon Wilder Penfield, who had gained a great deal of experience in the surgical treatment of epilepsy at the Montreal Neurological Institute. Penfield was dismayed at what Scoville had done to the inside of Henry's brain.[17] But he also realised that the damage might be of an instructive nature, especially since the patient had no psychiatric disorder and his intellectual powers seemed intact. He sent a member of his staff,

Brenda Milner, to Hartford to size up the situation. She became the first of a handful of neurologists and neuropsychologists who built their careers to a significant extent on experiments with Henry. The publication of 'Loss of recent memory after bilateral hippocampal lesions' – the often cited 'Scoville and Milner (1957)' – marked the start of Henry's life as H.M.

Milner first studied him on 26 April 1955. When asked, H.M. said that it was March 1953. He gave his age as 27, although in reality he was 29. He had completely forgotten speaking to another neurologist just before entering the room. In tests for intelligence, arithmetic and logic he performed excellently. In tests for remembering stories he scored badly, recalling nothing of the story, nor even that it had been told. Milner also visited the former doctor known as D.C., a schizophrenic patient who had been admitted to hospital after attempting to murder his wife. In his case, too, Scoville's silver straw had sucked out both hippocampi, and Milner concluded that he exhibited precisely the same disorder, with his intelligence and vocabulary spared, all his earlier medical knowledge still in place, but no memory at all of events longer than two minutes ago. When asked to draw an elephant, he denied shortly afterwards that he was responsible for the resulting sketch. He had no idea where he was, but no wonder, he said, since he had arrived only yesterday evening. D.C. had been in the hospital for six weeks at that point. Because of his psychiatric disorder, he was ineligible for a career in experimental research.

In Scoville and Milner's article, the very first to feature H.M. as a test participant, the reader can sense the authors' astonishment at how much remained intact despite the drastic nature of a disorder that made it impossible to form new memories. H.M.'s semantic memory had been spared. He retained his vocabulary, although it was that of 1953. To him astronauts were 'rocketeers' and he identified Cassius Clay (later to rename himself Muhammad Ali) as Joe Louis. He would never learn what an 'ayatollah' was. The fact that his working memory still functioned meant he did not have to give up his old hobby of doing crossword puzzles; in fact he remained passionate about them until his death and completed three or four every day. One of the last articles published before he died includes an analysis of almost 300 crosswords he filled in.[18] To the question that is often put to psychologists as to whether crossword puzzles are good for the memory, the response would have to be that you can carry on doing them even when your memory is seriously damaged.

Because of H.M., distinctions were introduced into the psychology of memory that have since become so firmly established it is as if they have always existed. Take long-term and short-term memory. Kurt Danziger, a historian of psychology, explains that psychologists began categorising memory in this way only in the second half of the twentieth century.[19] It did not become a distinction familiar to the public until about 1970. One early exception was William James, who in 1890 distinguished between 'primary' and 'secondary' memory. The first of these is really still part of consciousness, since it consists of sensations and perceptions that have not yet left the conscious mind. It is the type of memory that contributes to our awareness of what we are experiencing right now. James considered only secondary memory to be memory in the strict sense, producing recollections that are stored away apparently outside our consciousness of the moment. This distinction indicates precisely what was wrong with H.M. He was able to retain things that were still taking place in the window of his conscious attention, so he could carry on a coherent conversation on the most diverse subjects. When asked to estimate intervals of time he was as capable as anyone else, as long as those intervals lasted no longer than about 20 seconds. Outside that window he could not distinguish between a minute and a quarter of an hour, or between two minutes and an hour. The decisive factor was always his conscious attention. If something slipped his consciousness for a moment, perhaps because someone changed the subject or walked out of the room for a few seconds, he was unable to find his way back to it; all associative connections had gone. His memory never updated anything, so in studies he would estimate his own age as 'around 30', even when he was approaching 60. He forgot the ageing face in the mirror as soon as he walked away. In 1982 he failed to recognise himself in a photo taken in 1966 on his 40th birthday.[20] He could not transfer to his secondary memory any of the things that passed through his primary memory.

There is probably no one who has contributed so much to the distinction between long-term and short-term memory as H.M. His disorder proved that the hippocampus performs an essential function in holding information in readiness and then transferring it to the parts of the brain that are equipped for more permanent storage. Some of the material stored away before his brain was damaged could be retrieved by his short-term memory, so he was occasionally able to talk about the hunting trips of his youth. But that same one-way traffic meant he could not recall that he had already told the story.

In the early years after the operation it was assumed that this blockage between long-term and short-term memory affected all kinds of information. But in 1962 Milner presented a revealing finding. Healthy test participants can learn, over a number of sessions, how to draw mirror images. They might be asked to draw a star between two parallel lines, looking only in a mirror while doing so. Milner carried out this test with H.M. and was surprised to find that his learning curve was little different from that of a healthy person. He performed as well as anyone else; the only difference was that he forgot he had learned this new skill. Suzanne Corkin, then still one of Milner's students, showed a few years later that the same went for other motor skills. H.M. learned them, but forgot the lessons.[21] He also forgot the people who taught him. After 40 years of regular contact, Suzanne Corkin remained simply someone who seemed vaguely familiar. When asked who she was, Henry answered, 'Well, someone I went to high school with, at East Hartford High?'[22]

Skills such as mirror drawing are attributed to the 'procedural memory', in which we store our knowledge of how to cycle or swim. H.M.'s case made clear that this kind of memory can function even when the autobiographical memory is disturbed. The know-how remains, though the lessons have gone. The same goes for tasks that have to do with the distinction between explicit and implicit memory. Brenda Milner, Suzanne Corkin and MIT researcher Hans-Lukas Teuber showed H.M. a picture with parts missing and asked him what it depicted. If he was unable to say, they showed him increasingly complete versions until he could identify the subject. When the test was repeated a few days later, H.M. was able to say what the picture represented far sooner.[23] Once again, it seems that something had been stored in his memory, even though he denied ever having seen the pictures before.

In much that he did and experienced, H.M. was rather like someone suffering from Korsakoff's syndrome. His 'old' memories gradually shrank to become an endlessly repeated and increasingly limited repertoire of stories. There was that vague disquiet about what had just happened, which no one could relieve. Like many of Korsakoff's patients, he tried to fill the gaps in his memory. During one of the last studies in which he took part, someone asked him where his glasses were. H.M. said they had been stolen in the nursing home. In reality he had undergone laser treatment several years before, so he no longer needed glasses.

Even events that would be deeply engraved on any normal person's memory were wiped from H.M.'s within minutes. After Teuber picked him up one day for a new series of tests, the car in front of them skidded in the pouring rain, spun on its axis and landed on its side. Teuber stopped and ran over to the car, which had crashed in the verge. The mother and daughter inside were distressed but not seriously hurt. The police arrived a short time later, the car was righted and Teuber came back to sit, soaking wet, in his car with H.M. They discussed the accident excitedly for a moment and then drove on. Fifteen minutes later, Teuber asked whether H.M. knew how he came to be so wet. 'Because you got out,' H.M. said, 'to inquire about the way.'[24]

So for Henry Molaison the years went by in a life that was both empty and productive. His father died in 1966 and his mother cared for him at home until 1980, when she was 95. Finally he moved to a nursing home, where he shared a room with another patient, divided from him by a curtain.

Without knowing it, Molaison also made a major contribution to the career of William Scoville. H.M.'s increasing fame as a neurological case brought Scoville invitations to report on the operation and its consequences first hand. One of his articles begins 'I have been invited to give a brief description of H.M., a young man who has become a *cause célèbre* in the psychophysiologic study of memory'.[25] Scoville's reputation was in no way harmed by the disastrous operation on Henry, and no doubt on dozens of other patients who remained in obscurity. He went on to enjoy a glittering career, was awarded an honorary doctorate and saw a professorship of neurology named after him. The website of the Society of Neurological Surgeons states that he was honorary member or president of no fewer than 25 neurological societies at home and abroad. He died in February 1984, in a car crash.

Under the radar

Every era has its own conventions when it comes to dealing with neurological treasures. Railway worker Phineas Gage – who had an iron rod driven through his skull by an explosion in 1848, survived the accident and became walking evidence for theories about the function of the frontal lobes – is commemorated in the Warren Anatomical Museum at Harvard, where his skull and the rod are prime exhibits.

The aphasic cobbler Louis Victor Leborgne, nicknamed 'Monsieur Tan', had a lesion on the left side of the frontal lobe that in 1861 enabled Paul Broca to trace what is now known as 'Broca's area'. Leborgne lives on as a brain preserved in alcohol at the Musée Dupuytren in Paris.

Henry Molaison's brain is everywhere and nowhere. On 16 February 2009, on a flight from Boston to San Diego, Jacopo Annese sat next to a plastic box that occupied the window seat so that no one had to pass it.[26] After the box's arrival at the Brain Observatory its precious contents were laid in a gelatine bath for several months so the brain would harden prior to being deep-frozen. On 2 December 2009, exactly a year after Henry died, his brain was put under the knife for the second and last time.

In a session lasting 53 hours, streamed on the internet, Annese and his staff, using an instrument called a microtome, cut the brain into 2,401 ultrathin slices, vertically, from front to back, roughly parallel to the plane of the brow. The slices are 70 microns thick (7/100 of a millimetre). Then, in the summer of 2010, the slices were subjected to Nissl staining, so that the structure of the cells became more clearly visible. They have since been scanned and transformed into a virtual brain, an ethereal collection of measurements translated into a visual image, which can be consulted on the internet. Annese sees the project as a kind of neurological Google Earth; any researcher can zoom in to achieve the desired level of detail, all the way from brain areas to individual neurons. Alternatively, as he put it in an interview, the visitor might want to zoom in on the life itself. 'I see it in a romantic way – I think I am writing a biography. We will revisit his life by slicing through this brain and studying those structures that gave him the life he experienced.'[27]

Rather less romantic is the question of how Annese came to have Henry Molaison's brain. Who gave permission for it to be removed, sliced with the microtome and put online? In 2002 Suzanne Corkin reported that H.M. had assented to her request to place his brain at the service of science after his death.[28] His legal guardian, that distant nephew, had put his signature to her assent form too. A year later, Corkin heard that Annese had procured grants for the building of an apparatus that could be used to prepare and slice brains, making his lab a particularly suitable destination. Plans to move Henry's brain in due course to San Diego must have been finalised by 2006, since in the summer of that year Annese came to Hartford for lunch with the man who had so generously donated his brain. In California, Molaison's brain was received in an atmosphere of triumph. A colleague expressed pride at how adroitly Annese had operated, saying, 'Jacopo saw a research opportunity and pursued it – pretty much under everyone's radar'.[29] Annese was confident that Molaison's brain would attract donors. People who were willing to donate other organs to science had always been rather hesitant when it came to their brains. 'The way we approach the brain of H.M. will lead others to entrust cases to us. It could be seen as a beautiful thing that your brain becomes a book in this library'.[30]

Just how much Henry's brain will contribute to the science he hoped he was helping to progress is questionable. What appeared on the internet is a highly advanced virtual model of what was, in the end, an old and sick brain. The precise location of the lesion that caused his memory disorder had been determined by an early MRI scan in 1992. These new images and the sectioning in California made clear that a larger proportion of the hippocampus had been spared than Scoville's original drawings suggested. The brain of Henry Molaison was initially used in San Diego for quite different purposes. On the opening page of the Brain Observatory's website you were invited to click on a link to 'Help with Project H.M.'. This took you to a handy menu featuring three easy ways to designate your gift. Later a second phase began, that of staining and scanning, during which for 50 dollars you could sponsor the pieces of glass on which the brain slices were laid ('Sponsor a Slide').[31]

In the nineteenth century, no permission of any kind was required from Phineas Gage or Monsieur Tan. Their skulls and brains were simply taken and exhibited. Molaison was presented with an official request and Corkin is convinced that he consciously gave full permission for his brain to be donated. 'His wish to help other people will have been fulfilled', she wrote.[32] But what is the value of permission from someone who instantly forgets his undertakings? Or who by the end of a request has forgotten how it began? What can terms such as 'internet' or 'online' have meant to him?

H.M. will live on in other ways, of course, not merely as a virtual resource. In her book *Permanent Present Tense*, Corkin has woven her

Jacopo Annese, head of the Brain Observatory at the University of California.

memories of her experimental and personal dealings with H.M. into a superb history of the past 60 years of the neuropsychology of memory.[33] She had acted as both researcher and gatekeeper, scrutinising fellow scientists before allowing them access to H.M. Her memoir will serve as the basis for a movie; the film rights have been bought by Scott Rudin and Columbia Pictures. So far, no release date has been set.

CHAPTER FOUR

The Man Who Forgot Faces

You are standing waiting at the cinema box office. Next to you in the queue is a woman who seems vaguely familiar. She gives you a friendly nod. With some hesitation, you nod back. Meanwhile you are digging around in your memory. Who on earth is she? Halfway through the film it suddenly dawns on you: the woman who always serves you at the bakery. Embarrassed, you realise you must have seen her at least twice a week for several years.

Placing people when we meet them outside their usual context can often be difficult. Does an experience like this not make something else starkly obvious? All those times that you looked at the woman and asked for a sliced wholemeal loaf, you must have been paying far less attention to her face than you thought, since her face is the one thing that was precisely the same when you saw her in the cinema queue. How certain are we, then, that we recognise people mainly by their faces?

There is a neurological condition, popularly known as 'face blindness', that makes people unable to remember faces. They even fail to recognise individuals they interact with every day, such as colleagues or flatmates – by their faces, that is. People with this disorder do often correctly identify people they know, but by relying on clues that most of us, who do not have this particular handicap, use subconsciously, such as clothing, hairstyle, voice, or the knowledge that this is a person they are likely to encounter in certain surroundings. It is as if we recognise a portrait from its frame.

There have probably always been people who are unable to recognise faces, but the official identification of the disorder dates back only to 1947 and like many other neurological discoveries it was a direct result of the Second World War.

Soldier S.

During the war, a clinic for people with brain damage was set up in the small southwest German town of Winnenden, far behind the lines. Most of the patients came straight from the front. They had gunshot wounds to the head or had been struck by shrapnel, and often the bullets or shards of metal were still embedded in their brains when they arrived at the clinic. Among them was a 24-year-old soldier who is referred to as S. He had been wounded by a shell on 18 March 1944. His operation notes record that pieces of shrapnel the size of a 50-pfennig coin and a five-mark coin were removed from his brain. They were at the level of his ears. Pieces of bone had entered the occipital lobes at the back of his head. Both sides of the brain were badly damaged.

S. was treated by neurologist Joachim Bodamer, who knew what life at the battlefront was like since he had served as a medic on the front lines in Russia and France. In Winnenden he dealt with patients who sometimes stayed for months or even years before they were well enough to be discharged, which gave him an opportunity to observe their long-term progress. In most cases little more could be done about the lesions themselves. Bodamer concentrated mainly on the disorders and handicaps that resulted from their brain damage, a depressingly long list of neurological problems beginning with 'a': amnesia, aphasia, agnosia, alexia, agraphia. Two years after the end of the war he published three case studies about soldiers with a disorder that had never previously featured in the neurological textbooks: they had lost the ability to recognise faces.[1] He named the disorder 'prosopagnosia', from the Greek *prosopon*, face, and *agnosia*, absence of knowledge. His most important case was S.

Bodamer's report about S. is a shining example of the powers of observation and of experimentation with limited resources. What must have intrigued him from the start was the selective nature of the disorder. The patient's powers of concentration, his intelligence and motor skills all functioned without any significant problems. His memory was intact, so the fact that he could not recognise those he knew by looking at their faces did not seem to be the result of a memory defect. The disorder mainly affected his vision. S. now saw everything in black and white, 'like in the cinema'.[2] He could remember colours and even dreamed in colour, but he was disappointed every time to wake up in a drab, grey world. That would never change. He recognised objects he knew from before his brain injury, but was unable to imprint new objects. He also had difficulty integrating details into a coherent impression. In a picture of a petrol station he recognised the cars arriving and leaving, the people, the signs, but what customers were coming to do there escaped him. He could follow films only by listening hard to the commentary. He understood nothing at all of a film about country life on an island in the Bodensee that had a purely musical soundtrack.

The symptoms that convinced Bodamer he had discovered a new kind of disorder were barely noticeable, even to S. himself; he soon developed compensatory tricks and strategies and was almost unaware that he had ceased to recognise people by their faces. Only after Bodamer had put him through a long series of tests did the full extent of his handicap become clear. S. recognised a face as a face, and he had no difficulty identifying the separate elements: the nose, the eyes, the wrinkles and creases – it was just that he lacked the ability to add them together and perceive the unique appearance of that particular face. He was even able to observe changes in expression; it was just that he could not interpret them and was therefore unable to say whether someone looked angry or was smiling. One day Bodamer sat him in front of a mirror. S. thought at first that it was a painting, although he soon realised his mistake and understood that the face looking at him must be his own. He stared at it attentively for a long time but still did not recognise it. Months later, the face in the mirror was still unfamiliar to him. If he looked at it for long enough, he said, it was as if he had a vague recollection of a similarity to his own face. Bodamer asked some of the other people on the ward to stand in front of the mirror along with S., who was then asked to talk and laugh while the others remained silent and immobile. Even then he was unable to distinguish between his own face and theirs.

On one of his visits, Bodamer took along a drawing by Albrecht Dürer, a portrait of an elderly man wearing a velvet cap and fur coat. S. saw that it was a face and pointed to the nose and eyes, but he could not say whether the person portrayed was a man or a woman, old or young. Bodamer told him it was a portrait of an old man with a velvet cap. A few days later he showed S. the drawing again. This time S. said immediately: 'The old man with the velvet cap of the other day'. When Bodamer asked him how he knew, S. pointed to the cap. He had not the slightest recollection of the face. On his next visit, Bodamer once more took the drawing along, this time with the cap and coat covered. S. said he had never seen the face before.[3]

The paradox of S.'s disorder was that he still remembered the faces of his parents and sisters, but failed to recognise them when they visited him. Men who had lain in the same ward for months remained unfamiliar. He recognised the ward doctor who did his rounds every day by his spectacles. If he took them off, S. could no longer place him.

Bodamer discovered that all this also applied to the faces of animals. When shown a photograph of a long-haired dog, S. said it was a person, 'except that the hair is so funny'. Even after Bodamer told him it was a dog, he could not recognise it as such. 'I see it the same as before, but it could be a dog; it looked so funny'.[4] Bodamer went through an entire picture book of animal faces with him and S. did not recognise a single one. It was no better in real life. One day he stood for some time in front of a large animal that was harnessed to a cart, unable to decide whether it was an ox or a horse. Only when he looked at it from the side did he see that it was a horse.

S. dealt with his handicap remarkably well. In daily life he hardly ever made mistakes in identifying people – it was just that he used indications other than the face. Sometimes the crucial clue was the clothing, sometimes the spectacles or hairstyle, but mainly he relied on the voice or other sounds associated with a particular person. He became extremely adept at it. From footsteps in the hall or even the way the door handle moved he could tell who was coming into the room. But there were incidents that made painfully clear to him that something was wrong. When allowed out of hospital for a while, he happened to come upon his mother on the street. He failed to recognise her. Another unfortunate consequence, Bodamer noted, was that because he could no longer understand facial expressions S. ceased to use them himself. He had a fixed, glassy look, which suggested that generating expressions involves the same neuronal machinery as comprehending them. Even landscapes – before

being wounded S. had been a great nature lover – had lost their expressions. To him there were no longer any lovely or hostile landscapes.

Prosopagnosia, Bodamer argued, must be the result of a very specific
type of brain damage, which he located in the occipital lobes. Several self-
observations made by S. enabled Bodamer to come to this conclusion.
On a number of occasions the outlines of objects in S.'s field of vision
began, from one moment to the next, to tremble and flicker. Everything
appeared to vibrate for about 10 minutes. Bodamer was familiar with this
phenomenon in epileptic patients when electrical discharges occurred at
the back of the brain. He knew from the literature that they could be
caused experimentally by stimulating the surface of the occipital lobes
with an electrode. The odd thing was that in S. the outlines of faces
remained free of such vibrations.

A second indication that the damage was extremely specific arose from
an unfortunate incident when S. was again released from hospital for a
short time. He was obliged to report to the military authorities and when
he did so he was reprimanded for failing to salute an officer appropriately.
He apologised, saying it was because of his brain damage, but the officer
was not satisfied. An exchange of words followed during which S. became
extremely agitated. Fifteen minutes after the incident the faces of the
people around him suddenly became snow white. They lost all contrast.
The eyes and nostrils were deep black holes against the white. Nothing
else that S. looked at had changed at all.

Those two observations, taken together, were evidence of a double
dissociation: one function was disturbed while the other remained intact
and vice versa. In neurology this is a familiar argument for the independence
of a function, meaning that it has its 'own' substrate in the brain.

'Karl, is that you?'

Bodamer followed up his article with descriptions of two more prosopagnosia patients, Lieutenant A., wounded on the East Prussian front, and
Corporal B., hit in the back of the head at Normandy by shrapnel from a
shell. Like S., Lieutenant A. was able to recognise people from the sound of
their footsteps in the corridor. Like S., he looked attentively at his reflection
in the mirror without being able to place it. Like S., he was the subject of
experiments that, among other things, offer a glimpse of life in a

rehabilitation clinic. The head nurse said she had serious doubts as to whether A. was truly unable to recognise faces, since he always greeted her, even from a long way off. Bodamer tested this out. He asked the head nurse to stand silently in front of the lieutenant along with another nurse from the ward. The two women did not resemble each other at all facially and they differed in age by 20 years. A. looked from one to the next and back again for several minutes without being able to say which of them was the head nurse. The experiment ended when the ward sister could no longer stop herself from smiling and A. recognised her from her beautiful white teeth.

But what about his own wife? Surely, the lieutenant thought, he would be able to recognise her. A fresh experiment followed. Bodamer asked A.'s wife to put on a nurse's uniform, found a few nurses who were roughly the same height and lined them all up in front of the lieutenant. He slowly walked past the silent women, who were all staring straight ahead, and studied each face, but he passed his wife without showing any sign of recognition. He walked back along the row and again failed to stop on reaching his wife. Then, out of the corner of his eye, he caught sight of something in her eyes that seemed vaguely familiar.

In the literature Bodamer had come upon several patients who did not recognise faces, but usually there were other things wrong with them as well. Some were unable to recognise objects, or had memory disorders. One woman could not distinguish between her daughter and the maid, although the daughter was a full head taller. She recognised her husband only from his voice and had to ask all the men in the room one by one 'Karl, is that you?'[5] What was special about his own cases, Bodamer suggested, was that this specific disorder was virtually all that was wrong with them, rather than part of a general inability to recognise patterns, or memory loss.

Bodamer's account of soldier S., Lieutenant A. and Corporal B. was his last contribution to the neurological literature. As well as medicine, he had studied philosophy under Karl Jaspers, and for the rest of his working life he pursued a successful career as a philosopher of technology with an existentialist bent. Joachim Bodamer died in 1985 at the age of 75.

Face blindness

In that same year, Oliver Sacks published a book called *The Man Who Mistook His Wife for a Hat*.[6] The title was derived from his experiences with Dr P., a musicologist and teacher at a school of music. P. no longer recognised his students by their faces, although as soon as they began to speak or sing he knew who they were. Instead of picking up his hat at the end of his first consultation with Sacks, he grabbed his wife's head, intending to set it on his own head. 'His wife looked as if she was used to such things.'[7] In a postscript Sacks writes that only after he had finished his book did he find out that this case was not unique, that a number of people with the same disorder had been described in various languages and that there was a name for it. The fact that a well-trained and experienced neurologist had never heard of prosopagnosia shows the degree to which Bodamer's work had faded in the collective memory of neurology. Anyone searching through old volumes will find dozens of relevant case studies, but they were written in a variety of languages with little exchange of knowledge between them. German authors quoted Germans, French scientists only the French, and although the Swiss occasionally referred to both French and German scientists, hardly any of the work by them reached researchers in English-speaking countries. This has since changed. Practically all such studies now appear in English and the only German found these days is the obligatory reference to Bodamer's 'Die Prosop-Agnosie' of 1947.

It is now clear that Bodamer understood from the start that the 'forgetting' of faces was the ultimate consequence of a process that had gone wrong at a far earlier stage. His patients did not forget faces the way one might forget names or events. The problem was that faces did not enter their memories at all. There was nothing to be recalled. He also understood that the defect had nothing to do with the eyes or the optical nerves. It lay further back in the brain, in the area that integrates visual stimuli into patterns and then connects them with the knowledge of patterns laid down in the memory. The damage lies in the temporal lobes or the occipital lobes. So the currently popular term 'face blind' is misleading: we look with our eyes but see with the backs of our heads.

There are two main forms of prosopagnosia, and the distinction lies in the stage at which the processing of visual stimuli goes wrong. In apperceptive prosopagnosia the patient has lost the ability to integrate the elements that make up a face. It is an 'early' defect in the process of facial recognition. Patients with this disorder cannot say whether two photographs show the same face or different faces. Like Dr P., both soldier S.

and Lieutenant A. must have been suffering from apperceptive prosopagnosia. In associative prosopagnosia, by contrast, the patient can draw
faces and make judgements as to whether they are the same or different,
but can no longer connect a known face with their memory and knowledge of that person. Familiar faces have not disappeared from the memory,
it is just that they cannot be called to mind. When it comes to daily interaction with people the patient knows, the two disorders amount to the
same thing.

British neurologist A.J. Larner has identified an early case of the latter
affliction in Alice's meeting with Humpty Dumpty in *Through the Looking-
Glass and What Alice Found There* by Lewis Carroll, published in 1871.[8]
After an uncomfortable conversation with Humpty Dumpty, Alice feels
she ought to be going.

So she got up, and held out her hand. 'Good-bye, till we meet again!'
she said as cheerfully as she could.

'I shouldn't know you again if we *did* meet,' Humpty Dumpty
replied in a discontented tone, giving her one of his fingers to shake;
'you're so exactly like other people.'

'The face is what one goes by, generally,' Alice remarked in a
thoughtful tone.

'That's just what I complain of,' said Humpty Dumpty. 'Your face
is the same as everybody has – the two eyes, so –' (marking their
places in the air with this thumb) 'nose in the middle, mouth under.
It's always the same. Now if you had the two eyes on the same side of
the nose, for instance – or the mouth at the top – that would be *some*
help.'

So here we have an egg complaining about the extent to which all human
faces resemble each other.

For many years, prosopagnosia was presumed to be an acquired
disorder, the consequence of brain damage resulting from an accident, a
stroke, oxygen deprivation or – as was discovered in Dr P. – a tumour. But
ever since 1976, cases have come to light from time to time of people
suffering from the condition without any detectable brain damage, or of
people who were not able to recognise faces even when they were children. Over the past 10 years it has become clear that there is a congenital

form of the disorder, named 'developmental prosopagnosia'. Because it is present from birth, it often goes unnoticed, even by the child. Usually there will be some kind of incident that makes clear that facial recognition is absent. One five-year-old boy bit another boy who attended the same crèche and had been bullying him, but when reprimanded by a member of staff he was no longer sure whether he had bitten the right child. A girl of six lost her mother in a busy shop and started asking one woman after another whether she was her mother. In a 2003 article summing up the research to date, developmental prosopagnosia is described as 'a very rare condition'.[9] It has since been estimated that around 2 per cent of the population has so much difficulty recognising faces that a diagnosis of prosopagnosia would be appropriate. The internet has played a decisive role here. In 2001, Harvard University, along with University College London, set up a website on the subject (www.faceblind.org). It garnered an unexpected number of responses from people who recognised their own symptoms. Contact was made with some of them and research revealed that in many cases of developmental prosopagnosia, other family members had the same problem, suggesting there is a genetic factor that selectively disrupts the memory for faces.[10]

Developmental prosopagnosia might help to clarify certain aspects of autistic disorders, since people diagnosed with autism have trouble recognising faces and look at faces in an unusual way.[11] No one doubts there is a connection here, but in which direction? Is it that autistic children have problems recognising faces and therefore lack one of the important instruments for social contact, so that their autism is worse than it would otherwise be? Or is it, conversely, because of a lack of social orientation that their ability to recognise faces is insufficiently stimulated in a critical period and therefore fails to develop?

For someone who recognises faces to a normal degree it is hard to imagine the world of someone who cannot. To a great extent we remember faces automatically. It happens unconsciously, and it is so powerful a faculty that almost everyone can see faces in the famous portraits by painter Giuseppe Arcimboldo (c. 1527–93) with no effort at all, even though the face of his librarian, for example, is composed of books, while other faces are made up of vegetables, fruit or fish. Anyone with prosopagnosia will be completely thrown when confronted with these portraits, seeing only berries, apples and bunches of grapes. But there is

Giuseppe Arcimboldo, 'Portrait with Vegetables (The Green Grocer)', c. 1590.

one painting by Arcimboldo, 'Portrait with Vegetables', also known as 'The Green Grocer', that allows people who have no difficulty recognising faces to experience something of the world of those afflicted. We see a bowl filled with onions, turnips and other root vegetables, some still with their leaves. No matter how long we stare at it, no face appears. We are suffering from temporary prosopagnosia: the face becomes visible as soon as the image is turned upside down.

Not recognising faces, or 'forgetting' known faces – because that is the effect the observer experiences – can have far-reaching consequences for a person's social life. Prosopagnosia is not well known like colour blindness or dyslexia, so the embarrassing situations that arise cannot usually be solved by briefly mentioning the disorder. Interviews with patients show that the condition requires them to make adjustments in their daily lives.[12] They run the risk of introducing themselves to close colleagues, or of joining a group of strangers in the belief that they are acquaintances. Some may panic in crowds at the thought that they might lose track of the people they are with and be unable to find them again. One described a fear of taking the wrong child home from kindergarten. Walking past someone you know without greeting them will be interpreted as either indifference or arrogance. Most people with prosopagnosia develop tricks for avoiding these outcomes. Some try to avoid eye contact on the street. Others greet everyone with equal enthusiasm just in case. Sometimes a partner will be instructed immediately to say the name of any acquaintance they encounter. Those with the condition often prefer to avoid social situations, feeling insecure and shy, unable to decide whether this is an aspect of their character or the result of their experiences.

Nothing can be done about the condition itself. There is neither treatment nor cure. Patients are recommended to concentrate on learning to deal with the consequences. The tendency of many people to keep their condition a secret only makes matters worse. The first patient whose case was described in the medical literature, by a London family doctor named Arthur Wigan in 1844, was advised by him to be open about his handicap and simply trust that his friends and family would show understanding.[13] That remains the best advice.

CHAPTER FIVE

A Slope, Followed By an Abyss

Alzheimer and Korsakoff are both now remembered because their names have become attached to serious memory disorders. Of the two, neuropathologist Alois Alzheimer (1864–1915) is the better known. In 1906 he described a woman being cared for in his institution in Frankfurt who had forgotten just about everything she had experienced over preceding years. When she died he discovered deposits of protein in her brain that had obstructed the communication between brain cells and thereby caused her memory disorder. Today Alzheimer's disease is responsible for three-quarters of all cases of dementia. A number of biographies of Alzheimer have been written.[1] Far less is known about Korsakoff. To this day no biography has been written and knowledge of him among the general public is limited to the conviction that the disorder that bears his name is caused by alcoholism, which is not even strictly true.[2]

Sergei Sergeievich Korsakoff was born in 1854 in the Russian city of Gus-Khrustalny. After graduating from medical school, he specialised in neurology and psychiatry and eventually became medical superintendent at a psychiatric institution in Moscow. He gained his doctorate in 1887 with a study of the mental and physical consequences of alcoholism and in the years that followed he published not just in Russian journals but in German and French on the subject of what he called 'polyneuritic psychosis'. The term 'polyneuritic' referred to the inflammation of multiple nerves, known as polyneuritis, while 'psychosis' related to his

Sergei Korsakoff (1854–1900).

patients' acute confusion and disorientation. In its early phases at least, the disorder was accompanied by 'pseudo-reminiscences'. The patient invented all kinds of experiences but believed they had actually happened. Confabulation is still one of the most striking aspects of Korsakoff's syndrome.

The nerve damage might express itself in double vision, a drifting gait, cramps, paralysis and damaged reflexes. Because of these somatic symptoms, the fact that a serious psychological defect had arisen as well was sometimes overlooked. It included a complete loss of the ability to recall what had recently happened. The start of the illness was often marked by a crisis:

> The patient cannot rid himself of obsessive anxious thoughts; he expects something terrible to happen – either death, or some kind of seizure, or he himself does not know what; he is afraid to be alone, constantly calls for people to stand by him, groans, and laments his fate. At times there are wild shouts, hysterical-like episodes during which the patient is capricious, upbraids the people around him, throws things at members of his household, beats his chest, and so on. The agitation is particularly severe at night; patients are usually almost sleepless and disturb the sleep of others; they constantly call for help, demand that someone stay with them, help them to change position, entertain them, and so on.[3]

When the agitation subsided somewhat, patients regained self-control. They could gather their thoughts and after a while they entered a state of laconic indifference. They sometimes had the feeling that nothing was wrong. But their ability to remember did not return; they seemed not to have stored away anything that happened after the crisis.

Brown rice

Korsakoff pointed out that Swedish doctor Magnus Huss, who introduced the term 'alcoholism' in 1849, had observed a connection between long-term alcohol abuse and memory disorders, but according to his own research the same syndrome could occur without any history of alcoholism. Korsakoff reported on cases in which the damage had been done by typhus, tuberculosis or puerperal fever, or in which it resulted from poisoning with arsenic, carbon monoxide, lead or tainted grain. The cause surely had to be a substance that got into the blood and damaged the nerves. When Korsakoff hosted a major medical congress in 1897, his colleague in Berlin, Friedrich Jolly, proposed naming the syndrome after him. The disorder was confined to damage to the memory. The question of what caused it was left open for the time being, although all doctors believed it should be sought in some as yet undetected infection.

The discovery of the cause of Korsakoff's syndrome is a classic case of serendipity. In the 1890s, disquiet arose in the Dutch East Indies when more and more people, both native islanders and their Dutch colonisers, developed beriberi, a disease associated with damage to the nervous system not unlike Korsakoff's polyneuritis. It leads to the same disturbances of sensory perception and to muscle weakness, and it was threatening to affect the strength of the army. The decision was made to set up a laboratory in Batavia, under the leadership of medical officer Christian Eijkman. Eijkman noticed that some chickens kept as laboratory animals all contracted beriberi but later recovered. It transpired that a newly recruited cook had thought it wasteful to feed the chickens cooked white rice and had switched to local brown rice. After further tests it became clear to Eijkman that the chickens were not being made ill by something in the white rice but by the lack of something not found in it, a substance that had apparently been removed along with the brown husk. Beriberi turned out to be not an infectious disease but a deficiency disease. After controlled tests – this time with Javanese prisoners – the medical authorities were convinced. In 1911, Polish physiologist Casimir Funk succeeded in isolating the substance that cured polyneuritis in birds. In 1936 thiamine was synthesised; it is now better known as vitamin B1.

Sergei Korsakoff did not live to see that development. He died of heart failure in 1900, at the age of just 46. But he had already indicated that there was a connection between beriberi and 'his' syndrome. It was in fact a consequence of long-term vitamin B1 deficiency, often caused by alcoholism, although not by the alcohol itself but by a failure to eat a normal diet. If no vitamin B1 at all is consumed for a period of six or seven weeks, serious memory problems can result. The same deficiency may be a consequence of something else entirely. Symptoms of Korsakoff's syndrome have been described after stomach reduction, anorexia, hunger strike and diseases of the digestive tract. In all these cases, vitamin B1 supplements need to be given as quickly as possible.

Dual memory loss

A Korsakoff's patient, strictly speaking, suffers from two distinct forms of memory loss. The difference lies in the direction in time. 'Anterograde amnesia' means that the patient is unable to imprint new information. This is memory loss in a forward direction: whatever the patient may experience in the future, it will not enter the memory. 'Retrograde amnesia', by contrast, affects the patient's past: memories of things he or she has experienced disappear. The dividing line between the two always lies at the point when the brain damage occurred. What passes into oblivion is what came before or what follows after.

Or both. Pure forms of anterograde or retrograde amnesia are rare. With most brain damage, whether the result of injury or illness, some sort of mixture of the two occurs, permanent or otherwise. Depressive patients who have been subjected to powerful electroshock treatment to both sides of the brain will often have problems imprinting memories, but they may also lose parts of their past, perhaps stretching back three or four years. Memory disorders as a result of brain damage also tend to reach in both directions through time, but aside from those suffering from dementia, the largest category of patients with a combined form of memory loss are people with Korsakoff's syndrome. In their daily lives it is the anterograde amnesia that is the more obvious. They can no longer store away what they have just experienced, said or done in such a way that they can recall it later, even a few minutes later, so they repeatedly tell the same story or ask the same question, or fail to recognise someone who has been absent for just a few moments. Memories of a more distant past are often intact, so they still remember things they learned in high school

and retain their professional knowledge. They can recount their adolescent experiences. All those things seem still to be available to them,
forming the basis for long stories, often repeated word for word, which
may give the impression that their memory problems are limited to the
period since Korsakoff's syndrome struck.

Daily dealings with sufferers are not affected by endless repetitions
alone. Korsakoff treated a woman of 46 who recovered from typhus but was
left with a serious memory disorder. Not only had she become forgetful, her
memories of a more distant time had been affected as well. In her mind,
Korsakoff wrote, 'a certain emptiness prevailed.'[4] In the second year of her
illness this emptiness seemed to fill up again, although unfortunately not
with memories but instead with 'pseudo-reminiscences'. She became
convinced that her husband sometimes had affairs with women in the town.
Korsakoff described the man as 'a respectable doctor of advanced years' and
there was no reason to suspect him, but the woman would not allow herself
to be persuaded. From the details of her accusations her husband concluded
that stories he had once told her about the conduct of a young bachelor he
knew had been transformed into 'memories' of the behaviour of her own
husband. A little later she started to 'remember' other occasions on which
her husband had betrayed her, and each and every one of them could be
traced back to scenes in novels she had read. It put her husband in a difficult
position, especially since she was otherwise intellectually unimpaired. The
problem was that the woman could no longer connect the thoughts that
occurred to her with their true source. She was helpless in the face of whatever emerged from her memory.

Experimental research into the memories of people with Korsakoff's
syndrome can be complicated. The condition usually arises after a long
period of alcoholism, so an experimental group of Korsakoff's patients
with alcoholism needs to be compared to a control group of alcoholics
without Korsakoff's syndrome. There are plenty of those around, but it is
not easy to persuade them to take part in memory experiments. Another
problem is that researchers have limited knowledge of what test participants once knew. They can attempt to assess the depth and extent of the
forgetting, but they need to be reasonably certain that what seems to have
been forgotten really was in a person's memory before he or she became a
Korsakoff's patient. Much research is carried out using tests in which
photographs are shown of people who were famous in the 1950s, 1960s or

1970s, but no one can say whether a test participant's memories of a famous actor, say, date from the 1950s, when his films were first released, or from the 1970s when they may have been repeated on television. Failure to recognise the person at all may not necessarily indicate forgetting. Perhaps the patient was not particularly interested in films. Research into antero-grade amnesia is methodologically far simpler. The experimenter can present the material to be remembered – a list of words, photographs, a story – and later test how much has been retained. Even if the patient recalls very little, this does at least offer an opportunity to investigate whether the powers of retention for different types of information have been damaged equally severely. The first law of psychology applies here: the quantity of research is directly proportional to the degree of experimental accessibility. There has been very little research into retrograde amnesia compared to the wealth of experiments concerning anterograde amnesia.

Nevertheless, it is not entirely absent. Along with tests for recognition of famous faces, questions can be asked about important public events, television programmes or well-known voices. The results show that Korsakoff's patients are better at reproducing 'old' memories than more recent ones, although their performance is still far worse than that of the control group. It sometimes seems as if the distant past is still fully intact, but in reality much of that, too, has gone.

A second outcome is that the forgetting shows a temporal gradient. The more recent the event, the more likely it is to have disappeared. Even if the period about which much has been forgotten stretches back 30 years, there is still a contrast between memories of 30 years ago and those of 10 years ago. Korsakoff's patients will identify an actor from photographs of the early years of his career but not the later years, or be able to identify a person who was fairly famous 40 years ago more easily than a person who was a major international star 10 years ago.[5] This gradient also means that it would be wrong to speak of a 'gap' in the memory, except perhaps in the sense that there are more and more gaps the closer we get to the present.

The forgetting curve of Professor P.Z.

There is a consensus about thiamine deficiency as a cause of forgetting in Korsakoff's patients. Enzymes that are vital for the glucose metabolism of brain cells and for keeping intact the cell membranes and the myelin sheaths around a cell's axons are reliant on thiamine. The brain takes up almost all the available thiamine, which means that if the supply is interrupted, problems quickly arise; stimuli are conveyed less effectively, cell tissues begin to atrophy and some brain structures visibly shrink. MRI scans have shown that the hippocampus can lose around 10 per cent of its volume. Much remains to be explained, however. The same brain anomalies can be found in alcoholics who have no memory problems and the effect of a shrunken hippocampus is far from clear cut. The hippocampus is involved in the storage of memories, so damage to it might explain the anterograde amnesia seen in Korsakoff patients, but for the actual reproduction of early memories an intact hippocampus is apparently not required. In Henry Molaison it was largely removed, but he could still recover memories of his childhood.

One of the puzzling questions raised by this neurophysiological theory is why memories are more likely to be lost the more recent they are. It was once suggested that what presents itself as retrograde amnesia is in fact the result of anterograde amnesia that has been present for some time already.[6] Alcohol affects nerve tissue and therefore the ability to imprint memories. In the long history of alcoholism that precedes the acute phase of Korsakoff's, the memory might perhaps have been functioning increasingly poorly, so that many years later gaps seemed to appear, whereas in reality the amount stored away had steadily diminished. The progressive character of the brain damage might explain the gradient. In the memory of the alcoholic who later became a Korsakoff's patient, events would therefore be not so much erased from the memory as, over the years, 'written down' less and less.

This hypothesis was tested in the early 1980s by a professor, not as a researcher but as a patient and test participant who was given the invented initials P.Z.[7] Born in 1916, he began drinking heavily at the age of 30 but managed to acquire a prominent position in one of the sciences. He wrote hundreds of articles and a number of standard works, sat on the editorial boards of important journals, organised conferences, taught, supervised doctoral theses and gave lectures all over the world. In 1979 he published his autobiography. Two years later, when he was 65, he suffered a crisis that culminated in acute memory loss and he was diagnosed as suffering from Korsakoff's syndrome. He placed himself at the service of memory research.

First of all, tests confirmed what was already obvious: Z. was suffering from anterograde amnesia. He could not remember lists of word pairs like 'neck and salt' or combinations of numbers and geometrical shapes. A test for retrograde amnesia – those famous faces – showed evidence of severe damage as well, although he could recall a few well-known figures of the 1930s and 1940s. Z.'s prominent position in his field and the fact that he had written his autobiography enabled the researchers to develop a strictly personal test. They compiled a list of 75 'famous scientists'. Their names mostly came from Z.'s autobiography and they included close colleagues, fellow editors, co-authors and others he could be shown to have known well. The list was divided into three categories: those who had made their most important contributions to science before 1965, around 1965 and after 1965. Z. was requested to indicate for each name what their specific field was and what their most important contributions had been. His answers were given scores of 0, 1 or 2. He scored 1 if, for example, he knew the specialist's field but could no longer recall the contribution made to it. One of Z.'s colleagues, of the same age and an equally prominent scientist but without a past as an alcoholic, volunteered to go through the test as a control. The results are simple to relate. Although these were his own famous colleagues, Z. could generally say far less about them than the control could. Names that meant absolutely nothing to him were mainly in the 'after 1965' category, but he had also forgotten a good deal about many of those in the 'before 1965' group. Most puzzling is that only a few years prior to the crisis in 1981, he was able to relate all kinds of things about them in his autobiography.

Based on that same autobiography, a test was compiled that looked at what he could recall of experiences with family members, events during conferences, significant research results and books. The outcome can be seen at a glance. Set out across time – in this case his age – the percentage of correct answers declined rapidly. Even for memories from the relatively unaffected period up to his 15th birthday he scored no more than 70 per cent. The turning point came between 1940 and 1950, when Z. was aged 25 to 35 and his seriously heavy drinking began. He was able to give a correct answer to only just over 40 per cent of the questions about that period. The bottom of the graph was reached in 1960. About the 20 years between the ages of 45 and 65 he knew nothing at all. Again, the questions were based on what Z. had been able to commit to paper only a few years before he became a Korsakoff's patient.

The notion that such patients have severely damaged autobiographical memories while their professional knowledge, stored away in the semantic memory, is largely spared, led to the third and perhaps most distressing experiment conducted with Z. Thirty-five academic terms were taken from his own articles and books. He was asked to define them and to give as many examples and details as he could. The control took the same test. Sadly, many of the terms Z. had once known so well no longer meant anything to him.

The study involving Z. has introduced a more nuanced view than that derived from the rather simplistic distinction between two types of memory. His ability to imprint memories no longer functioned at all, but access to his own past was also seriously affected, and although his semantic memory worked a good deal better than his autobiographical memory, its content too was seriously depleted. He would have failed an oral exam on his own work, which is what the last test amounted to. The idea that retrograde amnesia is a veiled form of anterograde amnesia, the result of a memory steadily deteriorating during a long period of alcoholism, seems improbable. There was certainly a temporal gradient, but until a few years before the diagnosis, most of his memories were still accessible. Once Z. had passed the critical point of the acute crisis, many

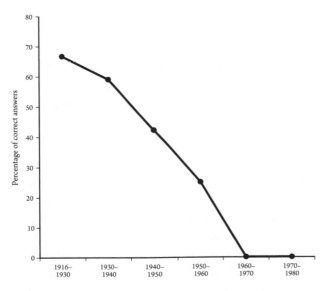

Memory loss in Professor P.Z., concerning information taken from his autobiography.

doors in his memory closed simultaneously. This is what makes the approach of Korsakoff's syndrome so treacherous. Its course is a slope, followed by an abyss.

The Claparède effect

Concentration on a single test participant made the experiments involving Z. rather similar to the case studies published a century earlier by Korsakoff himself, who tried to state precisely what had been remembered or forgotten by studying his patients' backgrounds in depth. Like the tests with Z., the resulting observations called into question the simple distinction between two types of memory. Nothing had been destroyed in an absolute sense in either one, Korsakoff concluded, not even the seriously and apparently irrevocably damaged ability to imprint memories. When he came to see a patient and asked who he was, the patient would claim to have no idea, but if he came in again after spending a few minutes out in the corridor, Korsakoff was not greeted like a complete stranger. After a number of visits he no longer needed to explain that he was a doctor, even though the patient would still be insistent about never having met him before. It seemed that something had been stored away, even though it was not in a part of the memory where the patient could consciously retrieve it.

Observations like these were confirmed by research elsewhere. In an asylum in Geneva, the Asile Bel-Air, neurologist Édouard Claparède had earlier attempted to provide experimental evidence for this 'unconscious memory'. A 47-year-old woman with Korsakoff's syndrome, admitted in 1900, retained a good deal of her earlier knowledge – the names of the capital cities of Europe, for example – but suffered from severe antero-grade amnesia. The nurse who cared for her every day remained a stranger to her ('madam, with whom do I have the honour of speaking?'), as did the doctors she had been seeing for years.[8] Claparède was intrigued by the contrast between what she claimed not to know and what she must know. She could not say where the toilet was but went there without hesitation. She said she did not recognise the corridors and wards of the asylum but found her way around them effortlessly. On one of his daily visits, Claparède hid a drawing pin in his hand. The woman was pricked by it but quickly forgot the incident. The next morning the doctor put his hand out to her again, without the drawing pin, and this time the woman swiftly and reflexively withdrew her hand. To his question as to why she had refused to shake hands with him she said, bewildered: 'Doesn't one have the right to withdraw one's hand?' When Claparède inquired further she asked:

'Is there perhaps a pin hidden in your hand?'

'What makes you suspect me of wanting to prick you?'

'That was an idea that went through my mind. Sometimes pins are hidden in people's hands.'[9]

Not for a moment did she recognise the thought as a memory.

This outcome – having an experience that is stored away but not accessible to the conscious mind despite the fact that it sometimes continues to influence thought and experience – later became known as the Claparède effect. It is part of the theory that in 1985 was termed 'implicit memory'.[10] Half a century after Claparède's study, tests with Henry Molaison showed that patients can suffer from severe anterograde amnesia yet nevertheless make certain skills their own – in H.M.'s case drawing mirror images – or unconsciously acquire knowledge about people or places. With retrograde amnesia, too, more memories may be spared than the patient has access to, as demonstrated by the case of a policeman with severe memory loss after a bout of meningitis.[11] He had forgotten where he spent his honeymoon and lost all memories of the birth of his three children, his career, the houses he had lived in, the cars he had owned and his friends. Of his time in the army he recalled only that he had been stationed in Egypt, not what he had done or experienced there. The infection had wiped out virtually everything. The Claparède effect came into operation as he was about to undergo an MRI scan. The procedure was halted when he had a panic attack. Being slid into a tunnel was, he said, 'like going into the pyramids'.[12]

In Korsakoff's day, the terms autobiographical memory, semantic memory, Claparède effect and implicit memory did not yet exist. But findings produced by studies of the Genevan woman, Henry M. or the British policeman would have strengthened him in his conviction that even in the most damaged memories something is spared, something unforgettable that cannot be remembered.

CHAPTER SIX

Your Colleague Has a Brilliant Idea – Yours

In *From the Earth to the Moon* by Jules Verne, first published in 1865, three gentlemen get into a space capsule and have themselves fired at the moon by the largest canon ever built.[1] It is really quite comfortable on board. There are divans, gaslight floods the padded walls and the men have a supply of brandy to last them for months. They have brought two hunting dogs with them, in case they are of use on the moon. Unfortunately, one of the dogs, called Satellite, suffers a nasty blow to the head during the launch and grows listless. The next day it is found dead on the floor. Sad. But what to do with the body? They cannot simply throw the dog over-board through a porthole, since they must not let any air escape from the capsule, but neither can they keep the body with them. They decide to take the risk. Two of them hold open a hatchway in the floor for a moment and the third lowers Satellite into his spacious grave.

No one expects what happens as a result. A few days later, one of the men looks through the window and to his horror he sees the dog. They had forgotten that anything you release into space will simply float along-side you. At the most inopportune moments, the dead dog drifts past the porthole.

Some people are just like that dog. You shut them out of your life, hoping never to see them again, wanting nothing further to do with them, yet they keep turning up one way or another and simply refuse to go away for good.

Satellite's body is lowered into its grave.

I have been on the point of using this metaphor in an article many times, but I could never shake off the uneasy feeling of having read it somewhere before. In a piece by Rudy Kousbroek, perhaps? I have never been able to find the source.[2] But I am keen to avoid committing plagiarism, even by accident. By using the metaphor of the dog floating in space I would run the risk of falling victim to a curious form of forgetting known as 'cryptomnesia': reading or hearing something from someone else and then later coming up with precisely the same idea, having forgotten it is not your own.

Cryptomnesia, which means 'hidden memory', is fairly common. A person may be firmly convinced he or she has thought of a solution that was in fact proposed by a colleague at an earlier meeting. Cryptomnesia has been suggested as an explanation for the publication in a plastic surgery journal of a 'new' surgical technique that in reality had been part of the training given to surgeons over many years.[3] Rather more everyday examples might include thinking you had invented a new cocktail, an original pun or an exercise for basketball training.[4] Bitter conflicts can arise in the workplace as a result of our tendency to come up with other people's ideas from time to time.

The most famous example of cryptomnesia concerns George Harrison. In 1969 he wrote 'My Sweet Lord', which topped the charts worldwide. A writ was issued against him by the production company Bright Tunes, pointing out the song's resemblance to 'He's So Fine', a major number one hit for the Chiffons in 1963. Bright Tunes accused Harrison of plagiarism, saying the melodies of the two songs were virtually identical. Harrison admitted that he knew the number by the Chiffons but denied having copied it. The judge – perhaps he had dabbled in psychoanalysis – issued a verdict that was worded in such a way as to spare Harrison's feelings. It must, he said, be a case of 'inadvertent copying of what was in Mr Harrison's subconscious memory'.[5] But unintentional or not, it was still copying. Harrison was ordered to pay more than half a million dollars in royalties. To be done with the whole business he later bought the rights to 'He's So Fine'. Anyone clicking on that song on YouTube can indeed sing along to it with the lyrics of 'My Sweet Lord'.

In the psychological literature of the past 20 years, cryptomnesia has been equated with 'unconscious plagiarism', but this is slightly misleading. Unconscious plagiarism may be a result of cryptomnesia, but they are not one and the same, and to assume that they are is to do an injustice to the rich history of the concept of cryptomnesia.

Subliminal memory

Around 1900 a peculiar collection of observations and findings was in search of an explanation and a name. Most had been garnered during spiritualist séances or at deathbeds. In December 1894, Genevan professor of psychology Théodore Flournoy met medium Hélène Smith, a sales assistant in a silk shop. He attended a long series of séances with the aim of finding out whether the messages she received and passed on had paranormal origins. In her trance the woman told of time spent on Mars. She spoke Sanskrit and conversed in antiquated French with people from the court of Marie-Antoinette. In some of her séances she indicated where lost objects could be found. Flournoy published the report of his findings in 1900.[6] It brought their affectionate relationship to an abrupt end.

Flournoy was convinced that all the medium's revelations could be explained in terms of psychological processes, as long as it was assumed she herself did not have conscious access to those processes. Smith was undoubtedly acting in good faith, but everything she said had its origins in her own mind. One day she lost a brooch. It was a much-loved keepsake and she placed an advertisement in the lost and found column of the newspaper. No response came. Ten days later, during a séance, she received extremely precise instructions as to where it could be found: one metre to the west of a white stone next to the path to the Rue des Bains. The entire gathering stood up, took a lantern and found the brooch beside the white stone. To Flournoy this was a case of cryptomnesia – the first time the term appears in the literature.[7] Smith must have been unconsciously aware that the brooch had fallen to the ground, but the memory was able to penetrate her conscious mind only during a trance. Her detailed stories about events at the court of Louis XVI could also be explained by cryptomnesia; things she had read as a girl in encyclopaedias and history books remained unavailable to her in a waking state but were recalled when she went into a trance.

In such instances of cryptomnesia, Flournoy saw confirmation of the theories of Frederic Myers, a British classicist who had been one of the founders of the Society for Psychical Research in 1882. Myers divided the human mind into a subliminal and a supraliminal self. Only those things above the threshold (the 'limen') were accessible to personal consciousness. The term 'subliminal' is his far better known contribution to the psychological vocabulary and it lives on in theories about subliminal messages, stimuli that are too fleeting or faint to be consciously observed yet do penetrate the mind. What had happened to Smith the medium, Flournoy wrote, was a perfect example of the kind of cases Myers had collected, 'in which the memory of a subliminal perception (i.e., registered immediately without striking the normal personality) appears as a revelation in a dream of ordinary sleep, or under some other equivalent form of automatism'.[8] Myers, for his part, defined 'cryptomnesia' in 1903 as the 'submerged or subliminal memory of events forgotten by the supraliminal self'.[9]

Doctors, too, made observations that seemed explicable only with reference to cryptomnesia. In 1902, Dr Henry Freeborn described in the *Lancet* the case of a 70-year-old woman who went into a delirium during a fever and suddenly started speaking Hindustani, a language she had not used since the age of four and could not remember ever having spoken.[10] When she recovered, the language was as inaccessible to her as ever. One of Freeborn's colleagues commented that this reminded him of a case described by Coleridge in which an illiterate maid in Germany was said to have recited Greek and Hebrew for hours during a fever and later turned out to have worked as a girl for a scholar who was in the habit of reading aloud. In all these cases, 'forgotten memories' once more penetrated the conscious mind, usually for only a short period.

Cryptomnesia was not at this stage associated with plagiarism. It was an explanation for phenomena that seemed paranormal but were in reality produced by memories that entered the consciousness only in exceptional circumstances, in a dream, trance or delirium. In the twentieth century,

parapsychology was marginalised by mainstream psychology, but cryptomnesia remained, preserving the idea that memories can disappear from
consciousness and later return to it without being recognised as memories.
Psychoanalysts eagerly seized on cryptomnesia when developing theories
about the processes of forgetting, as Freud himself had done as early as
1901. He was prompted by a personal case of cryptomnesia described in his
The Psychopathology of Everyday Life, in which he told his friend Wilhelm
Fliess how he had arrived at the insight that every individual starts out in life
bisexual. Fliess reacted in injured tones: 'That's what I told you two and a
half years ago at Br.[Breslau] when we went for that evening walk. But you
wouldn't hear of it then.'[11] Freud had no memory of such a conversation, but
later in the week it suddenly came back to him. In his book he writes good-
naturedly, 'Since then I have grown a little more tolerant when, in reading
medical literature, I come across one of the few ideas with which my name
can be associated, and find that my name has not been mentioned.'[12] Freud's
reputation as a combative guardian of the primacy of his ideas is not, it
would seem, derived from his self-image.

   In psychoanalysis, cryptomnesia only became more mysterious. A
dictionary of psychology published in 1934 defines it as 'a condition of
memory in which the original experiences are forgotten because of
unconscious motives and consequently appear as apparently new crea-
tions lacking the attributes of memory'.[13] So now, as well as forgetting,
there was a need to explain those 'unconscious motives'.

Cryptomnesia: the experiments

In 1989, two American psychologists, Alan Brown and Dana Murphy,
attempted to gain an experimental grip on cryptomnesia. They developed
an approach that set the pattern for later researchers.[14] In the first session,
test participants are asked to come up with ideas. Typically they have to
brainstorm about solutions to complex problems, such as a medical diagnosis. During the second session, several weeks or months later, they are
required to indicate what their contribution was on the previous occasion.
In a third and final session they are challenged to come up with ideas that
have not been proposed before.

   Several dozen experiments along these lines have been carried out
over the past 20 years and every time it turns out that in the second session

participants tend to present other people's ideas as their own. In the third session they often come up with ideas that they think are new but in reality have been proposed before, usually by one of the other participants. The cause is not simply confusion about ownership, since occasionally participants attribute their own ideas to others, although the number of times that happens is negligible compared to the times when ideas generated by other people are claimed by participants as their own. All this happens in good faith. Even when test participants have the chance to win considerable sums of money by attributing ideas correctly (and know this in advance), they still claim now and then to be the source of other people's ideas.[15] Sincerity is not the same as impartiality. The unavoidable consequence is that all individuals gain the impression that cryptomnesia is mainly something their colleagues suffer from. People who repeatedly see themselves cheated out of their own ideas must surely feel like an honest person surrounded by thieves.

The basic form of this kind of experiment is borrowed from earlier research into 'source amnesia', or forgetting the origin of things you recall. Source amnesia can mean that you tell a piece of juicy gossip you have just heard to a number of different acquaintances and eventually to the person who told it to you (who, you suddenly recall, impressed upon you that you must tell no one else). Cryptomnesia is rather different. With source amnesia you forget the origin of what you have heard or read, but you remember that there was a source. In a pure and authentic case of cryptomnesia you forget even that. The brilliant plan, the great invention, the timely bright idea that suddenly comes to you actually has its origins in your memory yet is not recognised as a memory.

It is of course true that forgetting who or what the source was will take you a long way in the art of coming up with other people's ideas. Research shows that the factors that contribute to source amnesia increase the likelihood of cryptomnesia as well. The longer the interval in time, the more cases of cryptomnesia there will be. If the sources closely resemble each other, because they are all fellow students for example, this too makes cryptomnesia more common. Even sex makes a difference; it is easier for women to appropriate the ideas of other women, men those of other men. There is a 'next-in-line' effect: those who came immediately before you in the brainstorming session run a slightly higher risk of having their ideas stolen by you, probably because you were already thinking about your own contribution as you listened. Ideas presented in chaotic circumstances, such as during brainstorming sessions or disorganised meetings, are also more likely to be incorrectly claimed at a later date.

Most likely of all to increase the occurrence of cryptomnesia is an invitation to participants to improve on ideas already proposed.[16] Nothing separates the true owner so rapidly and efficiently from his or her ideas as a minimal addition or insignificant variation. Even after just a few weeks, the slightest contribution is sufficient to convince you that you have improved upon an idea of your own.

From Zappa to Abba

All these elements can be seen in cryptomnesia 'in the wild', in cases that occur outside the lab but are convincingly documented. In the 1990s, one of those affected was the guitarist Steve Vai, who made his debut at the age of 19 in Frank Zappa's band, later became a solo artist and occasionally performed for touring bands as a guest guitarist.

While touring, Vai explained, he always tried to prepare new material for his next album.[17] This rendered up a pile of sheet music that he would sort through at home to see what was usable. While recording the album *Fire Garden* (1996) he came upon a piece that seemed vaguely familiar. Perhaps he had once played it, he thought. It was in his own handwriting. Vai decided to use it as part of his 'Fire Garden Suite'. After recording the track, he sent it to a friend. The reaction was swift: 'Ah, I see you recorded the song "Bangkok", from the play *Chess*'. Vai was astonished: 'What are you talking about? Bangkok? Chess? I never heard of that!' But his friend insisted, 'That's from this play, by Tim Rice and what's-his-name, one of the songwriters from Abba'. Vai thought: 'Hm. Well then they stole it from *me*!' But he rushed out to get the record. 'I listened and I almost dropped dead. It was the song.' It was indeed exactly the same piece, written by Björn Ulvaeus.

'How the hell did this happen?' Vai asked himself. Then he remembered that David Lee Roth, the singer with Van Halen, a band Vai was performing with at the time, had passed him a tape during the tour with music he wanted to play during a set change. Vai had written out the music, but that was all. The transcript ended up on the pile. Vai had his friend to thank for a narrow escape from the tricky situation George Harrison found himself in.

It was too late to remove 'Bangkok' from the album, since the master tape of *Fire Garden* was already finished, so he had no choice but to ask 'what's-his-name from Abba' for permission and pay for the rights.

This shows how a conspiracy of circumstances could get the better of even a man as honourable as Steve Vai. For a start, the origin of the music on the tape was unclear, which opened the way to source amnesia. He transcribed the music, no doubt by listening to the tape a number of times, so it became firmly lodged in his head, as well as being there on paper in his own handwriting. By the time the transcription came to light again many months later, the fact that this particular piece of music had a different origin from the rest of the pile had faded into the background. Vai summed up by saying 'I just thought I was adding to something else that I wrote', which, as we have seen, is the fatal road to unconscious plagiarism. I believe him.

What remains is your idea

The identification of factors that contribute to cryptomnesia is not the same, of course, as an explanation. What actually happens?

Imagine you were at a meeting last week about some kind of complicated problem to which you proposed a clever solution. Then the conversation moved on, no one picked up on your idea, a colleague presented a different solution and the decision was made to try that first. At the next meeting it becomes clear that the solution is not going to work. Fortunately your colleague has come up with a different idea in the meantime, a better idea, a brilliant idea: yours. You glance around the table. To your horror you see that you are the only person who realises it was your idea. What has gone on in your colleague's brain?

A case like this is the result of that intriguing difference between two types of memory: semantic memory and autobiographical memory. The semantic memory contains material we might tend to call 'knowledge' rather than recollection, such as knowing what 'incubation' means, what a 'joint and reciprocal will' is, or what the stretch of water between Britain and France is called. You once acquired that knowledge, but in most cases you will have forgotten the circumstances in which you learned it. Few people can say how or when they discovered that Stockholm is the capital of Sweden.

Autobiographical memory deals with the things we experience. This type of memory records the circumstances, or at any rate makes a valiant attempt to do so. Over time all kinds of things may be forgotten, but often you can still recall where something happened or who was there, whether it took place in the evening or during the day, at home, outdoors or at work. Recollections drawn from our autobiographical memories usually have a context.

When you presented your idea at the previous meeting you remained for a very short time in your colleagues' autobiographical memories as part of their recollection of the suggested solution. The solution itself went into their semantic memories and there, with yourself as the rapidly fading context, it became linked up with all the knowledge they already had of the issue at hand.

Cryptomnesia is therefore not simply the consequence of a failing memory. It arises because a different part of the memory – in the case of your colleague the semantic memory, in the case of George Harrison and Steve Vai the musical memory – has retained it extremely effectively. It is the discrepancy between the two memory processes that produces cryptomnesia. Seen from a broader evolutionary perspective, there is something to be said for such an arrangement. Confronted with a problem, it is not particularly helpful for the survival of the individual or group to remember just *who* came up with the brilliant idea, but it may prove invaluable to be able to recall *what* it was.

CHAPTER SEVEN

The Galileo of Neurology

Arthur Ladbroke Wigan, a British family doctor, died in 1847. After his death he faded back into the shadows from which he had emerged on the strength of a single idea and a single book. The idea was that the left and right cerebral hemispheres are not two parts of one organ but two separate brains, each with its own feelings, thoughts and impulses. The book was *The Duality of the Mind*, in which he had collected everything he could find to support his idea, whether psychiatric or neurological in nature.[1] It was published in the autumn of 1844 and briefly attracted the attention of the medical world.

Into the shadows again. To start with Wigan himself, no portrait of him exists. Of his personal possessions we have only one short letter. There is one signature, too, in the register of the Royal College of Surgeons. His name does not feature in letters, diaries or autobiographies of the time. No last will and testament has survived and we do not even know where he was buried.

The shadows stole across his book as well. Copies of the 1844 edition are extremely rare. In Britain, only the University of Cambridge has one. It is a collectors' item for which dealers ask fabulous prices.[2]

Even deeper shadows fell over the theory of two brains. Responses to the book were at best reticent, often condescending and sarcastic. After a first round of reviews, fewer than a dozen, no one ever mentioned it again. Wigan's one idea survived merely as a historical curiosity, an occasional note in the neurological textbooks. His work was not simply a path that became overgrown – it was barely a path at all.

In 1969 something strange happened to *The Duality of the Mind*. Suddenly a lamp was turned on above it, a few hands leafed hastily through the pages, then just as suddenly the light went out again. The occasion was a series of experiments with 'split brains' by American neurologist Roger Sperry. Tests with surgically divided brains showed that up to a point each cerebral hemisphere has its own repertoire of functions. A pupil of Sperry's, Joseph Bogen, believed he had found in Wigan a pioneer of the theory of hemispheric specialisation.[3] Wigan seemed to have been transformed from a fantasist into a forerunner, but his rehabilitation was short-lived. When a fleeting inspection made clear that Wigan meant something entirely different with his two brains, *The Duality of the Mind* was returned to the shelves.

That, roughly speaking, was the story of Wigan and his theory. And now his book has spent the past three evenings on the table in front of me, in a pool of light from my desk lamp. Delightful evenings. His psychiatric case studies, written with great empathy, are as absorbing as anything by Oliver Sacks. The autobiographical parts of the book are moving. Wigan was a sensitive observer of what went on in his own mind, and he had the courage to share even the most painful things with his readers. The stories about his patients prove that during long years spent running his practice he kept his eyes wide open. But what carries you along irresistibly once you start reading is the way that one idea can impose order on everything, if you have sufficient faith in it. In his foreword Wigan confides in the reader that over the past quarter century he has felt his hypothesis about the two halves of the brain ripening almost daily from conjecture to firm conviction. As a reader you know that something very different is going on. The dual brain became Wigan's sole means of understanding himself and the world.

Each of the two brains, Wigan came to believe, has its own memory, but the existence of two memories does not simply entail a doubling of capacity. Neither brain has access to the other, so there is a duality of memory loss as well. Each brain selects, interprets and registers at its own discretion, and each forgets according to its own laws. The adventures and experiences of one brain are not those of the other. If both brains are intact and healthy, then the discrepancies between their two memories remain within bounds; they engage in double bookkeeping, but without any major irregularities. Only if one brain is damaged in some way – or if both brains become sick – do problems arise. Then it may happen that the sick brain starts to rebel and the healthy brain has to relinquish leadership, with disastrous consequences for both performance and experience. Wigan's evidence was derived mainly from this rather morbid context. Motiveless bloodlust, incomprehensible personality changes, hallucinations or obscene impulses pounce upon the patient as if from nowhere. In reality they have their origins in a sick brain that was until that point safely under the control of a healthy, strong-willed, virtuous brain. Things that seemed forgotten, indeed altogether absent, suddenly pay a call on the conscious mind. With his two brains, Wigan was trying to bring order to pathological phenomena that two generations later would be divided along a different axis: that which separates consciousness and the unconscious.

Autodidact

The little that is known about Wigan's personal life comes from articles he wrote under the pseudonym Luke Roden for *The Illuminated Magazine*, published between 1843 and 1845.[4] We read that Arthur Wigan moved to London at the age of 15, in the final week of the eighteenth century. He was apparently apprenticed to a medical practitioner in Croydon for three years, though Wigan was always rather uncommunicative on the subject of his training. In *Duality* he admits that a lack of formal medical schooling always caused him difficulties, although he felt it was mainly an advantage, since he was at no risk of adopting the prejudices of the professors. Perhaps the young Wigan had authority issues, as we would call them now. He seems to have been impervious to good advice from older and more experienced doctors. When he was still working as a trainee doctor, he writes in *Duality*, Britain was hit by an epidemic of rabies.[5] Anyone bitten by a dog was advised to have the flesh around the wound extensively cut out. Wigan dealt with a number of such wounds himself, but with growing reluctance, since he had come to the conclusion that rabies did not actually exist. He bombarded the editorial boards of newspapers with letters in which he explained that rabies was a superstition, just as witchcraft had been. No one believed him, so he proposed a test. He would allow himself to be bitten by a rabid dog. Everything was in place for the start of the experiment; he had even bandaged his arm, leaving one space bare for the dog to bite. Only at the last minute did he allow himself to be dissuaded.

In 1807, Wigan became a member of the Royal College of Surgeons. He joined the practice of a family doctor in London by the name of William Cleveland, whose daughter Lydia he married in 1813. They had two sons and after Dr Cleveland's death Wigan took over the practice. In 1829 they moved to Brighton, then a rapidly growing seaside resort much frequented by the middle classes of London for the benefit of their health. As well as his practice, Wigan set up a free dispensary to distribute medicines to the poorest members of society. According to an advertisement in the *Brighton Gazette*, it was open for one hour a day, although 'persons decidedly dirty' were refused. This charitable initiative turned out to be a bad idea, since it ate away at Wigan's capital, but he stubbornly kept the dispensary open. In 1835 the inevitable bankruptcy ensued, although he carried on his commercial practice until 1841. At the age of 56 he retired as a practising doctor.

In the years that followed, Wigan travelled to France and Italy, visited madhouses and prisons, and wrote a book about Brighton. During this period he quietly added 'M.D.' to his name, although no one has ever been able to discover where he gained his qualification as a medical doctor. In 1843 he started writing *The Duality of the Mind*. It was published in 1844, by which time he was in his 60th year.

The reviews in the medical press were unanimous in their criticism of the overly chatty style of the book, which was written, as one of them put it, with the 'garrulity' of a 60-year-old. The style betrayed 'the old gentleman to whom composition and arrangement of a controverted topic are new employments'.[6] *The Lancet* wrote that Wigan had broached a subject that was too broad for one man and one generation. An anonymous reviewer in the *American Journal of Insanity* addressed the 20 postulates in which Wigan had summed up his theory and concluded that the most important of Wigan's claims about the dual brain were not new, since phrenology had already proposed them, and that the other claims were new but sadly unfounded. Not only had the author failed to establish their veracity, his book did not even contain much to support them. Yet the reviewer had enjoyed the book, he said in conclusion, because only a small part of it was devoted to the author's peculiar ideas and a relatively large part was reserved for 'very interesting acts and cases adduced by the author to illustrate his theory, though we are often unable to see their application.'[7] The reviewers, in short, were charmed but not convinced.

One can hardly blame them. The style is indeed that of an enthusiastic dilettante. Wigan was not afraid of encompassing lengthy digressions that end with a cheerful 'This, however, by the way.'[8] Three or four times he alludes to the revolution his theory will bring about in neurology and the resistance it will encounter from established medical men, hinting at Galileo, a comparison that had already been for two centuries what it is today: the hallmark of the autodidact whose revolutionary ideas meet with incredulity. We may also detect in it Wigan's insecurity with regard to his professional status. As a 'surgeon' he occupied one of the lowest ranks in medicine, barely above that of an apothecary.

After the publication of *Duality*, Wigan continued to search for further proof. He travelled to Naples, Sardinia and Lombardy, visited mental hospitals and prisons in the Netherlands and elsewhere, attended autopsies and inspected anatomical cabinets. On his travels he visited 'more than a hundred of the first men in Europe' to exchange ideas with them about his theory of the dual brain. In retrospect he concluded: 'I cannot remember a single objection, made by a man of that stamp, which has not vanished after my explanation.'[9]

The final years of this imperturbable spirit were lonely and racked by illness. His wife had died in the year that his magnum opus was published. One day in November 1847 he fell ill after standing too close to an open sewer near Regent Street. A friend, Dr Forbes Winslow, invited Wigan to come and stay with him in Hammersmith, on the outskirts of London. He remained there a few days but then, against all advice, insisted on returning to the city to attend a dinner. This was to be the last of the wise counsel he would brush aside. The next day he had a high fever. On 7 December 1847 he died as the result of a bronchial infection.

Two brains, one consciousness

In referring to the nerve tissue, 1,200 or 1,300 grams of it, that controls our thoughts, acts and feelings, we use the word 'brain' in both the singular and the plural. One might say 'Feel free to pick my brain' or 'I racked my brains'. An unfortunate friend might contract 'an illness that affected his brain' or be driven to 'blow his brains out'. The language reflects an anatomical uncertainty. Is the brain a single organ, like the heart, or are our brains paired, like our eyes and kidneys? Anyone looking at the brain from above will see two hemispheres lying symmetrically beside the central groove. Only if the two halves of the brain are gently eased apart do we find a strip of brain matter binding them together, the corpus callosum. It is the largest bundle of nerve tissue in the animal kingdom.

To Wigan the corpus callosum was not a link but a division. He pointed to the case of a man with hydrocephalus in whom the pressure of the fluid in the skull had severed the connecting tissue. At the autopsy it emerged that the two hemispheres had been completely separated, each pressed to its own side of the cranial cavity. This had no consequences for his intellect, so it seemed the corpus callosum was 'an organ of no importance'.[10] The first incident that had set Wigan thinking, 30 years earlier, about the generally accepted theory that the brain consists of two halves, concerned a boy of about 12 who lost his balance when trying to raid a rook's nest and in falling hit his head on the sharp edge of a section of railway track. The blow destroyed part of his brain. Wigan bandaged the wound as best he could and to his amazement the boy was completely clear-headed the following morning, felt no pain and recovered within a few weeks with no sign of any ill effects.[11] After that, Wigan came upon other cases of patients in whom an entire cerebral hemisphere had atrophied yet who still had all their intellectual faculties. The conclusion was irresistible: each brain houses an independent consciousness.

If each brain sustains an independent, conscious life, then the next question is, why do we not have a dual consciousness? Why are we aware of only one train of thought, one series of associations, one collection of sensory perceptions? Wigan's answer was that one of the two brains, usually the left, is dominant in normal circumstances, the other subordinate. The brain that rules determines our mental life and our actions.

Often there is a natural division of labour between the two brains. Simplification through doubling is the theme that unites many of Wigan's observations and findings. George IV could sign documents hand over fist and carry on a conversation about subjects of the greatest importance at the same time. In any London bank you could find clerks who were able to talk while adding up long series of figures. In times of anxiety and tension, Wigan wrote, he could not resist counting his paces, even if someone was with him and engaging him in conversation. Once he was rested, this strange ability disappeared again. All these phenomena flowed with perfect ease from the theory of the two brains. One brain does one thing while the other does something else, and if the more intelligent of the two is occupied by cares, then the subordinate brain has a chance to impose its curious talents and impulses on whatever it is we are engaged in. It is no accident that the number of things we can do simultaneously is limited to two. Even George IV could not, when both signing and conversing, fantasise about some third thing at the same time.

The dual brain also explained more remote phenomena for Wigan. Why are mathematicians rarely susceptible to insanity? The extreme concentration demanded by their discipline is achievable only if both sides of the brain can focus on the same thing. Both organs need to be in optimal condition. A slight congenital weakness in either one makes a person unsuitable as a mathematician. Moreover, the practice of mathematics increases the natural dominance of the leading brain to the point of absolute tyranny. After a while, no impulses at all from the subordinate brain will penetrate the mathematician's consciousness. It is a different matter, unfortunately, with artists. They deliberately cultivate their unusual ideas and fantasies. In the hope of profiting from their imaginations, they lay down the reins of rational thought and later find they are unable to pick them up again. They are constitutionally unsuited to concentrated study. Their tendency to submit to whims increases their susceptibility to madness.

An abundance of things in Wigan's own mental life and that of others could be explained in the most natural way by the presence of two independent brains. The rapid succession of confused images sometimes seen just before we fall asleep? One brain has dropped off and is starting to dream, while the other is still awake enough to look at the dream images. The inner struggles of a clergyman tormented by doubt? One brain believes, the other does not. Remarkable discrepancies between the actions of the same person at different times? One brain is courageous, the other cowardly.

Signed: Jesus Christ

Often we notice the presence of two brains in one head only when one of them is affected by disease, exhaustion or severe strain. Sometimes the dominance of the healthy organ can temporarily conceal the miserable condition of the other. Wigan describes an experience related by Paris psychiatrist Philippe Pinel. Along with a number of colleagues, Pinel interviewed a patient to see whether he had recovered sufficiently to be discharged. The man gave entirely reasonable answers to all the questions asked. The discharge papers were prepared and given to him to sign. When Pinel looked through them he saw the signature: 'Jesus Christ'.[12] Wigan had encountered a similar case in Edinburgh. A man who had been confined as a lunatic tried to secure his discharge by going to court. Allowed to represent himself, he was about to be discharged after long questioning, having shown no sign of insanity, when a witness who had been delayed by an accident rushed into the courtroom just as the case was reaching its close and casually asked: 'What news from the planet Saturn?' Addressed directly like that, the damaged brain could not keep silent and the healthy brain could no longer cope. 'He instantly relapsed into incoherence'.[13]

The long, muddled stories that the mentally disturbed often tell are muddled only on first hearing, Wigan decided. He wrote one of the stories down verbatim, numbered the sentences from 1 to 10 and asked his readers to look first at all those with odd numbers, next at all the even-numbered ones. In the first series the patient gave an indignant but coherent account of his admission to the mental hospital and the humiliations he had undergone there, telling how he, a gentleman of standing who could trace his lineage back 10 generations, had been brought to the place under the pretext that he was being taken in his own carriage to a hotel. He was driven by his own coachman no less, a man who had been in his service for 20 years, and he was then bound hand and foot to a bed. A fat housekeeper was the only person who had treated him with respect. The second series amounted to a summary of his delusions. He claimed he was the son of the sun and would bring pestilence down upon the earth, dry up wells and set forests ablaze so that all the pheasants would die. Clearly the confused monologue of the unfortunate man was actually an orderly dialogue between a healthy brain and a sick one.[14]

In Wigan's view, doctors, even the most distinguished among them such as Sir Henry Holland, personal physician to Queen Victoria, made the mistake of seeing in mental life merely a battle between higher and lower functions. Holland had remarked upon this in the last months of William Hyde Wollaston's life, a lengthy deathbed scene in which he was involved in late 1828. Wollaston, who had trained as a doctor but became famous as a chemist and physicist, was the discoverer of the elements rhodium and palladium. He made his fortune by developing a technique for processing platinum ore. While out hunting he noticed that he had lost all feeling in one of his fingertips. Holland wrote that Wollaston tested himself daily, took precise note of the progress of the disease and eventually came to the correct conclusion that one half of his brain was affected by a malignancy. The higher functions, Holland concluded, remained intact for a long time. But that was not what Wigan read into Wollaston's behaviour on his deathbed:

> The spirit of selfishness, which is certainly not one of the higher qualities of the mind, survived almost every other sentiment, and it was only in his last moments that Dr. Wollaston could resolve to part with his profitable secret as to the management of Platinum, by which he had already realized an enormous fortune. I cannot but think it a duty to record all the selfish littleness of great men as a warning to others, and therefore do I put the fact on record.[15]

Shortly before Wollaston died, another remarkable thing occurred. When all the doctors present thought that Wollaston was 'so near death as to be perfectly unconscious, and when he was unable to speak, he marked down a few lines of figures on the slate and added them up correctly, as a signal to them that he was still quite conscious of his state, and therefore able to appreciate their services'.[16] In Wollaston, Wigan explained, only one brain was dying, although this caused the death of both. It was not so much the 'higher' functions that were spared as the 'healthy' functions, those of the brain that was not sick. The arithmetic was performed by the intact brain and it was that brain that so anxiously held on to the lucrative secret to the last.

Wigan, it seems, was obsessed with the turn towards evil that a life can take if the good brain is affected by the sick brain. Slowly all a person's decency drains away. He describes with compassion the case of a gentleman who, during an exemplary career, had risen to a position in charge of a large office. He was a widower and his children had died young. He was well liked by his subordinates and treated them in a fatherly manner. Although he earned a substantial salary, his largesse kept him poor. As he approached

60 he tended towards garrulousness. His conversation, previously digni-
fied and reserved, occasionally took a dubious turn. The effect of admoni-
tions was short-lived. Eventually his remarks became downright obscene.
There was no option but to dismiss him. On his arrival home he packed a
few clothes, put some change in his pocket and began roaming aimlessly.
Everyone lost track of him. After three months he was found dead in a
remote part of the country, on a dung-heap where he had presumably
sought warmth. The immediate cause of death was hunger, but when the
skull was opened it became clear that there was a considerable softening of
the left cerebral hemisphere. The right hemisphere had been affected as
well.

Wigan found it hard to say precisely what had caused the decline.
Perhaps the right brain had mutinied or the powers of the left brain had
failed. Perhaps it was a combination of the two. But the self-control that
this excellent gentleman had cultivated in himself so early in life must
have masked the true extent of the ravages of disease for a long time: 'We
may conceive many struggles and victories before the contest was finally
given up, and he gave way to the full impulses of the grosser passions.'[17]

Phantoms

No case and no symptom was too bizarre to be given a place in Wigan's
book. He considered it a privilege to listen attentively to patients and to
trust their accounts, only later forming a judgement as to the explanation.
We have that approach to thank for the fact that in *Duality* early descriptions of disorders can be found that were only later taken seriously by
mainstream science.

Wigan also applied his theory to existing autobiographical accounts of
hallucinatory experiences. He writes about the case of a Berlin bookseller
called Cristoph Nicolai, who to his horror one morning saw 'a deceased
person' before him, 10 paces away. His wife, who was with him in the
room, could see nothing and immediately fetched a doctor. After about
seven minutes the figure disappeared. At the end of the afternoon it came
back, but then Nicolai began to realise that it must be a product of his own
mind. In the months that followed, such apparitions often came to him,
sometimes of people still living, sometimes of the dead, always at random
and without causing him any fear. He was clearly aware of the difference

between truth and illusion: 'I knew perfectly well when it only appeared to me that the door was opened and a phantom entered, and when the door really was opened and any person came in.'[18]

Another man, one Dr Bostock, had seen similar phantoms when he was feverish and exhausted. They moved as he moved his eyes and he too had no doubt they were generated by his own imagination. In the end he used them as a source of amusement: 'It appeared as if a number of objects, principally human faces or figures on a small scale, were placed before me and gradually removed, like a succession of medallions.'[19]

These innocent visual hallucinations call to mind the images that Swiss naturalist Charles Bonnet described in 1760. His observations passed into oblivion and were rediscovered only in 1936, by Georges de Morsier, a Genevan neurologist who gave them the name 'Charles Bonnet syndrome'.[20] They are attributed to under-stimulation of the brain, which starts to produce visual stimuli that are experienced as if they come 'from outside'. Of course that was not the explanation Wigan advanced. Here two brains were clearly at work simultaneously. In one brain, the sick one, the powers of observation must have been disturbed, so it began to process non-existent stimuli. The healthy brain quickly determined that in reality there was nothing to see, which explained the sense of reassurance after the initial shock. The healthy brain was perfectly capable of stopping the effects from occurring, but declined to do so because it was entertained by the vague images produced by the neighbouring brain.

Bonnet's description preceded Wigan's, but as far as we know, Wigan was the first to call attention to an extremely selective form of forgetting. One day a middle-aged man appeared in his consulting room with a curious complaint. However hard he tried, he could not imprint faces on his memory. He forgot them again immediately. Even if he had been sitting talking with someone for an hour, the next day he would be unable to recognise their face. His job depended on maintaining good relations with people and because of his unfortunate handicap, Wigan wrote, much time was spent 'in offending and apologizing'.[21] When he came across people he knew, he would recognise them only if they started to speak. He felt that the problem lay with his eyes and feared he would eventually go blind. Wigan was able to reassure him on that point, but he could be of no further help. The disorder must have its origins in the brain. The man was determined to hide his handicap as far as possible, against the advice of Wigan, who believed that open acknowledgment of it would be the best way to restore relations with friends who had become estranged from him. As we saw in the chapter 'The man who forgot faces', the disorder, now known as prosopagnosia, was not recognised in the neurological literature until 1947.[22]

Wigan made no connection between the forgetting of faces and his theory about the dual brain. It is not entirely clear how he could have done so, since if it was a disorder of one of the two brains, the other brain would take over the task. Perhaps Wigan thought that both the man's brains must have been affected. Over the last 20 years it has become clear that in roughly half of all cases of prosopagnosia there is indeed damage to both cerebral hemispheres. When the damage is on one side only, it is usually on the right. The forgetting of faces has awkward consequences, which go far beyond the loss of a single function, as illustrated by the case of Wigan's patient. It is the face, rather than a person's clothing or gait, that gives access to our memories of them.

Dissociation

Wigan dedicated *Duality* to Sir Henry Holland, the only author quoted with approval in the book. In his *Medical Notes and Reflections*, published in 1839, Holland had included a chapter entitled 'On the brain as a double organ', in which he considered the possibility that insanity might be the consequence of disharmony between the two halves of the brain.[23] That was not quite what Wigan meant – to him these were not halves, they were independent brains – but it was a step in the right direction. The celebrated society doctor received from Wigan the backhanded compliment that he 'has reasoned most acutely and correctly in a line *parallel to the truth*, and which, therefore, could not arrive at it'.[24] The italics are Wigan's. Holland had pointed to cases that appeared to corroborate the theory of the double brain. A young woman suffered from attacks that might last several hours or several days, in which another identity seemed to take over. In that condition she read different books from those she preferred in her 'normal' life and when the attack was over she recalled nothing of what she had read. She seemed to lay down different memories as well. Wigan had himself come upon this phenomenon of two mutually impervious memories. His patients often had a clear recollection of madness slowly creeping up on them but, once it had completely taken over, their experiences came to rest in a different memory. After they recovered, they no longer recalled anything they had experienced during their illness. This might sometimes occur even in brief interruptions to the clear conscious life. Wigan quoted a case described by the physician Dr John Conolly of a man who tried to make out a cheque and repeatedly failed to write what he wanted to write. After the first few words it was as if the pen took on a life of its own. The attack lasted half an hour. As soon as he came to his senses he saw that instead of writing 'fifty dollars, being one half-year's rate,' he had written 'fifty dollars through the salvation of Bra–'.[25] He could not imagine what he had meant.

An even more remarkable phenomenon, although one that was well documented and known to most in the medical world, concerned the way that people for unknown reasons suddenly plunged into a state that most closely resembled sleepwalking. They might remain in that condition for hours, all the time continuing to talk, write, sing or play a musical instrument as if they were entirely in their right minds. When they woke up they had no memory at all of what they had experienced in their somnambulant state. If they entered that state again, then all their memories from the previous occurrence of the phenomenon were immediately available to them and it was their recollection of waking life that had disappeared. This was usually called 'double consciousness', Wigan writes, but he preferred to speak of 'alternate consciousness', since in a sense the person was made up of two individuals.[26]

Two kidneys perform twice as much work as one, but that simple arithmetic does not apply to Wigan's two memories. Here the doubling is more like a halving, since one brain does not know what the other remembers. His 'alternate consciousness' would nowadays lead to a diagnosis of dissociation, or 'dissociative identity disorder' (DID) as it is officially known, the successor to 'multiple personality disorder' (MPD), a diagnosis that was common in the 1980s. One of the official diagnostic criteria of MPD was that the patient could not remember important personal information, and such memory loss could not be put down to straightforward forgetfulness. In most cases the other personalities or 'alters' each had their own memories (or have – the diagnosis is now rare but has not disappeared altogether). One difference between this and Wigan's cases of 'alternate consciousness' is that MPD or DID can involve any number

of alters. In this sense the theory of the dual brain implied a certain degree
of restraint.

Unnoticed

Wigan used flattering metaphors to describe the significance of his own
work. If you increase by half the length of the rope with which an animal
is tied to a post, you will double its freedom of movement. With his
research into mind and brain, Wigan said, he had done nothing more than
to add a few extra links to just such a chain. Later he compared his theory
to the first railway line, which will always remain the main line in the
much-branched network of the future, a cleverly chosen metaphor at a
time when Britain's rail network was expanding at a great rate. If they
thought about his work at all, his contemporaries saw things rather differently. Wigan was largely ignored by 'official' science. Whatever his meetings with 'more than a hundred of the first men in Europe' may have
amounted to, there is no trace of him in their work. *Duality* was dedicated
to Sir Henry Holland, with effusive compliments, but if Holland felt
honoured he never showed it. The social divide between the retired
family doctor and the personal physician to the royal family was far too
great for that. Wigan lacked any talent at all for what we would now call
'networking'. His doctrine was not actively ignored, it simply went unnoticed. Only the loyal Forbes Winslow wrote an article, in 1849, about the
legacy of his late friend, although it appeared under the heading 'The
unpublished manuscripts of the late Alfred Wigan, M.D.'[27] Wigan's first
name was Arthur.

Research into 'split brains' – in which an incision is made in the corpus
callosum for clinical reasons – led to renewed interest in Wigan's work but
brought him no late recognition. The corpus callosum, which Wigan saw
as a kind of fence between the two brains, is in fact a network of nerves
that enables communication between the left and right hemispheres.
Both halves are intensely involved in the processes that deal with perception, thought and actions. The case of the man with hydrocephalus in
which the corpus callosum was split in two was an 'experiment of nature'
and Wigan was right to conclude that the split had no perceptible consequences for the man's thinking or behaviour. A recent estimate suggests
that when the corpus callosum is cut completely in two, some 200 million

neuronal connections are severed. Only in the artificial conditions of 'split brain' experiments in the laboratory did it come to light that there is a degree of hemispheric specialisation.[28] Both halves perform the same functions to a large extent and where one of them does specialise, as with language for example, there is meticulous coordination between them. The anatomical symmetry of the cerebral hemispheres perfectly expresses their functional symmetry. It is simply not true that, as Wigan thought, each half can be either on or off, or that each has its own memories and ideas.

Wigan hoped that acceptance of his theory would lead to kinder treat-ment of those unfortunates who for their entire lives were forced to keep a careful watch on one of their two brains and despite their efforts some-times lost their grip, so that they 'committed acts of extravagance and folly' that were inconsistent with their lives in general and their charac-ters.[29] Their efforts were heroic but invisible. Only when they lost the battle did the impulses they had been fighting against become obvious. Such people deserved sympathy and encouragement, not punishment or disgrace. The young were particularly vulnerable. They had not yet been able to train their healthy brains to exhibit the virtue and willpower neces-sary for this kind of supervision. Wigan had lived long enough, he wrote, to know men who had committed follies and crimes when young but had been protected from the consequences by well-to-do parents. Later they developed into men of honour and reputation and it was as if their depraved youth had never existed. Those same deeds, performed by the poor, had ushered in lives of ignominy.

The language in which Wigan describes the relationship between the two brains is that of hierarchy and discipline. The leading brain gives the orders. It controls and keeps vigil, while the other brain is required to be subordinate. Throughout the book, reins are continually being laid down or taken up again, slackened or tightened. But the leading brain cannot do this by itself. It needs to be nurtured. The aim of education and training is to teach the leader to lead. In this sense, the interaction between the two brains reproduces something of the Victorian fascination with authority, control and willpower. A generation later, on the evidence of language disorders after damage to the left cerebral hemisphere, English neurologist John Hughlings Jackson pointed to the left half of the brain as 'the elder twin, the one in charge'.[30] If the right hemisphere managed to produce anything in an aphasic patient then it was a curse or a swear word. It was best for both halves if the left brain kept a firm hold on the reins of thought.

With his fascination for discipline, self-control and the lust and madness that burst free of them, Arthur Wigan vanished into the anonymity of Victorian undercurrents that would not surface again until the appearance of a book in 1886, oddly enough from the very publisher responsible for *The Duality of Mind*. But unlike Wigan's book, the novel *The Strange Case of Dr Jekyll and Mr Hyde* by Robert Louis Stevenson – neither a doctor nor a psychiatrist – placed a lasting stamp on the way we think about mental illness.

The theatre of the mind

Imagine a theatre. The spectators sit in eager expectation of a surprise performance. Naturally they try to guess what they are about to see. Someone spots a spangled shoe sticking out from under the curtain and thinks the play will start with a ballet. Someone else sees the silhouette of a hat and expects a tragedy. The experienced theatregoer has an advantage with guesswork of this kind, and Wigan was such a theatregoer:

> I *have* been a close and attentive observer, and a constant frequenter of this great theatre of the mind, and fancy myself able, in some cases, to anticipate the nature of the performance. The curtain is the bony cranium which hides the proceedings; but a close attention to your own theatre, your own little microcosm, will enable you to foretell your own performances, and to give a shrewd guess at those of others.[31]

This theatre metaphor appears in the opening of a case study in which Wigan introduces an 'intimate friend', but the experiences of this friend were so similar to those of Wigan himself in his financially precarious years in Brighton that it is difficult to avoid the impression that we are dealing here with an autobiographical fragment – all the more so given that the 'friend' entertained an identical revolutionary notion of the brain's duality. At Wigan's request this friend had committed his account to paper.[32]

It concerned a man with a sincere and truth-loving character, who found himself in difficulties after a long series of disasters and setbacks.

They had placed him in some of the most humiliating positions imagi-
nable. He was tormented by the thought that he was now regarded as a
man who had lost his honour, and although in his quieter moments he
realised that this was a delusion and his friends still treated him with
respect, he could not escape the feeling that he had committed some
dreadful crime. In this state he saw with great clarity what awaited him:
the crowded courtroom, the jury, the death sentence. In his mind he was
already writing a plea for clemency addressed to the sovereign and both
houses of parliament. All this time he knew he had not perpetrated any
crime and that all this was no more than a horrible fantasy, yet he felt as if
he was hovering above an abyss, certain he would descend into madness
if he let go of the reins even for a moment.

One thing he could not understand was that in good company and
after a few glasses of wine he was actually very cheerful, to the point of
elation. In such moments he liked to tell of all the things he had experienced in an eventful life and a varied career. It was not uncommon for a
circle of listeners to gather around him and beg him to tell them more. But
suddenly the old illusion arose and from one minute to the next a curtain
came down across all those cheerful scenes: 'I could say no more; felt as if
the eyes of all the world were upon me, was wretched and miserable;
every disagreeable event of my life came again before me, and I in vain
tried to recall one single incident or reflection of a different character.'[33]
Such experiences had reinforced his sense that a double identity must
exist within him, with memories that were not interchangeable between
the two.

One evening, in a state of mental anguish and needing to be alone, he
walked to the beach. In the moonlight he made his way across the
seashore. Somewhat calmed by the murmur of the waves and lost in
thought, he realised too late that he had been caught out by the tide. He
hurriedly waded back to dry land. Cold and shocked, he felt all control
over his thoughts ebbing away. He looked out over the glistening streak of
moonlight that stretched off across the water to the horizon and said to
himself: 'That shining path is the road to happiness, I will follow it'. He
walked to a boat that had been pulled onto the beach, intending to drag it
into the water and float away along the gleaming path. But suddenly he
became aware of the absurdity of the plan and ran away. At the same time
he felt a powerful urge to return to the boat. He heard a clear voice

repeating his own words: 'That shining path is the road to happiness, follow it'. He noticed that despite himself he was walking closer and closer to the boat. The water had risen so high now that it would be no effort at all to pull the boat into the sea. In the end, in desperation, he threw himself on the ground. Only then did he feel safe from his own impulses. After more than an hour lying on the pebbles he was calm enough to return home, knowing that if he had gone out in the boat he would almost certainly have drowned.

Did Wigan wander over that beach at night himself, in despair at the scandal of bankruptcy and fighting the urge to end his own life? We will never know. His 'friend' wrote that he hoped his testimony would meet with compassion from people who try with all their might to keep their disordered brains in check. That was exactly what Wigan was hoping to achieve with his book.

Those two brains of Wigan's – one sound and strong-willed, the other subservient and confused; one reproving, soothing and sensible, the other impulsive, sensual – make us wonder what kind of demons Wigan had to exorcise. Near the end of the book he quotes two lines by eighteenth-century Scottish poet Robert Burns.[34]

What's done ye partly may compute,
But never what's resisted.

They are the closing lines of an indictment of hypocrisy and our tendency to be too quick to judge others. In the calculus of emotional life, Wigan saw urges and temptations and took them into account in his verdict on the outcome of the struggle. Almost always that verdict was mild and forgiving, even when the battle was lost. Reading *Duality*, you sometimes feel as if you are sitting in Wigan's consulting room, where your story has found an understanding ear, even though you have just mentioned something of which you feel ashamed. He finds precisely the right words: 'Each man knows his own bad volitions, which he has been able to suppress; but he knows not which of his neighbours, whom he thinks so pure, have had the same difficulties to encounter; still less does he know those who have indulged their evil propensities undetected of all but One.'[35]

In that 'suppress' we can detect something of the axis along which half a century later many of the phenomena introduced in *Duality* would be divided, the axis of consciousness and the unconscious. It ceased at that point to indicate a neurological dichotomy, although for a long time such a thing was sought, even by Freud himself. Consciousness and the unconscious became instead a psychological dichotomy. After Wigan the axis was rotated through 90 degrees. He was trying to understand the interaction between left brain and right brain, positions on a horizontal axis, whereas 'high' and 'low', on a vertical axis, were the positions of the conscious and unconscious mind. It was now the lower passions that had to be held in check, and they arose from the depths of the unconscious or even the subconscious. It did indeed take a good deal of pushing to keep them down.

In Wigan we can already read, between the lines, the insight that what needs to be pushed away does not truly disappear. As part of his long story about the 'friend' who almost sails off on a gleaming path of moonlight, we come upon an unforgettable description of the man's emotional state. As he walked along the beach, confused and distraught, he felt a strong urge to scream. He had a strange feeling that it would do him good, that it would bring relief and that afterwards he would be able to control himself again. But he resisted the urge, fearful that one of the coastguards would hear him. Even at the sea's edge, in the middle of the night, amid the roar of the crashing waves, he had to restrain himself.

In his despair and confusion he sought comfort and soothing words, but instead his friends and family admonished him and gave him sensible advice. He was unable to reply. Had he tried to say anything in response he would immediately have lost his footing:

> I felt that to begin to give reasons would put one into a state of excitement, and my disordered brain would presently betray itself – I should be mad! So, like the bird that has entirely exhausted itself in the vain attempt to escape from his cage, I folded my wings, and lay down with a panting heart and stupefied brain – not to think – not to consider – not to reason – not to complain or remonstrate, but to endure, *ipse meum cor edens*, to gnaw my own heart in silence.[36]

CHAPTER EIGHT

On Repression

Any psychologist of memory who occasionally addresses a general audience rather than a gathering of colleagues knows to expect at least these three questions after the break. First: can you train your memory? Then: does a woman's memory work differently from a man's? And finally: do repressed memories really exist?

The first two questions need not detain us long. The training of memory has been exhaustively researched and as soon as it is clear which type of memory we are talking about, it becomes possible to explain to the audience the degree to which training leads to better performance. Many studies have looked at the significance of gender, too, and they suggest that the differences between men and women are negligible compared to those between individuals irrespective of sex. No one interested in variation within the human species will become much the wiser by comparing men and women. Their memories work in exactly the same way, although they will as a rule remember different things.

So what about the third question? The problem is not a lack of research. For at least a century, psychiatric and psychological journals have been publishing reports on repression. Such research may produce contradictory results, but that is not much of a problem either, since psychologists are commonly faced with incompatible conclusions and usually, after a bit of sorting and selecting, they can form a view as to which position has the best arguments. Not so with repression. For a start, so many definitions and attempts at definitions are in circulation that to all intents and purposes we have none. It is of little use turning to Freud – who to this day has a powerful influence on ideas associated with psychological repression – since his own definition changed from one publication to the next. Even in a special article devoted to the subject, in which he presented graphic descriptions intended to make plain to the reader exactly what repression is, the wide diversity of instances chosen created all kinds of confusion about what Freud actually meant by the term.

A second complication is that repression, however we may define it, overlaps untidily with terms like 'motivated forgetting', 'psychogenic amnesia', 'dissociation' and 'selective forgetting'. Each of these in its turn triggers a metaphor or semi-metaphor intended to explain what is thought to be going on in the memory: blocking, splitting, banishment, cutting off, suppression, burying, hiding. Even if there were no problems of variation and demarcation, one issue would remain that verges on the insoluble. In practically every definition of repression we find the terms 'trauma' and 'the unconscious'. Attempts to define those two terms lead to circular descriptions such as 'the unconscious is the part of the mind where repressed traumatic memories are retained' or 'repression is the blocking of traumatic memories'. We are left with a shadowy concept suspended between two others that are no less shadowy.

Concepts whose meaning has shifted over the past century can be found not just in psychiatry and psychology but also in the natural sciences. Until 1967, one second was defined as one 86,400th of an average solar day, but then it became linked to vibrations of the caesium 133 atom. The current definition is a further refinement again, but at least a definition existed, and it was shared by researchers and their journals. Psychology and psychiatry are disciplines lacking central authorities, although the leading figures in these fields – and their professional organisations – compete for primacy. The *Diagnostic and Statistical Manual of Mental Disorders* (DSM), first published in 1952 and now in its fifth edition, represents a sustained effort by the American Psychiatric Association to make binding agreements about terminology and diagnoses. For historians, however, the DSM is a valuable source precisely because it demonstrates the changing theoretical orientations and social relationships that make reaching a wide consensus impossible. When physicists deliberate the definition of a second, they need not take account of what people outside of their field think it should be. Clinical psychology and psychiatry are in a very different position, since the way clients and patients imagine the relationship between trauma, the unconscious and repression is a factor of significance in every form of therapy.

In view of all this, it would be misleading to begin any discussion of repression with a definition, whether established or freshly minted. Definitions are partisan, coloured by the theory that gave rise to them and the era in which they were formulated. They are part of the problem. It is more productive to investigate the scientific and therapeutic practices within which the concept of repression is or has been deployed. The questions then become a good deal more manageable. In which theoretical or experimental contexts is repression to be found? How is it thought to be caused and what are its presumed effects? Is repression damaging or beneficial, and can it be reversed? Attempting to answer questions like these gives us a chance to see repression at work in the wild, in its own habitat.

From the long history of controversy surrounding repression I have chosen three episodes. In 1905 Freud published the case history of 'Dora', a young woman who had entered into analysis with him because of symptoms of hysteria. She had repressed all sorts of things without knowing it, Freud explained, and her analysis was intended to deal with the symptoms by helping her to make those memories conscious again. A hundred years later, 'Dora' has become more than anything else a case study of Freud's beliefs about repression.

The second episode began in America in about 1990 as a controversy concerning 'recovered memories'. At stake was the issue of whether it is possible for someone to be abused as a child, repress memories of it, forget about the abuse completely for 10, 20, 30 years and then 'recover' those memories in therapy. The need to answer that question arose when cases came to court in which recovered memories were presented as evidence.

The third episode began at around the same time, again in America, when psychotherapist Francine Shapiro started using a new technique for dealing with traumatic memories. Her procedure, known as eye movement desensitisation and reprocessing, or EMDR, seems on first acquaintance rather bizarre. The client is asked to call the traumatic memory to mind as vividly as possible and at the same time to follow the therapist's hand or finger as it moves rapidly back and forth. This is thought to remove harmful emotions from the recollection of the trauma, so that it can be stored in memory as a more or less neutral image. A number of studies have shown the effects to be beneficial. In many Western countries, EMDR and cognitive behavioural therapy are recommended as the treatments of choice for trauma-related disorders.

Placing these three episodes, with their widely differing historical backgrounds, side by side serves to show that the special type of forgetting known as repression, which is in fact understood as *not* forgetting, has deep roots in widely diverse constellations of trauma, unconscious processes and ideas about the usefulness or necessity of bringing repressed memories back to the surface.

Dora

For 11 weeks, six days a week, 18-year-old Ida Bauer came to 19 Berggasse to undergo psychoanalysis. The sessions followed a fixed routine. Ida was invited into the consulting room, lay on the couch and started to say whatever came into her head. Freud sat by the head of the couch in his armchair and occasionally made notes.

On the last day of 1900, Ida announced she had had enough. She said she was terminating her analysis with immediate effect. Freud was unpleasantly surprised. He asked when she had reached that decision. Around a fortnight ago, Ida told him. The period of notice to which a maidservant is entitled, thought Freud to himself. He felt the treatment proper had not even really begun.

In the first weeks of the new year, Freud threw himself energetically into working up his notes, although it would take him until the autumn of 1905 to prepare his case study about Ida for publication.[1] It appeared under the title *Fragment of an Analysis of a Case of Hysteria*, 'fragment' not just because the analysis was suddenly broken off but because Freud saw himself as following 'the example of those discoverers whose good fortune it is to bring to the light of day after their long burial the priceless though mutilated relics of antiquity'.[2] Every analysis is to some extent a reconstruction of that which has emerged only partially from the unconscious. Freud gave Ida the name 'Dora' in his case study and it was under that title that the case became famous.

Dora had been referred to Freud by her father, Philipp Bauer, a rich Viennese cloth manufacturer who had been in treatment with Freud as a result of syphilis, having contracted the disease before he was married. Dora was troubled by a stubborn nervous cough and sometimes lost the ability to speak. When a letter was found in her room that contained allusions to suicide, Bauer acted, taking her to see Freud and asking him to 'bring her to reason'.[3]

Dora was 'in the first bloom of youth – a girl of intelligent and engaging looks'.[4] When she told her story, a picture emerged of tangled sexual relationships. Her parents' marriage was not happy. Bauer had infected his wife with syphilis. They had entered into an intimate friendship with a couple by the name of K. Ida spent a lot of time with Mrs K., with whom she discussed her deepest secrets. Mrs K. and her father had begun a love affair, and after a while all those involved accepted the situation. Of her mother Dora said little more than that she suffered from an obsessive cleaning compulsion. There was little affection between them.

The problems started when Mr K., a man later identified as a business agent called Hans Zellenka, began making advances to Dora. He wrote letters to her and gave her presents and flowers. When Dora was 14 he invited her to watch a religious procession from the top floor of his shop, but when she arrived it turned out that all the staff had been sent away and she was alone with him. He lowered the blinds, suddenly pulled her to him and kissed her on the mouth. Dora wriggled free and ran off.

Two years later, the two families spent a holiday together in the Alps. During a walk by a lake, K. made advances again. His wife meant nothing to him, he said. When Dora realised he was hinting at a relationship, she slapped him in the face. As soon as she got home she told her parents everything.

When K. was called to account, events took an unfortunate turn for Dora. He hotly denied everything, saying Dora was sexually obsessed; his wife had told him the girl had asked all kinds of intimate questions about their love life and had devoured Paolo Mantegazza's *Die Physiologie der Liebe* (*The Physiology of Love and Other Writings*). To Dora's dismay, Mrs K. supported her husband. Her parents believed him as well. Her story was dismissed as a young girl's fantasy and Dora gained the impression she had been given to K. by her father, just as K. had given his wife to Bauer. From that moment on, Dora's symptoms worsened. In October 1900 she entered into analysis with Freud.

Dora expected little to come of it. She had obtained no relief at all from consultation with doctors about her throat and she had gradually come to treat all members of the medical profession with barely concealed contempt. During analysis her main concern was to convince Freud that the incident with K had actually taken place. She succeeded. Freud was the first person ever to believe her. He also thought he could cure her of what he saw as 'hysterical symptoms': her nervous cough and her throat trouble. After just two weeks he wrote to his friend Wilhelm Fliess that the case was not particularly difficult, in fact it had 'smoothly opened to the existing collection of picklocks'.⁵ The key was sexuality, of which Freud remarked that no one who disdained it could unlock the door.

The previous year, Freud had published *The Interpretation of Dreams*. Dora's analysis would, he believed, prove the therapeutic value of dream interpretation. The dream, he explained, 'is one of the roads along which consciousness can be reached by the psychical material which, on account of the opposition aroused by its content, has been cut off from consciousness and repressed, and has thus become pathogenic. The dream, in short, is one of the *detours by which repression can be evaded*.'⁶ The italics are Freud's. By interpreting Dora's dreams, he gained an insight into what she had repressed. If he could share that insight with her, the symptoms would disappear. One of Dora's dreams occurred in an identical form three nights in a row:

A house was on fire. My father was standing beside my bed and woke me up. I dressed quickly. Mother wanted to stop and save her jewel-case; but Father said: 'I refuse to let myself and my two children be burnt for the sake of your jewel-case.' We hurried downstairs, and as soon as I was outside I woke up.⁷

As part of a long dialogue with Dora, who was requested to describe the circumstances in which the dream had taken place, Freud presented his interpretation. He asked whether Dora was aware that a jewellery box – *Schmuckkästchen* – was a common euphemism for the female sex organ. Dora replied: 'I knew you would say that'. To which Freud responded: 'That is to say, you knew that it *was* so'.⁸ Indeed, fire was symbolic of the sexual act; the box had to be saved from the nocturnal fire. Not long before, Dora had been given an expensive jewellery box by K. and now,

Freud argued, her feeling – or no, her desire – must be that she should offer him her own 'jewellery box'. 'That is the thought which has to be repressed with so much energy'. 'You are afraid of Mr K.', Freud suggested to her, 'but . . . you are still more afraid of yourself, and of the temptation you feel to yield to him'.[9]

The lock had burst open. Dora had powerful sexual desires. They caused feelings of guilt, so they must be repressed. In her dream Dora was actually pleading with her father to protect her from the temptation to give herself to K.

Dora rejected this interpretation. She seems to have been unhappy with other explanations as well. During one of the sessions she fiddled idly with a cloth purse she wore around her waist. A few days before, Freud had brought up the subject of masturbation. He said that in the past, as a child, she must have masturbated and he had no doubt that the urge to masturbate was still present as a repressed desire. Dora disputed this fiercely, saying she could not recall ever having masturbated. Now Freud watched her playing with her purse as she lay on the couch, pinching it open, slipping her finger inside then back out, closing it again, opening it, finger in and out. He remarked that she was miming her repressed desire, adding with pride that he had learned to watch each person for even the most hidden symbolism, since 'if his lips are silent, he chatters with his finger-tips'.[10] Dora said nothing. From then on she left her purse at home.

A similar interpretation caused Dora's nervous cough to disappear. Freud claimed that Dora had fantasised about the relationship between her father and Mrs K. and imagined them performing fellatio. Those fantasies too were repressed, but in the closed system that is the mind, they had forced their way out by symbolic and somatic routes, specifically the cough and the sore throat. As with the purse, Dora controlled herself in response to this interpretation, barely coughing at all after that.

If you looked closely then, you could see that a huge amount had been repressed. When Dora told Freud of the sudden kiss in the shop, she said she 'could still feel upon the upper part of her body the pressure of Herr K.'s embrace'. Freud claimed she had felt something very different at first:

> I believe that during the man's passionate embrace she felt not merely
> his kiss upon her lips but also the pressure of his erect member against

her body. This perception was revolting to her; it was dismissed from her memory, repressed, and replaced by the innocent sensation of pressure upon her thorax, which in turn derived an excessive intensity from its repressed source.[11]

Dora's fierce reaction to the embrace was, Freud believed, evidence that even at the age of 14 she was 'thoroughly hysterical'. Freud knew K. He was 'still quite young and of prepossessing appearance' and an embrace would have caused a 'genital sensation' in 'a healthy girl'.[12] Now that feelings of revulsion had arisen, it seemed a 'reversal of affect' had taken place – and reversals of this kind are in fact veiled expressions of hysteria.

His Dora study, Freud told Fliess, was 'the most subtle thing I have yet written'.[13] Few have concurred with that verdict. Dora must have felt assailed by all Freud's interpretations, every one of them of a sexual nature and pressed upon her by a man of roughly the same age as her father and Mr K.[14] Freud ascribed to her, among many other things, an unconscious lesbian love for Mrs K., an unconscious love for Mr K. and an oedipal love for her father. And because analysis is intended to rid a patient of hysterical symptoms through insight into repressed feelings, Freud shared all this wisdom with Dora. He felt hurt by her sudden decision to terminate her analysis, but he did have an explanation for it: she must have identified him with Mr K. and her father. The ending of her analysis was revenge for what those two men had done to her. On that point he may well have been right.

Dora returned to Freud on one occasion, 15 months after her abrupt departure. In May 1901, one of the children of the K. couple died. Visiting them to offer her condolences, Dora had an open-hearted conversation with K. and his wife. She said to Mrs K., 'I know you have an affair with my father'[15]. No denial was forthcoming. Mr K. admitted that he had made advances to her beside the lake. The acknowledgment of what had happened cleared the air to some degree. After that last visit, Freud lost track of her.

More than 20 years later, in the autumn of 1922, physician Felix Deutsch was called to examine a patient with a severe headache. Ida Bauer began reeling off a litany of problems in her marriage: her husband had deceived her, her son had abandoned her; all men were egotists. Then she talked of her childhood. Her father had been unfaithful to her mother and she had been sexually assaulted by the husband of her father's mistress.

Deutsch was Freud's personal doctor. He was sympathetic to psychoanalysis and familiar with its classic texts. He made a cautious reference to the case study. Indeed, yes, she was Freud's 'Dora'.[16] She too knew her classics.

Ida's health problems had persisted: coughing fits, migraine, shortness of breath. In the 1920s she worked as a teacher of bridge and became a bridge master, with Mrs K. as her partner. After the *Anschluss*, now a widow, she tried to emigrate to America, finally succeeding in 1939 but only by leaving all her money and possessions behind. Destitute and in increasingly poor health, she lived in New York for a few more years. Ida Bauer died of intestinal cancer in 1945.

Freud's case studies amounted to a demonstration of psychoanalytical methods and they gave a broad public, not just doctors and psychiatrists, a chance to look at his ideas about sexuality, memory and repression. Freud had that lay readership very much in mind. These are accounts that read more like psychological novels than professional case histories. But with each case Freud was also providing a self-portrait. The reader sees him hard at work, captivated by what amounts to the opportunity to present his patients to an audience. He questions them, points to symptoms, suggests diagnoses, thinks aloud, interprets, explains – and he is far less conscious than elsewhere in his work that he too is being observed. His case studies in particular show, as if in a mirror, just what it was that drove Freud. His hidden agendas, blind spots and unspoken assumptions emerge time and again. 'Dora' conceals less than any other case.

The 'Dora' case has been dissected in detail dozens of times.[17] French psychoanalyst Jacques Lacan believed Freud identified with the virile Mr K. and was therefore no less surprised by the sudden end to the analysis than K. was by the slap he received on that walk. In feminist interpretations, too, it is above all Freud who is analysed. He is seen as having fallen prey to the male fantasy that a girl will experience feelings of lust if an older man expresses sexual interest in her. Others point to the heterosexual male bias concealed within Freud's claim that 'a healthy girl' will be aroused when a man makes advances. French writer Hélène Cixous went a step further, refusing to see Dora as a victim. In her play *Portrait de Dora*, Dora is the heroine.[18] By means of hysteria she puts herself at the place from which everyone was trying to dislodge her: the centre of attention.

She disrupts the order of an existence tailored to the wishes of her father and Mr K., and when her father, via Freud, tries to make her see reason, she takes measures of her own, rejecting his interpretations and guarding her secrets, just as she guarded her virginity in her dream. After 11 weeks she leaves him perplexed, just as she left K. beside that Alpine lake.

These are responses that, as it were, tell the old patriarch to go and lie on his own couch. His innermost feelings are interpreted according to the principles he formulated: identification, repression and projection. At the head of the couch sit analysts who have learned from Freud how to listen. A person's choice of words, hesitations, inconsistencies, slips of the tongue, dreams – any or all of these can be clues. No psychiatric theory has drawn so much criticism of its ideology as psychoanalysis, nor is there any psychiatric theory that has offered its critics, of its own volition, so many useful tools.

Memories are ultimately the raw material with which psychoanalysis works, but in them Freud saw above all what was missing. It began with anamnesis. Nothing of what the patient told him could be taken at face value. Even before Freud began writing his case study about Dora, he explained that patients will keep quiet about certain memories out of shame or shyness. Other memories will simply not enter their consciousness during analysis, and what has truly been forgotten will often be replaced by invented memories. The analyst must therefore watch out for, in succession, 'conscious disingenuousness', 'unconscious disingenuousness' and 'a falsification of memory'.[19] But amid all this deception and semi-deception there was one thing to hold onto: what the patient had forgotten – in whichever sense of the word – was at least as significant as what he or she remembered. The gaps could provide clues for a successful reconstruction. Freud did not speak of archaeological relics for nothing.

Freud thought about repression as one angle of a triangle of which the other two are hysteria and trauma. For Dora it was the affront implicit in K.'s advances that turned out to be the repressed trauma, and at the same time she had repressed the fact that she desired him. But things that are repressed do not thereby disappear. A trauma or forbidden desire concealed in the unconscious can cause mischief in the form of somatic phenomena that at first seem inexplicable. Symptoms of hysteria in his patients, Freud wrote, are 'the expression of their most secret and repressed wishes'.[20] Conversely, psychoanalytical interpretations could clarify what had been repressed and so end the memory loss. Removing the symptoms by turning unconscious thoughts into conscious thoughts ultimately amounted to doing away with memory disorders. One could hardly expect the patient's approval during that process; in fact resistance and opposition were proof that the analyst was on the right track. Dora was no exception. She responded to Freud's interpretations of her fiddling with her purse, her nervous cough and the pressure on her upper body that she could still feel when she remembered K.'s embrace with either silence or protest, but Freud was untroubled by her denials. 'The "No" uttered by a patient after a repressed thought has been presented to his conscious perception for the first time does no more than register the existence of a repression and its severity; it acts, as it were, as a gauge of the repression's strength.'[21] A good analyst must possess a certain imperturbability.

In classic psychoanalysis patients relinquish command of their own minds, handing it over to the analyst who, because of his or her expert knowledge of the unconscious and how repressed material within it can be drawn out, knows the patients better than they know themselves. The analyst commands a symbolic language, can interpret dreams, understands the origins of slips of the tongue. Even if the patient has forgotten something, the analyst can guess from the shape of the hole it has left what the missing element must once have looked like. All these interpretations were just so many hypotheses, even Freud acknowledged that. They needed to be checked – but against what? Not against the patient's own verdict. Resistance to an interpretation did not prove the analyst wrong, so agreement could not be accepted as evidence of its validity. If Dora's 'no' could be explained as a 'yes', then a 'yes' no longer carried any weight.

Freud's theories would now be considered unverifiable, but that was not his intention. To Freud, the disappearance of the hysterical ailment after an interpretation was shared with the patient indicated that the interpretation was correct. He must have leaned back satisfied in his chair when Dora's nervous cough stopped after he outlined to her the repressed fantasy that had caused it. But this form of confirmation leaves matters unresolved. If a physical complaint disappears after an interpretation that the analyst experiences as successful, there is still no evidence that it has disappeared because of the explanation, whether in Dora's case or in anyone else's. Conversely, the persistence of an ailment does not necessarily mean that the explanation of its origins was wrong.

To these doubts about the verification of psychoanalytical interpretations we can add uncertainty about the precise circumstances of the repression. Freud was not the discoverer of repression, nor did he invent the term. His biographer Ernest Jones has pointed to passages by philosopher Johann Friedrich Herbart from 1824 that describe *Verdrängung* (repression) as the exclusion from consciousness of thoughts that are in conflict with ideas already present in it.[22] Freud introduced a specific meaning, although over the course of his long career his definition was not always precisely the same. In an article written in 1915, called 'Die Verdrängung', he did his best to present the concept as relatively uncomplicated. The essence of repression, Freud wrote, in italics, '*lies simply in turning something away, and keeping it at a distance, from the conscious*'.[23] Because repressed material needs to go somewhere, the unconscious and repression are defined in terms of each other: without the unconscious, a trauma or forbidden desire would be unable to leave the conscious mind. No doubt in the hope of clarifying this, Freud used a whole series of metaphors for repression. In that same article he writes that it is possible to imagine repression as getting an unwanted guest to leave your sitting room. You might even try to stop him from coming back in by putting a guard at the door. Elsewhere Freud described repression as 'banishing', 'intentional forgetting', 'splitting off', 'dissociation', 'suppression', 'fending off', 'inhibition of thought', 'avoidance of thought', 'attention-withholding' and 'debarring'. The 'guard' at the door to the room appears in other metaphors as a 'censor'.[24] Freud cannot be reproached for using metaphors, but their diversity is such that they each prompt a slightly different range of associations. With 'dissociation' and 'splitting off' it seems that access to the conscious mind has gone and there is no way back for the repressed material. A 'guard', by contrast, suggests that the conscious mind needs to be protected against continual efforts by the unwanted guest to re-enter the sitting room, while a 'censor' needs to stay alert to avoid being circumvented.

Debates about the most appropriate definition of repression continue to this day, although they have gradually shifted from differences of opinion between practising psychoanalysts to controversies argued over by historians about the exegesis of Freud's conceptual apparatus. At stake are questions about the exclusive or otherwise connection with sexuality, the interpretation of the symbolic language by means of which repressed material tries to get past the censor, and the finer points of the difference between dissociation and repression. The most radical question that could be asked about repression arose at a much later date: does it exist at all?

Recovered memories

'It must be around now that the term "repression" celebrates its centenary,' wrote legal psychologists Hans Crombag and Peter van Koppen in 1994, with a feeling for the historic moment.[25] It is the opening sentence of an article in which the authors ask a question that approaches the ongoing debate about repression from a completely new angle. The questions that had been asked for quite some time already were: does repression really exist? Is it true that painful traumatic events can be driven out of the consciousness? Do they nevertheless continue to influence our acts and experiences from the unconscious? Can memories, through repression, end up in a 'split off' part of the consciousness? Can a therapist, using special techniques such as hypnosis or dream analysis, retrieve 'forgotten memories'? Memory researchers had given a wide range of answers to each of these questions. For some 20 years, the controversy had taken the form of trench warfare.

Crombag and Van Koppen asked what at first sight appears to be an indirectly related question. They wanted to know whether or not people *believe* that repression exists. Their method of finding an answer seems rather simplistic. They used a questionnaire. This approach was inspired by what might be thought of as an application of the Thomas theorem: 'If men define situations as real, they are real in their consequences.'[26] Even if repression did not exist, Crombag and Van Koppen reasoned, the conviction that it does exist would still influence the way we deal with situations involving presumed repression. They soon got down to work.

Suppose a woman makes an accusation, after coming to believe through therapy that she was abused in early childhood. She had forgotten about the abuse for a long time, it was repressed, but now the forgotten memories have been 'recovered' and she wants to hold the perpetrator to account. If the public prosecutor decides to pursue the case, a complicated situation arises. The suspect denies the allegation and there are no witnesses. The judge will have to decide whether the recovered memories can be accepted as evidence, and may call in an expert witness. At this point the situation becomes even more complicated. If the judge invites memory researchers such as Harald Merckelbach or Ineke Wessel of Maastricht University, they will explain that up to now no one has ever managed to demonstrate anything resembling 'repression' under controlled conditions in a laboratory.[27] But if the judge instead decides to call on Bernardine Ensink, of the same university, she will testify that her research shows that of women seriously abused in childhood, one in three forgets the abuse for a time, so 'recovered' does not necessarily mean the memory is untrue.[28] Confronted with expert but conflicting opinions, the judge will have to rely on his or her own pre-existing beliefs. So it is important to know to what degree judges – and lawyers, prosecutors and other judicial functionaries – *believe* that repression exists.

In their questionnaire, Crombag and Van Koppen pose two questions that require yes or no answers:

Do you believe that 'repression' (the forgetting of traumatic events over a long period) occurs?
Do you think it is possible that you have yourself repressed the memory of a traumatic event?[29]

One group of respondents was made up of 134 students and staff from Maastricht University's Law Faculty, 'the legal group'. A second group of the same size, 'the psychology group', was composed of psychologists, remedial educationalists, paediatricians and other care workers who took part in a congress on sexual abuse of young people. Of the legal group, 87 per cent said they believed that repression occurs. The figure was higher still for the psychology group: 95 per cent. Even among their colleagues, therefore, or at least these particular colleagues, the belief held by Merckelbach and Wessel is very much a minority view. But the real surprise lay in the answers to the second question. Only 56 per cent of the legal group and 47 per cent of the psychology group thought they themselves might have repressed something. This is a curious result. Roughly half of respondents seemed to believe that repression was something other people did and that it was unlikely to have happened to them. This puts into perspective the overwhelming 'yes' to the question of whether repression exists, but around half of those asked believed in repression as a universal quality of human memory. In a later study that looked at the views of psychotherapists, Merckelbach and Wessel ascertained that 96 per cent of them were convinced repression occurs and 84 per cent that it causes psychological problems.[30]

Evidence, not of repression but of belief in repression, also emerges from actual court cases. In 1995, memory psychologist Willem Albert Wagenaar appeared as an expert witness in a civil case in which a woman was demanding 50,000 guilders in damages from her brother for a rape she believed had taken place 31 years before.[31] She was four years old at the time, her brother eight years older. Wagenaar argued that both parties could find support for their views about the authenticity of 'recovered memories' from this court case. One side would see it as proof that memories can be inaccessible for decades and then called back through therapeutic intervention. The other would see in the same story proof that such 'memories' were fabricated. Both parties engaged expert witnesses to give evidence in court. This was precisely the scenario outlined by Crombag and Van Koppen, in which judges are thrown back on their own beliefs in choosing which of the conflicting explanations is right. After the verdict, one of the two parties involved can claim the case as support for its theoretical stance. Wagenaar concluded that this produced a disastrous form of circularity, in which the verdict rendered support for the theory that led to the verdict. It was a clear example of the Thomas Theorem: beliefs have real consequences.

Crombag and Van Koppen described repression as 'the involuntary and abrupt banishing from the autobiographical memory of a traumatic event, with the result that the memory of it cannot be made conscious again for a long time'.[32] It is a definition that attempts to encompass the associations attached to 'repression' today, but it also underlines a significant change since Freud first described repression a hundred years ago, in that it narrows down the cause of repression to trauma alone. Freud believed that forbidden desires and guilty feelings might also be repressed. The association with hysteria, which to Freud was both a cause and an effect of repression, has been lost entirely over the past hundred years. The examples given by Crombag and Van Koppen, which were intended to explain why it is sensible to investigate what people destined to become tomorrow's lawyers and judges think about the concept of repression, reflect with great precision the time in which their article was written. In the mid-1990s the controversy about 'recovered memories' was at its height. In professional journals and in courtrooms, fierce conflicts arose over the issue of whether traumatic events – which in fact generally meant sexual abuse – really could be excluded from the memory for so long that they seemed forgotten. That conflict has died down again of late. A study group set up in the Netherlands in 1994 by parents accused of abuse was dissolved in 2004 for lack of new cases, but an internet resource about 'false memories' still offers hundreds of links to websites that demonstrate the fierceness and intensity of a battle that went on for more than 10 years about the relationship between memory, trauma and forgetting.[33] The arguments exchanged there can be of help if we prefer not to leave completely unresolved the question of whether or not repression truly exists.

The arena of trauma and forgetting

In her early thirties, Laura Pasley sought help. Since the age of 10 she had suffered from the eating disorder bulimia nervosa. She was overweight, had broken off her education and felt insecure and ugly. On the advice of her church minister she consulted a psychotherapist, Steve. During their very first session, Steve asked Laura whether she had ever been sexually abused. She confirmed that she had. When she was nine, a boy at the swimming pool suddenly wriggled a finger inside her. Out of embarrassment she had never told anyone. Steve said that was not what he meant. It seemed she had always remembered the event at the swimming pool. He was looking for something deeper, something that would have to be dug up from the depths of her memory. Eating disorders, he explained, always pointed to serious abuse. Together they must go in search of the hidden trauma.

In the sessions that followed, Laura sat with her eyes closed and listened to Steve as he worked on her. She could not understand much of what he said, but that was not a problem, Steve insisted, since he was talking directly to her unconscious. The frequency of the sessions increased. Her insurance company refused to continue paying for her treatment, so Laura went without a car and got into debt. One day she was vacuuming when she suddenly saw the image of a little boy of about three trying to suffocate a baby with a pillow. In the next session Steve tried to convince her that her brother had tried to kill her. Under hypnosis she saw herself sitting in the bath as a child and her mother putting her fingernails into her vagina. Later she had flashbacks of her mother abusing her with a coat hanger. As the therapy went on, her condition worsened. At one point she had to be admitted to hospital after taking an overdose.

Then group therapy began. With Laura and 10 or so other women, Steve arranged meetings that lasted for hours, with hypnosis, flashbacks and role-playing. When Laura's turn came, he shouted at her endlessly, saying she was keeping quiet about the worst things. One of the women described a memory of satanic rituals, which set off a fresh round of stories about torture and rape. Eventually Laura began to 'see' scenes of gang rape and sex with animals. She was admitted to hospital after another overdose, developed insomnia, still had bulimia and had gained almost another 50 kilos in weight. After four years in therapy she was in a worse state than ever. When Steve told her she was not trying hard enough, something snapped. She decided to stop seeing him.

The real turnaround came two years later, when she read an article about false memory syndrome. It included an interview with an elderly couple accused of satanic abuse by their daughter, who happened to have been one of the women in Laura's therapy group. Laura got in touch with them. She found it impossible to reconcile the terrible stories she had heard about them in the group with her personal impression of this friendly couple. Slowly she began to lose faith in her own accusations and flashbacks. She says it was as if a light went on in her head. As soon as she realised what had happened to her, she decided to sue her therapist. Steve was eager to keep the case out of court and proposed a settlement, which she accepted. Laura felt that her life was now in her own hands again. The bulimia ceased.

The story of Laura Pasley is one of many vignettes in *Victims of Memory* by Mark Pendergrast, himself a father accused of incest.[34] Pasley was one of the first retractors; since then, more and more people have come to believe they were misled by their therapists, and many have successfully taken legal action. Although there are hundreds of them, their numbers are negligible compared to the tens of thousands of women who, during therapy, have retrieved 'memories' of abuse taking place long ago and confronted their fathers, brothers, uncles and others, often going on to make formal accusations.

Pasley's case is not representative in every sense. Most of the therapists treating women with problems like hers were women. The accused was almost always a man, usually a member of the family. But in other respects Pasley's story is a distillation of thousands of others: a woman with psychological problems enters therapy; the therapist suggests a background of sexual abuse; 'forgotten memories' are brought to light by hypnosis, dream interpretation or regression therapy; the woman becomes convinced she has been abused and decides to confront the perpetrators, if they are still alive, with her accusations. The result is almost irreparable damage to family relationships.

A case like Pasley's makes clear that it is virtually impossible to tell such stories in neutral, unbiased terms, which in turn indicates the polarised character of the debate about 'recovered memories'. The word 'recovered' suggests both salvage and cure, and implies that it is indeed possible to recall things that were forgotten for many years. Those who doubt this use the terms 'pseudo-memories' or 'false memories'. The interest group set up in the United States in 1992 by falsely accused parents resolutely opted for the name False Memory Syndrome Foundation. It is unfortunate that there is still no neutral term. A number of writers of monographs have made an attempt at impartiality by choosing titles that include both.[35]

Many different academic fields, organisations and disciplines have become involved in the debate: psychiatry, clinical psychology, memory studies and medicine, to name only the most obvious among them. Every case of recovered memories, however intimate and personal in origin, has sent ripples through a whole web of social institutions, including insurance companies, employers' organisations, hospitals, mental health services, the legal profession, child protection services, state-financed welfare organisations and victim support services.

There is no disagreement about the origin of the 'recovered memories' movement. It dates back to the publication in 1988 of *The Courage to Heal* by Ellen Bass and Laura Davis, who were active as therapists in a grass-roots movement of women who had suffered sexual abuse.[36] They presented a checklist for women wondering whether they had been abused as children, with questions such as:

Do you feel powerless, like a victim?
Do you feel different from other people?
Do you have trouble feeling motivated?
Are you afraid to succeed?
Do you often feel confused?

A 'yes' to one or more of these questions, they wrote, addressing their readers directly, is an indication of traumatic events in your youth, even if you do not currently have any memory of them. Often the knowledge that you were abused begins with no more than a vague suspicion, an inner voice. Listen to it. They had never come upon anyone with a vague suspicion of this kind who later found out she had not been abused after all. No suspicion without confirmation. In bringing back forgotten memories, hypnosis was frequently helpful, but the severed connection could also be restored through creative therapy, regression therapy, dream analysis and body-orientated therapy. Treatment often culminated in a confrontation, which meant seeking out the perpetrators and telling them of the damage they had done.

In less than two years, America became the scene of memory wars – in the plural, because there were many different battlefields. The internet was one. On thousands of websites launched by therapy groups, self-help groups, retractors, workshops and damages claims assessors, virtual battles raged. Courtrooms soon became the stage for a battle of experts. In scientific circles the number of books and articles about memory, trauma and repression increased exponentially. How was this explosion to be explained? If *The Courage to Heal* was the spark, where had the powder keg come from?

The answer given by the 'recovered memories' movement was simple: sexual abuse was far more common than previously thought, it mostly affected women, and therapy by specialists offered a safe environment in which memories of abuse could be 'dug up'. Other women were inspired by all this to seek help, and growth was then self-reinforcing. But if sexual abuse happened everywhere, why did the recovered memories movement have such a selective geographical distribution? What kind of social factors were behind this particular pattern?

Elaine Showalter, professor of English literature at Princeton, has tried to look at the memory wars with a degree of historical detachment.[37] Her earlier books included *The Female Malady*, a study of the history of hysteria as a psychiatric diagnosis.[38] She placed the rapid rise of the 'recovered memories' movement in that same category, seeing the therapies that came into being around it as examples of ways of legitimising what were actually social and mental problems, contemporary manifestations of what used to be called hysteria in women and neurasthenia in men. An important aspect of her argument concerns the narrative character of modern forms of hysteria. Stories about recovered memories – and indeed about Gulf War syndrome or multiple-personality disorder – can spread rapidly via the internet, newspapers and other media, like viruses in an epidemic. Books, films and documentaries provide prototypical stories about recovered memories. People who have never even heard of recovered memories become familiar with the psychological complaints they can cause and wonder whether their own disorders are the result of events they have repressed. The mere fact that therapists travelling together on an educational trip to America happen to learn about therapies for recovered memories might mean that a comparable movement arises in their own country. The stories people then tell and the clues therapists then look for come to resemble each other closely. Here too a dangerous kind of circularity arises; the remarkable similarities between all those stories can create the impression that the recovered memories related in them are authentic.

The issue of recovered memories split the therapeutic community. The reliability of checklists like the one given by Bass and Davis was questioned from the outset, and far from all therapists believed traumatic memories could be buried or thought it would be therapeutically valuable to try to recover them. The women's movement was divided as well. Assistance for women who had been abused was deeply rooted in feminism and for a long time it faced an unwillingness to accept the seriousness and extent of abuse. Gloria Steinem was among those who supported the recovered memories movement, but there were also feminists who felt that legal action based on pseudo-memories was having a damaging effect on cases dealing with real abuse.

The sciences of memory became a battleground too. American psychologist David Holmes wrote in 1990 that back in 1974 he had concluded there was no reliable evidence at all for the existence of repression and that since then nothing had been published to change his mind.[39]

Experiments in the 1930s seemed to show that unpleasant events were recalled in less detail than pleasant events, but in later studies it turned out there was an underlying factor that determined how well events were remembered, namely the intensity of the emotions that accompanied them. In this instance at least, the pleasant events were experienced more intensely.[40] Holmes also pointed to more recent research that seemed to show that we take longer to recognise words that evoke stress than neutral words, as if at a sensory level we repress certain words to protect ourselves. Later it transpired that the 'stress words' used in the experiment were less common than the neutral words, which explained the difference.[41] Other attempts to find proof of repression in laboratory conditions used slides of simulated accidents.[42] Again no repression was found.

What these experiments show above all is that research into trauma and repression does not lend itself to laboratory investigation. Ensink wondered, with good reason, just how traumatic slides of accidents could be for someone who regularly watches television.[43] And in a polemical reaction to an article by Merckelbach and Wessel about recovered memories, Onno van der Hart wrote with some irritation that 'phenomena don't exist only if they have been replicated in the laboratory'.[44] Ethics sets boundaries to the type of stimuli test participants can be subjected to in an experiment, and even the most indulgent ethics board draws the line roughly at the level where an experiment turns slightly nasty. Experiments certainly never come close to inflicting real trauma.

As far as many clinicians and therapists are concerned, there is no need to search in laboratories for repression; they encounter it every day in their practices. In their consulting rooms they see people seeking help after traumatic events and it often takes a great deal of effort to gain access to memories of what happened. Sometimes it is not just a matter of a single event. The memory loss may be far broader, covering long-term abuse, torture or time spent in a concentration camp. 'All these convergent studies,' Van der Hart writes, 'confirm the existence of total amnesia for traumatic events'.[45] He himself points out, however, that they are clinical studies, and that from the perspective of experimental psychology there might be all kinds of objections to be made. In the controversy about repression, this is indeed part of the problem. Generally speaking, clinicians and experimental psychologists deploy different styles of methodology. Clinicians often report their findings in case studies, a form that experimental psychologists do not regard particularly highly. Questions arise as to how representative a single case is, given the impossibility of replication and the fact that opportunities for anyone but the therapist-researcher concerned to check the findings are limited. It is often argued that research of this kind is not real science. Experimental psychologists favour studies involving larger numbers of test participants and carefully controlled conditions, but it is hard to counter the reproach that they are not looking at real traumas. In the debate about recovered memories, a familiar shift takes place: differences of opinion about facts turn into differences of opinion about what counts as a fact. The controversy moves to the level of criteria, definitions and methods.

The only place where real science can come upon real traumas is where individual or collective disasters take place: earthquakes, plane crashes, serious traffic accidents, fires, kidnappings, robberies or rape. These are loosely referred to as experiments of nature and they put researchers in a position to observe as far as possible the responses of the memory. What can we learn from traumatic events about repression and forgetting?

No support has been found for the theory that shocking events can lead to 'dissociation', such that memories are split off, as it were, and therefore become hard to access. A study of 115 police officers, each of whom had been involved in major shooting incidents, investigated whether their memories of those events had indeed been 'repressed'.[46] That turned out not to be the case. In fact they tended to find themselves reliving the incidents and to be troubled by flashbacks, phenomena that had already been found among Vietnam veterans and soldiers returning from the Gulf War. Survivors of Auschwitz said they had not experienced anything that could be described as dissociation; their memories did not seem repressed, in fact if anything they crowded in upon them, at unpredictable moments and with unsettling effects.[47] This did not mean that such memories (where it was possible to check) returned to consciousness as exact replicas – shifts and distortions can take place in traumatic memories as in any other memories – but they were not repressed or forgotten.

In research that concentrated specifically on children – of relevance to the controversy about recovered memories – roughly the same reaction to trauma was observed. Sixteen children aged between five and ten who had witnessed the attempted murder of one of their parents retained extremely vivid memories of that event, which came back time and again, causing them to relive the experience.[48] Similarly, 10 children aged between five and 17 who had witnessed their mother's rape said that images of the crime returned to them regularly.[49]

Research into recovered memories has often begun with whatever could be reconstructed out of the scraps of memory that did remain, which are used as clues to what actually happened. The studies just mentioned begin at the other end; the troubling or traumatising event is well documented and from there the researchers investigate how it has been remembered or forgotten.[50] The outcomes converge towards the conclusion that there is a degree of forgetting, so that details disappear from the memory and discrepancies gradually creep in, but there is no repression or splitting off. What traumas seem to demand of memory is their recurrence rather than their repression.

Trauma and eye movements

At the age of 24, firefighter Marita went out with her team to deal with a blaze in an old church. Her commander ran into a narrow street about 10 metres ahead of her and at that moment a wall fell. He could not get out of the way in time and was killed instantly. Marita saw it happen. After the incident she felt guilty that the commander, a family man, had died while she who was childless remained alive. Too fearful to continue on active duty, she found herself confined to a desk job, and five years later, still plagued by nightmares and detailed memories of her colleague's death, she went to see a psychotherapist.

Marita's is the first of 25 case histories to be found in the *Casusboek EMDR*, published in the Netherlands in 2009.[51] It gives a clear idea of the procedure used by client and therapist during a course of eye movement desensitisation and reprocessing (EMDR). In their first session, the therapist asks about the worst memories Marita associates with the accident. She names three, and the therapist proposes treating the first of them, namely the image of the falling wall and the feelings of sadness and powerlessness that went with it. When Marita, at the therapist's request, calls that image to mind as vividly as possible, she becomes terribly distressed. The therapist asks her to indicate on a scale of 0 to 10 just how bad she feels and Marita answers 9 (in EMDR jargon: SUD 9, or 9 Subjective

Units of Distress). She puts on headphones, and while clicks are sounded in her ears, alternating between left and right, she says whatever comes into her mind about how the memory makes her feel and what bodily sensations it evokes. From time to time the therapist interrupts by posing a question and then asks her to concentrate on the recollected image again. Gradually the SUD goes down to 7 ('seems as if I'm breathing quite differently'), then 5 ('feel that I'm looking at the photo of someone else altogether'), then 4 ('nothing, I feel neutral') and 0 ('I can deal with looking at the picture now').[52] A week later she says she has been trying to recall the image of the falling wall but that it has become more vague, and she feels less emotional when doing so. In the sessions that follow, other painful memories are dealt with. Four sessions prove sufficient.

EMDR is a technique in search of a theory. Even therapists who use it every day have no idea why it works. Despite the unambiguous reference to eye movements in the name, there is now a firm consensus that the clicks used in Marita's case, for example, can work just as well. Uncertainty also surrounds the other elements of the name, 'desensitisation' and 'reprocessing': no one really knows what they contribute to the therapeutic effect.

EMDR was first introduced in 1989 by Californian psychotherapist Francine Shapiro.[53] She had been walking in a park when she found herself thinking back to an unpleasant experience and noticed that her eyes were moving rapidly back and forth as she did so. Afterwards it seemed as if those memories had lost their distressing emotional charge. She decided to try it as a technique in the treatment of people who were plagued by traumatic memories. Her 1989 article was an account of her doctoral research, in which she treated 22 patients suffering from post-traumatic stress disorder with EMDR. All were cured.

Post-traumatic stress disorder (PTSD) was first included in the third edition of the DSM, in 1980, and it has been there ever since, with a few small adjustments. The current diagnostic criteria specify that the sufferer is troubled by nightmares or flashbacks and tries as far as possible to avoid stimuli associated with the trauma. Patients also tend to be excessively vigilant and sensitive, a combination known as hyperarousal, which can lead to problems in sleeping and concentrating. The use of EMDR increased rapidly against the background of an equally rapid increase in the number of people diagnosed with PTSD.

There are major differences between the technique as it was first formulated and the way it is applied today. The R in EMDR was added later, in 1991. Shapiro was initially convinced that the eye movements helped to accelerate desensitisation, a phenomenon familiar from traditional treatments for trauma and phobias that involve repeated exposure to the feared stimulus, either in actual fact ('in vivo') or in the imagination ('imaging'), as a way of gradually reducing the anxiety. Later she came to believe that memories of traumatic events were stored away in neural networks as dysfunctional information and that this started off a natural process that led to adjustment, except that occasionally it became stuck or took too long. Rapid eye movements could speed up reprocessing.

Another difference is that EMDR has now become institutionally embedded. In her early publications, Shapiro wrote that the technique could be applied by anyone who took the trouble to read her 1989 article and follow the instructions contained in it. The technique was so simple that no special expertise was required. A year later she came to regret this, it seems, since in 1990 she set up the EMDR Institute Inc., which provided a two-day training course leading to a diploma in EMDR therapy. Before another year was out, the technique had become so complicated that a level II diploma was required to qualify a person to use EMDR. Those who took the course had to sign a declaration saying they would not teach it to others. After the publication of her own handbook, Shapiro dropped that restriction.[54] There are now EMDR institutes outside America as well. In the UK, training and accreditation is in the hands of EMDR UK & Ireland Association. Only after taking courses recognised by the Association can a member apply to be registered as an 'EMDR Europe practitioner'. There are currently over 400 British therapists attached to the Association.

The therapy itself has changed too, partly as a result of attempts to explain why it works. Shapiro's own explanation was never really taken seriously. Just where those 'dysfunctional networks' were located and how eye movements could facilitate 'reprocessing' remained unclear. Some claimed that the movement of the eyes replicated the 'rapid eye movements' seen during dreaming and that REM sleep consolidated memories of daytime or, conversely, removed them from the memory (see chapter 2). Sleep researcher Robert Stickgold suggested that trauma caused deprivation of REM sleep, so that the processing of memories stagnated. Perhaps EMDR created a condition similar to REM sleep in which memories could be processed.[55] But experiments showed that moving the eyes up and down was just as effective, as for that matter was staring straight ahead, or even keeping the eyes closed. Moreover, the eyes move far more quickly during REM sleep than the windscreen-wiper speed used in EMDR. It was soon discovered that the eye movements could be replaced by clicks in headphones or taps to the hand, as long as these were administered on the two sides of the body alternately.

One explanation that, according to the *Casusboek EMDR*, 'is often used when dealing with clients', attributes the effectiveness of the technique to improved communication between the cerebral hemispheres. As the editors put it: 'Because a larger area of the brain is activated and because communication between left (reasoning) and right (emotion) is improved, the processing of the traumatic event can take place more quickly and effectively.'[56] They go on to say that this theory 'is probably not tenable in the long run' since vertical eye movements, which do not lead to better communication between left and right, are just as effective.[57]

A rather more convincing explanation suggests that the limited capacity of the working memory is responsible for the therapeutic effect. If the unpleasant event is 'loaded' into the working memory and that memory is simultaneously engaged in processing clicks, taps or a waving finger, the traumatic experience cannot be brought to mind so vividly and in such detail. It will therefore not be stored away so vividly in the long-term memory when the session is over. Research along these lines indicates that counting backwards from 1,000 in steps of 7 or even 'mindful breathing' works just as well as a means of distraction – which disposed of the last remnants of the bilateral explanation.[58] One of the implications of the working memory hypothesis is that clients who are good at multitasking will benefit less from EMDR, which does indeed seem to be the case.[59]

'The theories described thus far,' the *Casusboek EMDR* concludes, 'do not generally contradict each other.'[60] It is a surprising conclusion, since the summary actually shows that the effectiveness of EMDR is associated with the most diverse therapeutic tasks. The horizontal eye movements that were at first essential for 'reprocessing' and later for improved communication between the cerebral hemispheres could be replaced by vertical eye movements or even by no eye movements at all, while the clicks left and right were no more effective than sums, which have no special effect on the left brain (reason) or the right brain (emotions). The information that ought to be 'often used when dealing with clients' is that nobody has any idea why EMDR works.

So does it work? Various answers are possible. There can be no doubting that many people have been helped by EMDR, sometimes after a range of other therapies brought them no relief. Examples of successful treatments can be found in EMDR casebooks and manuals. As far as the individual client is concerned, no further research is needed as long as treatment is helpful, but effect studies compare groups of clients with similar symptoms who undergo different treatments (or remain on the waiting list) and then try to determine the degree to which each group has been helped. Camille DeBell and R. Deniece Jones compared seven studies looking at the effectiveness of EMDR and concluded that in four of the seven, the treatment achieved better results than the control conditions of no treatment, treatment without eye movements or asking patients to talk about their traumatic memories.[61] In the remaining three studies, EMDR proved as effective as relaxation therapy and 'imaging'. In a much larger meta-analysis of 61 studies concerning the effectiveness of treatments for patients with PTSD, psychotherapy was shown to be better than medication, and of all the various psychotherapies, behavioural therapy and EMDR were the most effective.[62] In 2007, a decidedly mainstream periodical, the British Journal of Psychiatry, came to the conclusion that these two types of therapy should be accepted as the recommended treatments.[63]

Twenty years after its introduction, EMDR has come a long way from the time when it was purely a treatment for PTSD. Among those on whom it has been used successfully are, according to the Casusboek EMDR, 'a four-year-old girl who refused to go to sleep', 'a borderline client with serious PTSD judged to be criminally insane', a woman with 'chronic phantom pain for the past seventeen years', a boy 'with swallowing anxiety after the death of his grandmother', someone suffering from 'a failed cure for smoking' and a woman with 'obesity and relationship problems'. Elsewhere in the extensive literature we read that EMDR has been effective against a fear of public speaking, a fear of flying, compulsive disorders, panic attacks, depression, stagnated grief and multiple personality disorder. What all these applications have in common, the reports say, is that based on the symptom or disorder it is possible to isolate a specific memory image in which the emotional impact is concentrated. When that emotional burden is removed, the pathology caused by the image disappears.

The literature on EMDR emphasises that it is not a 'technique of forgetting'. The traumatic memory is not erased but returned to storage without the negative emotions that were attached to it. What goes back into the memory is no longer something that will trouble the client in the form of flashbacks or nightmares. The traumatic event itself is not forgotten. But neither is it unforgotten.

The metaphors used by clients featured in the *Casusboek EMDR* to describe their memories after treatment have more to do with forgetting than with remembering: 'the image I always had on my retina seems simply to have disappeared'; 'a painful memory has been cleared away'; 'each time a bit of that horrible photo goes'. One therapist says that in his client the memories 'slowly faded, as it were. He can remember less and less about those situations and no longer re-experiences them'.[64] Disappear, clear away, fade – this is the language of forgetting. It seems that for the clients themselves the traumatic event is at least partly forgotten. That appraisal is correct. The autobiographical memory does not simply conserve raw data. Each recollection has an emotional significance, associations that can revive it, things that add up to what we might call the colour or sentimental value of a memory. If all these elements are removed by EMDR treatment, we cannot claim that the troublesome recollection is not forgotten, since in its original form it has indeed been forgotten, if only in the sense that it is no longer accessible. To say that EMDR is not a technique of forgetting is to fail to appreciate precisely those elements of a memory for which clinical psychologists have always shown more understanding than anyone else.

Occasionally therapists themselves will admit, if only implicitly, that EMDR has the effect of erasing memories. One example is the case of a 15-year-old autistic girl called Gea.[65] At the urging of two friends she stole a pair of earrings. When the sales assistant caught her, Gea panicked and stabbed her with a pair of scissors, seriously injuring her. Gea was taken to a detention centre and from there to a psychiatric ward. She had regular nightmares and flashbacks of the woman bleeding profusely. PTSD was diagnosed and EMDR treatment was recommended for the relief of her symptoms.

The ensuing discussion was interesting. Should Gea's trauma in fact be treated at all? After all, her symptoms 'might deter her from committing another crime and always remind her of her dreadful act, so that she would always be on her guard. Is that such a bad thing?'[66] Since Gea exhibited insight into what she had done and regretted it terribly, the decision was made to try to relieve her of the traumatic memories. Treatment had a beneficial effect on her behaviour. In this specific case the decision to offer treatment seems right. But what about a rapist tormented by memories of his terrified victim? Or a robber suffering nightmares in which he sees the face of the person who had the barrel of a gun put to his head? Traumas are not dysfunctional by definition and treatment might remove their signalling function. That ethical question need not be resolved here, but the fact that we come upon a moral dilemma is further evidence that we cannot simply say that EMDR leaves 'the memory itself' intact.

What people believe

A century later it is almost impossible to read Freud's 'Dora' without a shake of the head. The report is blatantly sexist and it puts a positive gloss on the liberties taken by an adult man with a girl of 14. Freud both played down the repeated sexual advances and bombarded Dora with interpretations she must have experienced as sexually intimidating. It is no accident that this case history has drawn more criticism than any other from feminist historians. The mere fact that Dora was regarded as ill seems remarkable today.

The irony is that help for abused women first took off within the feminist movement, but therapeutic insights about recovered memories resemble psychoanalysis more than anything else. For a start they share its metaphors. The abuse suffered by women when they were children is a hidden trauma that needs to be freed from what Freud called its 'long burial'. This is a laborious process, and the techniques deployed to achieve it have their origins in psychoanalysis: hypnosis, regression to early childhood, the analysis of dreams. What comes to the surface at the start of therapy is no more than a collection of 'mutilated remnants', and a great deal of work and inventiveness is needed to rebuild, out of all those shards and fragments, the memories that were there before they were repressed.

As in psychoanalysis, the patient has no authority at all. The fact that Laura Pasley could not remember any serious sexual abuse taking place in her childhood was interpreted by her therapist as evidence that she had repressed the memory. It was the same story with thousands of other women. The absence of memories pointed to 'denial' and the more strongly the client denied having been abused, the more probable it seemed to the therapist that further digging would produce results. This meant that the therapist's suspicions could not be measured against the woman's own judgement. That authority had been taken from her. She found herself in the same position in relation to the therapist as Dora did when she said she could not recall ever having masturbated: her 'no' was actually a 'yes' – you only had to watch her fingers. Something else the therapists of recovered memories have in common with psychoanalysts is their belief that memories can cause harm by the simple fact that they are repressed. Their temporary invisibility in the unconscious causes problems that are all too obvious, whether eating disorders like Laura's bulimia or the sore throat and coughing that afflicted Dora. Their expression is somatic and symbolic, and it needs to be interpreted by a therapist, since the patient cannot be expected to know the language of the unconscious.

The most important similarity, however, concerns that which both movements regard as the effective component of the therapy. Freud believed that the healing effect of psychoanalysis lay in the recovery of the memory, in other words in resolving the memory disorder. By removing or attenuating the burdensome emotions attached to the repressed material, he tried to make the memories return to the conscious mind where they could gradually be whittled away. This natural erosion by time worked only on memories that had been brought back into view. In the unconscious they remained intact and dangerous. The same went for women with repressed memories of abuse. They had a chance of recovery only if they could face up to the trauma and fill that suspect void in memory, with the help of a therapist. The route to healing led from unconscious to conscious, from hidden to open, from fragmentary to complete.

It is precisely here that the contrast with EMDR is at its most acute. People suffering from PTSD who come for therapy feel tormented precisely because their memories do not allow themselves to be repressed, let alone forgotten. The flashbacks and replays of horrific events, which sometimes go on for years, retain their painful vividness. Many patients must surely feel that if only there were such a thing as repression, they might not need therapy at all, whereas in fact they need treatment with EMDR to take the sharp edges off the memories and then store them in a form that is no longer tormenting. Flashbacks to traumatic events therefore do not have the symbolic guise adopted by repressed memories in their efforts to creep surreptitiously back into consciousness. Events are re-experienced in a raw and realistic form; no interpretation is necessary.

Dora had been in analysis with Freud for 11 weeks – hour-long sessions six days a week – when she suddenly refused to go on. Freud believed that analysis had not yet even begun. The lock had been sprung, but now he needed to bring the repressed material carefully back into her conscious mind. The interaction between analyst and patient normally lasted for years, as it still does. Treatment with EMDR takes hours, spread over a limited number of sessions. Freud, for his part, would have shaken his head in disbelief at how in such a short time, with two waving fingers, a traumatic memory could be transformed, its intense negative emotions removed. In his own theory, those emotions were the cause of repression, and luring memories back out of the unconscious was a time-consuming process. With the removal over recent years of psychoanalysis from the list of therapies for which health insurance companies are willing to pay, an approach to trauma involving a combination of introspection and interpretation that lasts for years has been replaced by a quick fix.

So the relationship between trauma, repression and forgetting has been interpreted in astonishingly diverse ways over the past century. A trauma could be the cause of repression, or of the impossibility of repression. Troubling recollections might end up in the unconscious, or they might stubbornly refuse to leave the consciousness. Traumatic memories had to be reconstructed laboriously to recover their original form, so that they could then serve as evidence for the prosecution of those responsible, or they had to be made paler and vaguer before being stored away again. When traumatic memories popped up in the conscious mind, they might have a symbolic character, or they might be all too painfully realistic. Articles have regularly appeared in the psychological or psychiatric literature with titles that express some astonishment on the part of the authors, like 'What people believe about memory despite the research evidence'.[67] Yet it is impossible to blame 'people' for this, since the 'research evidence' differs with each practice, as do the criteria for what counts as evidence.

No matter how trauma, repression and forgetting were classified and arranged in all those scientific and clinical practices, guaranteed throughout was that the therapist was essential. A patient was reliant on a psychoanalyst because the repressed material had attempted to get past the censor by adopting a disguise. Such attempts could be interpreted only by someone who was at home in the secret language of the unconscious: without an analyst, no insight into the trauma; without an analyst, no hope of a cure. This same relationship between therapist and patient was a feature of all cases involving recovered memories. The patient had forgotten the abuse and the therapist gradually helped to bring memories of it back to the surface. As with Dora, this involved a laborious process of reconstruction, because the buried material came to light in the form of shards and fragments. With PTSD, the therapist does not need to study the symbolic language of the unconscious or learn the skills of the archaeologist. There is nothing to interpret and there are no gaps to fill, since the memory forces itself upon the conscious mind already vivid and complete. Yet the therapist is still indispensable, because he or she commands the technique of allowing the memory to be stored away again in a relatively harmless form. Along the meandering course that characterises the acquisition of new insights in psychology and psychiatry, it is pleasing to see a simple straight line from time to time.

CHAPTER NINE

The Myth of Total Recall

Glaciers can sometimes hold on to the bodies of people who die in accidents on the mountains for a very long time. Climbers who reached the summit in a morning may take 70 or 80 years to come down. Some time in the summer of, say, 1927, a man might climb to a height of 4,000 or 5,000 metres and sit down for moment, perhaps to enjoy the view, to have a snack or to take a brief rest. Then something goes wrong. Perhaps he dozes off and freezes to death in his sleep. As evening falls, it starts to snow. The seated climber no doubt sticks up out of the white landscape for a while, but eventually the snow reaches his waist, his shoulders, his scalp and he is blanketed, invisible. There may be a few summer days when his head shows again above the melting snow cover, but a few months later that too is over. Winter arrives and the man is buried under a layer of snow measuring two, then seven, perhaps eventually ten metres deep. The long descent begins.

A glacier is essentially a river. A time-lapse film would make this obvious: it meanders, carves out bends, squeezes through gorges, overflows its banks. Bodies that end up in glaciers are sometimes deposited at one of the bends before being carried onwards a decade later, all in a stony, frozen tempo.

In what form do bodies reach the bottom? What do they look like at the foot of the glacier? It depends what happens along the way. During his long journey, the seated man may have been compressed to a midget by the ice layer above his head, but someone who falls through a crevasse and is carried onwards at the bottom of the glacier may be pummelled and kneaded against the rock into a thin giant. Another will seem perfectly preserved, emerging at the bottom exactly as he disappeared at the top, in tasselled knickerbockers, sometimes still with his climbing gear, touch-ingly innovative equipment from the 1920s. When identified he may be found to have living relatives, even grandchildren, who are finally able to bury their 30-year-old grandpa. Sometimes you realise intuitively: this must be a metaphor for something. But for what?

Rudy Kousbroek saw glacier corpses as a metaphor for what time can do to a reputation. Little trace may be left half a century later of people who were great names in their day. Others, barely noticed when they were alive, grow to be revered as men or women of stature. Time hammers and crushes and renders up figures that have changed beyond recognition.

Does time do this with our memories as well? Are our brains like glaciers that crush and squeeze and flatten and stretch until one memory becomes a giant and the other a dwarf? Not as a rule. If our memories really did systematically deceive us, we would have no powers of recollec-tion at all. Our memories could not have developed through our evolu-tionary history if they did not, broadly speaking, reflect reality. Evolution has little patience with nonsense.

The problem lies, of course, in the term 'as a rule'. It admits of excep-tions. The problem lies not in those exceptions themselves but in our inability to know in a specific case whether we might be dealing with an exception. The fact that our memories can sometimes deceive us erodes the value of recollections which we would otherwise be ready to stake our lives on – an overconfidence that is knocked out of us as we get older. Any sensitive observer will be conscious of examples of memories that changed under the pressure of later memories piled up on top of them.

There is another contrasting intuition about what time does to memories. The passage of the years can sometimes have a protective effect, tucking them up and guarding them from distortion. Metaphors describing this intuition point to depth, burial, layers. In 1902, Freud visited Pompeii with his brother Alexander and there he walked through his own metaphor.[1] At various points in his work he had compared the tracing of a traumatic memory during psychoanalysis to the excavation of Pompeii, the city hidden since 79 AD under a layer of ash five metres thick until it was carefully laid bare in the second half of the eighteenth century.

Only after the city was exposed to the air and the weather did natural erosion set in. The real destruction of Pompeii, Freud wrote, began only after the protective layers were removed. What the patient dug from the depths during psychoanalysis was the intact memory, authentic, unchanged, protected all that time by the 'screen memories' covering it. Memories that entered the unconscious survived precisely because they were buried.

In *The Interpretation of Dreams*, Freud flirted with an even more radical theory. In dreams, day residues sometimes emerge, memories of trivial events of waking life that seem to have been recorded even if we paid no attention to them at the time. This surely proves that none of the things we have done or experienced are ever completely forgotten, that our memories are absolute. He expressed agreement with the German psychiatrist Friedrich Scholz, who wrote that the dream memory teaches us that 'nothing which we have once mentally possessed can be entirely lost'.[2] Freud and Scholz were far from alone. Many contemporaries involved with the sciences of memory – doctors, psychologists, neurologists, psychiatrists – held the view that every perception, every sensory experience, indeed every thought, contemplation or dream leaves traces in the brain that can never be expunged. American physiologist and photography pioneer John William Draper wrote in 1856 that the ganglion cells, which bundle together stimuli from other cells, store away a permanent record of our experiences.[3] Those traces remained present in a latent form, resembling a photographic plate that had been exposed but not yet developed. He saw the memory as a 'silent gallery' with, on the walls, 'silhouettes of whatever we have done'. In daytime those inner images are invisible amid the mass of sensory impressions in the waking consciousness, but while we are dreaming or in a feverish delirium, and especially 'during the solemn moments of dying', the mind turned inwards and all those images became visible.[4] Although he used a different metaphor, Sergei Korsakoff said exactly the same; not even the serious memory disorder to which his name is attached could wipe out the original traces. Within the patient's memory 'the vibration of all the strings that have ever reverberated continues, a soft echo of everything he has ever thought'.[5] In *The Interpretation of Dreams* Freud quoted with approval Belgian psychologist and philosopher Joseph Delboeuf, who wrote in 1885 that in our brains 'even the most insignificant impression leaves an unalterable trace, which is indefinitely capable of revival.'[6] Plenty more examples are available in the literature of the time. The notion of total recall is an old one.

It is still very much with us. In 1980 memory psychologists Elizabeth and Geoffrey Loftus presented their test participants with two assertions regarding memory and asked them which best reflected their own view as to how memory works:

Everything we learn is permanently stored in the mind, although sometimes particular details are not accessible. With hypnosis, or other special techniques, these inaccessible details could eventually be recovered.

Some details that we learn may be permanently lost from memory. Such details would never be able to be recovered by hypnosis, or any other special technique, because these details are simply no longer there.[7]

The vast majority of those questioned responded that they were convinced everything we experience is permanently stored in the brain and that what we call forgetting is actually just the inability to retrieve what has been recorded. It is all still there. Strikingly, of those who had studied psychology or were still doing so, 84 per cent endorsed the first assertion, whereas among non-psychologists the proportion was 69 per cent. In justifying their answers, the psychologists sometimes pointed to hypnosis, occasionally to psychoanalysis, but mainly to the tests carried out by Canadian neurosurgeon Wilder Penfield, the man who contributed more than anyone to the theory that our brains contain a complete record of everything we have ever experienced. To Draper, Freud, Korsakoff and all those other nineteenth-century scholars, given the limited means available in their day, this was little more than a suspicion. Penfield gave it the status of an experimentally confirmed hypothesis.

Burnt toast

One episode of *The Heritage Minutes*, a series of minute-long films about significant moments in Canadian history, deals with Penfield's work.[8] The story starts cosily enough. It is a morning in 1934 in Montreal. A man is sitting reading the paper at the kitchen table and his wife is standing next to him holding a plate. She says she can smell burnt toast. Her husband replies absently that he cannot smell anything. He is startled when the plate falls and smashes on the floor, but he manages in the nick of time to catch his wife, who is having a severe epileptic fit. In the next shot she is lying on the operating table. The camera zooms in on the surgeon. He has the partially exposed brain before him and in his hand an electrode with which he is carefully dabbing the cerebral cortex. 'Every time she has a seizure,' he says to his team, 'she smells something burning. Now if we can provoke that smell by probing the surface of the brain, we'll find the source of the seizures.'

Next comes a shocking image. The camera moves a little lower. Suddenly we are looking straight into the woman's face. She is conscious! A sheet has been stretched between her face and her exposed brain.

'Mrs Gold, do you feel anything?' the surgeon asks.

'I can see the most wonderful lights!'

He moves the electrode.

'And now what do you feel?'

'Did you pour cold water on my hand, Dr Penfield?'

The doctor does not reply.

'Now what?' Her face takes on an anxious look.

'What is it, Mrs Gold?'

'Burnt toast! Dr Penfield, I can smell burnt toast!'

Penfield exchanges knowing looks with his colleagues. The spot has been found. Then we hear the woman speaking as a voice-over: 'Dr Wilder Penfield. He cured my seizures, and hundreds more. They say he drew the road map of the human brain. We just called him the greatest Canadian alive!'

Penfield became a Canadian only in that same year, 1934, when he and his wife were naturalised. Wilder Graves Penfield was born in Spokane, Washington, in 1891, the son and grandson of doctors.[9] He began studying philosophy but soon switched to medicine. Then he moved to Oxford, where he specialised in neurology under Charles Scott Sherrington. In 1928 he was invited to come to Montreal to take up a combined appointment at the medical faculty of McGill University and the Royal Victoria Hospital. His passion already lay with a field that had only just begun to develop: the surgical treatment of epilepsy. In the years that followed, he worked hard to create what he had in mind from the moment he arrived, a special institute where the best neurophysiologists,

Wilder Graves Penfield (1891–1976) at the age of 67.

neurosurgeons and neuropathologists could come together, combining clinical work and research. He received a substantial donation from the Rockefeller Foundation and in 1934 the Montreal Neurological Institute (MNI) opened its doors.[10]

On the lower floors of the eight-storey building were wards, each with space for 50 beds. The upper floors were equipped with laboratories. On the fifth floor, between treatment and research, were the operating theatres, the heart of the MNI. They were much like theatres in the everyday sense. Around the operating table ran a glass gallery, so that spectators could observe the surgical procedures, practically over Penfield's shoulder. At the head end was Herbert Jasper's apparatus. Jasper was an authority in the field of EEG measurements and during operations he took EEGs directly from the exposed brain surface. Below the gallery was a booth for the photographer, who could make pictures of the brain via a mirror. A stenographer took dictation from the surgeon. A system of buzzers allowed staff to be called in whenever Penfield felt there was something special they ought to see. The MNI developed within a few years into a centre of excellence, before the term was invented. Specialists came to Montreal from all over the world for periods of study.

Before moving to Montreal, Penfield had spent six months studying under German neurosurgeon Otfrid Foerster, regarded as the king of European neurology. Penfield learned German so that he could communicate with him (although after they met it became clear that Foerster was eager to practise his English on Penfield). In Breslau, Foerster had operated on patients whose epilepsy was the result of brain damage suffered during the First World War. Penfield observed a technique he would later refine and that would eventually go down in history as the Montreal procedure. First, EEG measurements on the shaved scalp were used to find the global position of the focus of epilepsy. Then Penfield removed part of the skull under local anaesthetic, exposing the brain surface. The brain itself is without feeling. The patient remained conscious and was asked to describe the experiences that resulted when the surgeon prodded at the brain, one convolution at a time, with an electrode that repeatedly delivered a charge of two volts lasting five milliseconds. It was an extraordinarily demanding operation that required the patient to have great faith in the doctor. Penfield always stressed that the Montreal procedure must be confined to clinical applications, such as treatment for epilepsy that could not be controlled by drugs.

The sensations experienced by the patient varied according to which part of the brain was touched. Stimulation of the motor cortex could lead to tingling or movement in fingers or toes. Stimulation of the sensory cortex could make the patient see flashes, stripes or stars, hear a buzzing sound, clicks or whistling, smell strange odours, or feel as if cold water was dripping onto his or her hand. The patient's responses were recorded by the stenographer and Penfield marked the places he had touched with tiny bits of numbered paper that he laid on the cerebral membrane. Then a photograph was taken. As soon as the stimulation caused an epileptic fit or a sensation that had consistently preceded a seizure, the real operation could begin, which usually meant that a small amount of brain matter was removed at that spot. Penfield was of the 'no brain is better than bad brain' school.

By the early 1950s, Penfield had carried out hundreds of operations. His carefully documented wanderings over the surface of all those epileptic brains found their way into standard works on the functional anatomy of the human brain and various types of epilepsy.[11] His contribution to the topography of the brain is hard to overstate. Many of us will be familiar with Penfield's homunculus, his drawing of a human figure with proportions that correspond to the size of each body part's representation in the brain: enormous lips, a large tongue, short legs and thin arms with giant hands. Much of the knowledge gained before the rise of imaging techniques about the representation of functions can be attributed to Penfield's methodical tracking of the surface of the brain (and to the courage of his patients).

By the 1940s, Penfield had established a reputation in the surgical treatment of epilepsy, but his reputation outside neurosurgery was not directly connected with his clinical work. Alongside his articles and monographs about epilepsy and the topography of the brain, a second stream of publications started up, in which he reported on findings that drew the attention of a far wider public.

Tape recorder

Stimulation of the sensory and motor cortex prompted reactions that were only to be expected based on existing knowledge about the neurological representation of functions. But in some patients stimulation of the temporal lobe provoked odd responses. When that part of the brain was prodded with an electrode, they reported a feeling that they had experienced the same situation before in precisely the same way, or, conversely, said that everything seemed strange and unreal, like in a dream. Some suddenly saw with hallucinatory clarity a scene from their childhood, or heard voices. Others, or the same patients when touched at a slightly different spot, heard a song so clearly that they could sing along. Out of the hundreds of reports published by Penfield about the stimulation of the temporal lobe, the case of M.M. can serve as an example. It concerned a 26-year-old woman with epilepsy that had become unresponsive to medication.[12] Her attacks began with a sense of déjà vu, sometimes followed by a flashback in which she seemed to experience some part of her life again, such as waiting for a train at a railway station. She underwent an operation based on the Montreal procedure and the places where the electrode was applied were photographed.

Stimulation at number 11 prompted an auditory memory. 'Yes, Sir, I think I heard a mother calling her little boy somewhere. It seemed to be something that happened years ago'. When asked to explain, she said: 'It was somebody in the neighbourhood where I live'.[13] A little later, when the same spot was stimulated, she again heard familiar voices, the same woman calling, not in her neighbourhood this time but in a lumber yard. She added with some surprise that she had 'never been around the lumber yard much'. After stimulation at number 13 she said: 'Yes, I hear voices. It is late at night, around the carnival somewhere – some sort of travelling circus'. And when the electrode was removed: 'I just saw lots of big wagons that they use to haul animals in'.[14] A touch at number 15 gave her the feeling she had experienced the operation before and knew exactly what was going to happen next. Stimulation at 17 took her into an office. She saw desks and a man leaning on one of them with a pencil in his hand. When Penfield announced he was about to touch her brain but didn't, there was no response. When he stimulated it without warning she reacted. Everything she 'saw' and 'heard' seemed familiar.

The fact that epilepsy with a focus in the temporal lobe can cause déjà vu and dreamlike experiences had been discovered in the nineteenth century by British neurologist John Hughlings Jackson, who introduced the term 'dreamy state' to describe it. But the fact that touching the brain with an electrode also seemed to activate memory traces was a revelation. Those memories felt much clearer and more detailed to the patients than ordinary memories. When sounds were involved they felt as if they were listening to a tape recorder that had been working away in the brain unnoticed, recording everything they had ever heard. It was like recalling a 'forgotten memory': a snatch of a conversation, children playing outside, a train in the distance – sounds that had been forgotten almost immediately at the time. The memories were so vivid that patients had the feeling the sensations were being experienced in the present. Often it was only when talking to the doctor after the operation was over that they realised these were in fact fragments from the past.

In interpreting his findings, Penfield relied on the experiences of his patients. The temporal lobe must contain reports of everything that had ever caught their attention, no matter how briefly and fleetingly, everything they had ever seen, heard, thought, dreamed, imagined – an immense archive of impressions and experiences. Using a term derived from William James, Penfield explained in *Science* that the 'stream of consciousness' left a neuronal trace that could later be reactivated by electricity.[15] In fact his theory was even more radical. It sometimes happened that he activated a memory in a specific part of the brain and was later obliged to cut out precisely that area, yet after the operation the memory was still present. This could be explained only by assuming that the temporal lobe on the other side of the brain also recorded everything. So our brains are engaged in double bookkeeping. We possess not just one absolute memory but two. Expressing himself in the metaphors of his time, Penfield declared that our brains store away experiences 'like a wire-recorder or a tape-recorder'.[16]

What Penfield did not claim was that the memory traces activated electronically were the same as ordinary, natural memories of the kind

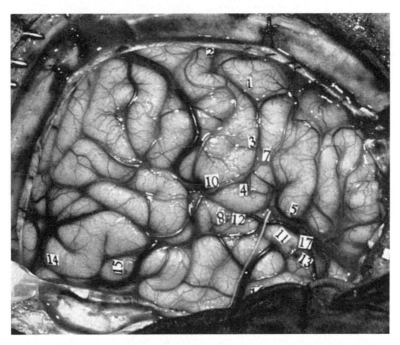

The exposed right hemisphere of M.M.'s brain. The places Penfield stimulated with his electrode are marked with numbered pieces of paper.

that simply pop up in the consciousness, prompted or unprompted. The traces in the temporal lobe represent what was once experienced in that form, and the reactivation of those traces happens 'in real time', as it would be called now. A once-heard song is recalled in its original tempo. Ordinary memories have a far more general character, are shortened in time, have gaps, add similar experiences together and are not as detailed as a precise record. In fact the memory would not work at all well if it replayed the tape recording. Those two absolute memories, left and right, provided at best the raw material for ordinary recollections, which is the most practical arrangement.

Penfield also declined to comment on the precise location of those memory traces. He could not be certain whether they lay at the surface of the temporal lobe and were activated by electrical stimulation as if the electrode turned them on, or whether the electrical stimulation actually turned off structures in the surface with the result that more deeply placed circuits that were normally blocked became active. He was convinced that the electrode caused a tape somewhere in the temporal lobe to be replayed, but he could not be specific about exactly what the connection was between that effect and his electrical pulses.

Nuances such as these were soon lost. One image commanded all the attention: the brain as a tape recorder. From the 1940s onwards, Penfield published dozens of papers that all had the same structure. They began with a short explanation of the Montreal procedure, then came a few case studies with the kinds of flashbacks and memories seen in M.M., then the presentation of the tape-recorder hypothesis and the experimental evidence for it that he had meanwhile collected. When Penfield lectured, as soon as he took the stage – perhaps for the opening talk at a major conference, the Sherrington Lecture, the Lister Oration, the Maudsley Lecture or the Gold Medal Lecture – the discovery of the absolute memory was the central theme. In 1963 it briefly seemed that Penfield, now 72, was working towards a conclusion. In the British journal *Brain*, he and his colleague Phanor Perot published an analysis of 1,288 successive operations during which the surface of the brain was stimulated.[17] The article was 100 pages long and bore the subtitle 'A final summary and discussion', but Penfield carried on writing regardless and, right up until the mid-1970s, articles and books continued to appear with increasingly grandiose titles, such as 'Engrams in the human brain',[18] 'The electrode, the brain and the mind'[19] and *The Mystery of the Mind*.[20]

In 1900, Freud was still comparing an intact memory trace to an archaeological find. Penfield turned to the most advanced artificial memories of his day as a source of metaphors, which then emerged in the excited articles that appeared in the press about his discoveries. 'Movie film in brain: Penfield reveals amazing discovery' was the headline in the *Montreal Star* in 1957.[21] In the same year, *Time* published an article about his work, saying that Dr Penfield had recently provided the National Academy of Sciences with proof that parts of the brain work like 'an audio-visual tape recorder, preserving the details of everything a man sees and hears'.[22] One subheading ran 'Built-in Hi-Fi'. In an era in which tape recorders and film cameras were appearing in many American households, these were seductive analogies that enabled people not conversant with neurology to form a clear impression of what modern science said was going on in their brains. Although from the 1970s onwards the computer became the dominant metaphor for the human brain, the theory of absolute memory would forever be known as the 'tape recorder view'.

Perdu?

In 1951, Penfield presented his theory about the brain and memory during a symposium held by the American Neurological Association.[23] His account ran along familiar lines: the stimulation of the temporal lobe, the reactions of S.B., D.F., L.G. and a handful of other patients, the 'forgotten memories' that came to light, the various electrically activated memories and ordinary memories, the conclusion that in the two cerebral hemispheres a dual register of all experiences is kept. First to take the microphone in the debate that followed – and he was not quick to let go of it again – was Lawrence S. Kubie, a prominent psychoanalyst from New York. He said it was many years since he had been as excited by a scientific contribution as he was now by Dr Penfield's. At last, here was a meeting point between psychoanalysis and neurosurgery. What Kubie believed we could learn from this work was that

> electrical stimulation of the temporal cortex can produce the equiva-
> lent of hypnotically induced regressions into the past, with a reliving
> of the past as though it were the present. It is important that this can
> occur both on the operating table and in the experimental psycho-
> logical laboratory. Here is a proof that the past can be as vivid as the
> present; or that, as Freud put it, in the unconscious there is no such
> thing as time and space. It proves also the literalness with which past
> moments are permanently stored as discrete units.[24]

Using Penfield's technique, the memory could be directly manipulated: 'This is Proust on the operating table, an electrical *recherche aux temps perdu*. Yet is it *perdu*? It will be important for Dr Penfield and his group to ascertain how often the recovered experiences were forgotten (repressed) memories.'[25] Ordinary memories, retrieved without electrical stimulation, resembled Freud's 'screen memories'. A psychoanalyst, using hypnosis, dream analysis and free association, had to labour away for months or years to penetrate the layer of screen memories, whereas the neurosur-geon could get through that layer in a few moments. It turned Kubie into something of an experimentalist. Surely dreams and free associations should be collected from these patients before the operation, so that they could be compared with the material that emerged on the operating table. And would it not be interesting to compare neurotic symptoms and dreams from before and after the operation? Perhaps that would be a way to find out whether the reliving of the past through electrical stimulation influenced the 'emotional storm centers'.[26] Kubie rounded off his long monologue by complimenting Penfield on his important contribution to 'the neurophysiology of the unconscious and of repression'.[27]

We may well wonder whether those compliments were appreciated. After Kubie, Penfield's fellow neurologists spoke and he responded only to their comments, not mentioning Kubie's enthusiastic contribution. But to Kubie the idea that in Montreal the neurological mechanism behind the unconscious might have been discovered was too enticing to let go. Was this not the historical moment when archaeological meta-phors about buried memories could be replaced by the reality of neuro-logical processes in a clearly described part of the temporal lobe? Kubie asked Penfield for permission to watch some of his surgical procedures. It was granted. Scrubbed sterile and in operating theatre garb, the psycho-analyst entered Penfield's theatre armed with a dictaphone to record everything the patient had to say. It resulted in a long article two years later about what psychoanalysis could learn from modern brain science.[28] In his published work, Penfield kept his distance from psychoanalysis, but in private he seems to have believed that traumatic memories will not fade if they are covered up, only if they are brought to the surface. He had a second home where he spent his summers and accommodated colleagues and friends as guests. In 1942, a young Englishman stayed there who had barely escaped with his life when his ship was torpedoed. A good friend had been killed. In a biographical portrait of Penfield we read how the young man arrived in a state of extreme nervousness and everyone tried 'to help him to forget his experience'.

> When his nerves did not improve, Dr. Penfield's advice was asked. Instead of avoiding the subject, Dr. Penfield persuaded the young man to try to recall and record every detail of the tragedy, the crash and turmoil, the confusion following the failure of electricity, the terror at finding his cabin door jammed while he was inside trying to pick up valuables, the long

seasick hours on a raft before he was rescued. Copies of this record were sent to his parents at the Rockefeller Foundation. And then he was suddenly free of his nervous condition and began to enjoy himself as normally as the others.[29]

Those who read Penfield's reports of what all those hundreds of patients had to say will rarely encounter anything that seems worthy of repression. They present him with snippets of respectable but humdrum lives: the sound of a ball bouncing off a wall, a car coming up the drive, a neighbour calling a small boy indoors. No memories of peeping at the woman next door, no incestuous desires, no masturbation fantasies, no glimpse of 'the beast with two backs', nothing that gives the impression of ever having been 'buried'. The hoped-for collaboration between Penfield and Kubie never came about, let alone a uniting of neurosurgery and psychoanalysis.

Led Zeppelin

It was in 1933 that Penfield derived the first electrically stimulated flashbacks from epileptic brains. For almost half a century after that he was challenged remarkably rarely. The problem was not that he was the only person with access to the means to carry out such experiments; in fact the Montreal procedure was applied all over the world as a way of discovering the focus of an individual's epilepsy. On operating tables far from the MNI, patients reported fragments of sound and images they felt to be memories. Current brain science has dispensed with the notion that Penfield discovered a neuronal tape recorder, but this was as a consequence of new interpretations rather than new facts.

Some of the arguments used against Penfield demonstrate merely that his original work has been read carelessly. Neurosurgeon George Ojemann operated according to the Montreal protocol on a man with temporal lobe epilepsy and discovered that stimulation at a particular place caused highly specific musical flashbacks: songs by Led Zeppelin. If the electrode was removed, they disappeared; when the electrode was placed at the same spot again, the music came back. Ojemann removed tissue at that spot, cheerfully commenting later 'Now, I am not a great fan of rock music, and this was an epileptic brain, so of course I took it out!'[30] When the man came back several years later, it turned out that his memories of Led Zeppelin were still completely intact. Ojemann presented this as a decisive refutation of the tape-recorder theory.[31] But Penfield had come upon results exactly like this himself and took them as proof that all experiences are recorded in duplicate.

A more convincing refutation emerges if we look closely at the frequency of the experiences of Penfield's patients. In the article in *Brain* in which he summed up his findings, reports of an uninterrupted series of 1,288 operations were analysed. All the reactions that had to do with memory were connected with the temporal lobe alone, but only 40 of the 520 patients in whom the temporal lobe was stimulated immediately before the operation reported any response. The others, more than 92 per cent, experienced nothing at all. If there was a tape recorder in their brains, then Penfield did not succeed in switching it to 'Play'. No explanation has been found for the difference and nowhere does Penfield state that he feels one is needed. Of the 40 patients who did report the relevant phenomena, 24 described hallucinations, usually of the type they had experienced during a seizure. Sometimes the result was a strange mixture of hallucination and flashback, as seen in a boy of 12 who found himself listening to his mother phoning his aunt and could hear his aunt's voice as well as his mother's. In an analysis of Penfield's reports, neurobiologist Larry Squire points to the fact that stimulation of this part of the brain could produce two very different experiences, while stimulation of two widely separated places sometimes yielded two that were almost identical.[32]

Questions also arise about the nature of the patient's subjective experiences. Take M.M., the woman who 'saw' a travelling circus in the night and 'heard' a neighbour calling her young son. Penfield included that response in publication after publication, always using virtually the same form of words to describe it. Virtually, because in all those repetitions discrepancies crept in that give us reason to stop and think about what the woman actually 'remembered'. According to a report from 1958, M.M. heard the same woman shouting again after the stimulation was repeated, but this time in a lumber yard. She added that she had 'never been around the lumber yard much'. 'This was an incident of childhood,' Penfield writes, 'which she could never have recalled without the aid of the stimulating electrode. Actually she could not "remember" it but she knew at once, with no suggestion from us, that she must have experienced it some time'.[33] According to a report from 1963, however – that 'final summary' in the journal *Brain* – the woman actually said: 'I have never been around any lumber yard'.[34] The comment that the electrode had brought back a forgotten memory is missing this time. And in the report about M.M. in *The Mystery of the Mind*, the lumber yard has disappeared altogether.[35] To be able to classify an awareness of hearing someone shouting something in a lumber yard as a forgotten memory, it is of course essential to have been in a lumber yard at some point. Even if that is the case, we might still wonder whether two memories have been combined here, of hearing a shout and of the time she was in a lumber yard, so that it is not so much that a bit of tape is being played as that fragments of memories are being juxtaposed, a process more accurately described as reconstruction than as reproduction.

Doubts about the precise status of the experiences Penfield prompted – memory, hallucination, fantasy – are reinforced by the strange shifts in time. For quite a few patients, simply the experience of lying on the operating table brought about a sense of déjà vu, as if they vaguely recalled having already been through exactly the same procedure. Might it not therefore be that experiences of sounds or images were likewise incorrectly experienced as memories? Even in the version in which M.M. says she has 'never been around the lumber yard much', it seems more a conclusion of some sort than a statement of fact when she says she 'must have experienced it some time'. Another temporal shift took place in the sense that the 'memories' were so clear and vivid that the patient had the feeling of having experienced them in the past. Penfield writes that it was often only in their conversation afterwards that a patient was able to say that the event had once taken place. This immediately introduces a knotty problem: the patient has to recall not only the experience but whether or not it was already a memory when experienced during the operation. The fact that many patients felt when being touched by the electrode as if they were 'in a dream' makes it hard to rely on their judgement as to the origin of all the things that passed through their minds.

In 1982, Pierre Gloor and four fellow neurologists reported on a new series of experiments on epileptic brains.[36] These too were carried out at the MNI, but with a rather different technique. Twenty-nine patients with temporal lobe epilepsy had electrodes implanted deep in their brains. In the weeks before the operation, their anti-epileptic medication was reduced, the hope being that the electrodes would record the location of any seizures. The electrodes remained in place for several weeks and could be read by telemetry. They could also be used to produce small electrical pulses. Whereas Penfield had stimulated only the surface of the brain, some of these electrodes penetrated as far as the hippocampus and the amygdala, which lie deeper within the temporal lobe. The hippocampus and amygdala belong to the limbic system, a part of the brain that is particularly ancient in evolutionary terms, involved in consciousness, hormone regulation, smell and emotions. In 62 per cent of patients the same phenomena occurred as Penfield had reported: déjà vu, the sense of being in a dream, flashbacks and visual hallucinations. But the most commonly reported experience was fear, ranging from a slight unease that something bad was about to happen to a sense of panic and the urge to flee. What patients experienced as the cause of their fear varied markedly, both from patient to patient and in the same patient from one moment to the next. Sometimes the fear could be linked to a childhood memory of being pushed under water, other times to anxiety about not having finished an assignment that ought to have been delivered two weeks ago. Slight anxiety might be connected with a sensation of sitting on the edge of a fountain and accidentally falling into the water, severe anxiety with a feeling of standing on a cliff high above the sea. The situation seemed to suit itself to the intensity. In no case did the experience form more than a single scene, an isolated image. The researchers characterised them as 'snapshots', in which no time elapsed.[37] They certainly did not give the impression of being part of a tape that was being played back. All these sensations were prompted by the stimulation of structures in the limbic system. Stimulation of the surface of the temporal lobe had produced no experiences at all.

These findings gave a new interpretation to the reports collected by the MNI's founder. The real origin of the sensations almost certainly lay in the limbic system. Only electrical discharges there, whether deliberately caused or spontaneous, produced déjà vu, dream states and flashbacks. Penfield had prompted them for years by stimulating the surface, but that was probably because the electrode caused tiny seizures that disturbed underlying structures. Activation of the amygdala and the hippocampus caused the strange shifts in time that made the sensations seem familiar. This gave all the experiences, including hallucinations and fantasies, the character of a memory. Even if patients thought during a seizure that they were somewhere they had never been, they still felt as if they were remembering something. What goes on during an epileptic seizure is very much like what happens during a dream just before waking. In a flash a scene is put together that fits the emotion, and what ends up as part of that scene depends on what is available at that moment in the way of fragments of fantasies and memories.

Total recall

Gloor presented his results in the First Wilder Penfield Memorial Lecture in 1981, five years after Penfield's death. There were no stirring articles in the papers, no headlines such as 'Recent research proves there is no tape recorder in the brain'. It is questionable in any case whether articles along those lines, had they appeared, could have done anything to alter the conviction so many people still have that our brains record everything that passes through them. The ineradicable traces Penfield believed he had found seem to have perpetuated themselves in the collective memory. There they lie, next to other favourite neuromyths such as 'we use only 10 per cent of our brains', or 'women are better at multitasking because they have more connections between the two halves of their brains' – myths that are believed not because the evidence is convincing but because people want to believe them.

'Recall is essentially total,' is how Kubie summarised Penfield's work in 1952.[38] That formulation is close to the title Paul Verhoeven gave his science fiction film about memory manipulation.[39] In *Total Recall* a builder called Quaid, played by Arnold Schwarzenegger, goes to a company called Rekall to have memories of a journey to Mars implanted in his brain. He chooses a two-week package, including memories of a luxury hotel and excursions, but stripped of memories of lost baggage, rainy days, rip-offs by taxi drivers and other miseries that apparently have yet to be eliminated from Mars in 2084. The memories are transferred to his brain as complete files, and it later turns out they can be removed just as neatly, should the need arise. The implicit metaphor here is the computer, but the idea that memories can be introduced or erased as separate entities, independently of memories already present, is in fact the digital version of Penfield's tape recorder. Only memory traces imagined as actual copies of experiences can be transferred to any brain at random. The fact that memories of an event are always marked by earlier experiences – so in that sense two people can never experience the same thing – makes them quite different from mechanised recordings by a tape recorder.

Sometimes the metaphors used to express the theory of absolute memory – Penfield's tape recorder or today's computer hard drive – are turned around and deployed as evidence. If a machine can record stimuli and store them away indefinitely, why would a far more refined organic instrument like the human brain be unable to do so? We now know that memories are stored in the form of possible connections between brain cells, and with its estimated 100 billion brain cells, the number of connections in a single brain is so astronomical that there would be room for the experiences of many lives. This certainly means the memory can never be 'full', but it is that very notion of storage in brain tissue that makes the theory of absolute memory so improbable. Every day we lose an average of almost 100,000 brain cells, some 30 million a year. Brain tissue does not escape decay and atrophy. A brain is not a machine but an organ. It consists of continually changing networks and circuits, modulated by chemical processes. It has rhythms of day and night, states of wakefulness and rest, changes in levels of hormones, cycles of growth and death. The brain, in short, is more like a steaming and dripping stretch of rainforest than a computer's hard disc. Memory traces are not conserved permanently in a sterile environment like information in the artificial memories we have invented. Instead they are subject to the neuronal equivalents of rot and untamed growth.

The belief in an absolute memory was not an after-effect of the invention of devices such as tape recorders and video cameras. Freud and Korsakoff alluded to it even before film was invented, using quite different metaphors. Anyone who traces the history of absolute memory backwards will soon encounter the mesmerists, hypnotists and spiritualists who claimed that during a trance a person has access to memories unavailable to the waking consciousness that therefore seem forgotten.[40] Such claims were taken as proof that nothing is ever lost. Moving further back in time we find ourselves in the Romantic era, when poets and philosophers gave voice to the idea of the human mind as an immense reservoir of impressions.

When Loftus and Loftus demonstrated in 1980 that 84 per cent of those schooled in psychology, when asked, think that our brains store everything permanently, the study by Gloor and his colleagues had yet to be published. But more recent studies show that this theory still remains popular, with almost four in ten people believing in this version of absolute memory.[41] An inquiry among psychotherapists showed that more than half believe hypnosis gives access to such memories, all the way back to birth if need be.[42] Where does this persistence come from? What makes the idea that our brains store away everything that was ever in our consciousness so attractive?

Part of the answer must be that we have our own experiences of 'forgotten memories'. You can wake up convinced you have slept a dreamless sleep and later in the day see or hear something that suddenly brings back the supposedly forgotten dream. It may even be that you are convinced you have forgotten something – such as the name of the family that lived next door when you were five – and a week later see that name on the back of a truck and immediately recognise it as the one you were sure you no longer knew. Older people can testify that they may abruptly recall things they have not thought about for 50 years, things that were stored away all that time and never brought to mind. What Freud wrote about day residues in dreams does indeed reflect a familiar experience. Even the most trivial of experiences seem to be recorded. It is, in short, rather perilous to insist that something is definitely no longer in your memory. There is always a chance that, via associations you do not have access to at the moment, it will return to your consciousness.

But being unable to prove that something has gone for good does not constitute proof that everything is still there. What makes discussions with those who adhere to the theory that the brain records everything somewhat hard going is their assumption that a theory that proves impossible to refute must be true. This is a small but fatal step beyond logic. A theory that is immune to refutation falls outside the sphere of testing and investigation.

Penfield would not have chosen to use Freud's arguments and Freud did not see himself as a modern Romantic. Both men spoke in their own time with the authority of the 'scientist', but each mobilised his own techniques, metaphors and studies to support the theory of absolute memory. That so many people inside and outside science, however we define it, believed and still believe in a memory that retains everything perhaps proves how difficult it is to for us resign ourselves to the idea that most of what we experience passes through our brains without leaving any trace, as if it had never happened. We might be able to accept having a memory like a sieve if we could be certain that only the dust and debris were shaken through it and everything of real value remained within, but unfortunately our brains are not set up like that. The traffic coming towards you on the motorway when you drove to Wolverhampton on 12 April 1982 has gone from your memory, but the same is true of a conversation you had with your father in the car, the delicious oxtail soup your mother made and the walk you took with your three-year-old daughter. The myth of absolute memory comforts us by suggesting that nothing has really been lost, even if it cannot be recalled right now. The ancient Greek idea of the *horror vacui*, dismissed by physicists in the seventeenth century as an anthropomorphism, remains more than welcome in psychology as an explanation for the belief in a brain that registers everything and forgets nothing.

CHAPTER TEN

The Memory of the Esterházys

We rarely see novels presented as historical sources. It seems unlikely that a study of the Victorian fascination with the occult and spiritualism would list *Affinity* by Sarah Waters (1999) as one of the works consulted or that Ian McEwan's *Saturday* (2005) would find its way into the footnotes of a historical analysis of the US invasion of Iraq in 2003. A novel belongs to the fiction genre, and history, however indulgently we may draw the boundaries, is non-fiction. For an article about the controversies surrounding the Iraq War, a historian is more likely to consult congressional records, newspaper articles, radio reports, news footage and other sources that record the factual circumstances of events, or were at least created for that purpose. So historians end up in the usual locations: in library newspaper collections, among the files in town council basements, in audio-visual archives and in all those other places that help to give society a memory.

Yet we cannot be completely at ease with such a firm divide. Anyone wishing to study the relationship between the social classes in early nineteenth-century Britain will find nothing in the archives about those aspects that are precisely the most fascinating: the implicit codes of daily interaction, the unspoken rules of behaviour, all those protocols that set out what was proper or improper yet are not themselves set down anywhere. The historian will have to seek other sources, such as novels. In *Pride and Prejudice* or *Sense and Sensibility* we see those codes and rules in operation, still implicit and unspoken, but revealed in ways that advance our understanding of the class-based structure of the society of the time. The fact that *Pride and Prejudice* is as much a product of the imagination as *Affinity* or *Saturday* does not mean it has no historical insights to offer. A novel can sometimes be a better source of historical material than any archive.

On further reflection, the novel has a rather ambiguous position in relation to the archive, which is one thing it has in common with the human memory. The keepers of archives like to compare them with memories, and we often hear memory being referred to as an archive, but recollections are not arranged in rows, nor are they stored in chronological order or categorised by topic. Memories do not have the all-or-nothing character of a file that may or may not be available; they can be readily to hand at one particular moment and not at another. Memories erode, they fall apart, they end up scattered or on top of each other. The most important difference of all is that memory is finite. An archive will not disappear into thin air from one moment to the next when its compiler dies.

On the face of it we might even characterise memory and archives as opposites: memories are flexible, subject to revision, temporary, whereas files in an archive have a degree of permanence, can be put back exactly the way they came out, survive across generations and remain unchanged over time. It is tempting to say that what comes out of our memory is subjective whereas what comes out of an archive is objective. Unfortunately this notion of memory and archives is, once again, an oversimplification.

Celestial Harmonies

'I didn't so much "experience" the war,' Dutch author Harry Mulisch once wrote. 'I *am* the Second World War.'[1] With a Jewish grandmother who was gassed at Sobibór, a Jewish mother forced to go into hiding and a German father who worked for the much-feared 'robber bank' Lippmann-Rosenthal, in Mulisch all the major themes of the war years came together.

His fellow author, Hungarian Péter Esterházy, born in 1950, might be equally entitled to say, 'I *am* Hungary'. In him and his family, five centuries of Hungarian history come together. Esterházy studied mathematics and worked for a while as a systems analyst, but he soon made his name as a

novelist and essayist. In 2000 he published *Celestial Harmonies* (*Harmonia Caelestis*), a novel he had been working on for almost 10 years.[2] *Celestial Harmonies* is many things combined. It consists of two 'books'. Book I is a lively chronicle of the Esterházy family, introducing us to counts and electors, princes and barons, bishops and chancellors, every one of them referred to by Esterházy as 'my father'. The Esterházys were major landowners, with property on an almost inconceivable scale, sometimes described by Péter with a wave of the hand as 'a quarter of Hungary'.[3] Any 'father' taken at random owned 'fields so vast, the wild geese could not traverse them in one night's flight'.[4] The Esterházys' wealth was acquired mainly in the sixteenth and seventeenth centuries. During the Counter-Reformation, the Catholic Esterházys were given a great deal of the land confiscated from Protestants. When they sided with the Habsburgs in the war against the Turks, they were rewarded with aristocratic titles and large estates. The family's loyalty to the House of Habsburg can be measured in centuries. In 1683 it was Count Paul Esterházy (1635–1713) who came to its aid during the Turkish siege of Vienna. In 1809 Prince Nicholas Esterházy II (1765–1833) led a regiment of volunteers to liberate Vienna from the French army, rejecting Napoleon's offer to have him crowned king of an independent Hungary. From generation to generation the Esterházys engaged the most excellent artists, architects and craftsmen to build and furnish their citadels, castles, hunting lodges, summer residences, stately homes and city palaces.[5]

Péter Esterházy.

'Father' Nicholas Esterházy (1583–1645) married money, twice in fact, and in 1625 he was elected Count, the highest political position in the country. But the most famous 'fathers' are probably Prince Paul Anton (1711–62) and Prince Nicholas Esterházy (1714–90). In 1761 Paul

Anton took 29-year-old Joseph Haydn into his employment as Vice-Kapellmeister. Haydn was given responsibility for the court orchestra, music lessons and the library, but his main task was to compose music, often for Paul Anton, who was himself a creditable player of various stringed instruments. After Paul Anton died, his brother Nicholas became the musician's patron in his turn, and in the autumn of 1771, Haydn composed the renowned 'Farewell Symphony'. The members of the court orchestra, who spent every summer season at Esterházy Castle in Eisenstadt, separated from their families, had been waiting in vain for several weeks for Nicholas to declare the summer season over. The musicians asked Haydn to make clear to the procrastinating prince, with the utmost tact, that they would like to return home. Haydn wrote a symphony towards the end of which the players stand up one by one, blow out the candle on their music stands and quietly leave the stage. When the symphony was played for Nicholas, only two musicians were left at the end, first violinist Luigi Tomasini and Haydn himself. Nicholas got the message and promised his musicians they would soon be allowed to leave. Princes Paul Anton and Nicholas were not the first Esterházys with musical talents. Prince Paul Esterházy (1635–1713) is regarded as the most important Hungarian composer of the seventeenth century. In 1711 he published a *Harmonia Caelestis* of his own, a collection of religious songs.

All those 'fathers' helped to write the country's history. They were involved with the Reformation and the Counter-Reformation and they engaged in the delicate game of strategic marriage. They were generals in times of war and envoys in times of diplomacy. They negotiated matters of tax, excise and landed property, entered into conspiracies or fell victim to them, dictated treaties and received petitions, lost sons in battles against the Turks and danced at the Viennese court. They travelled to the Vatican as imperial envoys and held receptions for ambassadors. Their position was such that many of their activities were recorded in writing. The Esterházys began keeping archives in 1626 and the first official archivist was appointed in 1747. Biographers of Haydn who consulted the archive in Esterházy Castle long afterwards could trace exactly which rights and duties the Esterházy princes granted and imposed during over 30 years of their patronage. The family has an extensive paper memory made up of treaties, tenancy agreements, inventories, catalogues, marriage contracts, petitions, last wills and testaments, and dozens of other documents that have in turn found their way into historical studies of the role of the Esterházys in the cultural and political history of Hungary. This has allowed for a detailed reconstruction of the period during which the family was headed by Paul Anton and Nicholas: how they treated their staff, organised their household, dealt with tenants and instructed architects, as well as how they led their daily lives of audiences, travel and receptions.[6] It was in part that wealth of documents and their use in historical publications that enabled Péter Esterházy to write so vividly about his many ancestors.

I say in part, because in *Celestial Harmonies* the documents from the archive are really above all places where a dancing Péter Esterházy allows his feet to touch the ground for a moment. The *Harmonia Caelestis* written by his musical 'father' and published in 1711 is truly a collection of religious songs, but aside from that, the events Esterházy has him experience are largely fictional, as are the conversations between Prince Nicholas and Haydn, the battlefield manoeuvres of even earlier 'fathers' and the many versions of how his 'father' met his 'mother'. Anyone taken in by all the historical names, places and events is put straight from time to time by a cheerful anachronism, such as a stopwatch in the seventeenth century or a photograph in the eighteenth.

As well as his imagination, Péter Esterházy drew on two kinds of memory in writing Book I of *Celestial Harmonies*: that of the archives and that of his family, which took the form of stories handed down. In Book II a third kind of memory joins them: that of Péter Esterházy himself. The centre of gravity slowly shifts to the fate of Esterházys he has known: his grandparents, his uncles and aunts, his parents, his brothers and younger sister. This shift from ancestors to relatives and then to his own immediate family makes the stories more personal, although they are still rooted in historical events. For the Esterházys, history took several dramatic turns in the twentieth century. After the First World War, the Austro-Hungarian dual monarchy of the Habsburgs fell apart and the Hungarian Democratic Republic was founded, replaced in 1919 by the Republic of Councils under Béla Kun. Extensive expropriations followed, but they were later reversed. The transition to a republic left the Esterházys' property largely intact. That changed after – and because of – the Second World War. In 1944, Hungary was occupied by German troops and after the Red Army took Budapest in February 1945, the country came to lie within the Russian sphere of influence. Further expropriations took place in 1948 and this time they were permanent. Péter's grandfather Count Móric Esterházy, a former prime minister, was allowed to retain a few acres of land in recognition of his anti-German stance during the war, but the state seized all the family's castles, palaces, landed estates, art collections, libraries and wealth. All its privileges were annulled and its titles abolished. Péter's father, Mátyás Esterházy, born in 1919 as heir to one of Hungary's greatest personal fortunes, was transformed after the war from a count into a penniless 'class enemy', the product of a centuries-old line of class enemies. In Book II, Péter describes how the Esterházys dealt with this change in their fortunes.

Celestial Harmonies takes a tragic turn at this point, but the tone remains playful. There is a witty description of a historic meeting in 1917 between Péter's grandfather, Hungarian premier at the time, and the German emperor Wilhelm II: 'The emperor expressed his disapproval of various Hungarian and Austrian affairs of state. He had nothing to do with either, I had nothing to do with the latter. I told him. His eyes flashed so murderously, I could hardly suppress a laugh.'[7] The dialogue goes on for another few pages, until Péter Esterházy brings it to a mocking conclusion: 'In his book *The Tragedy of Europe*, Ashmead-Bartlett, English journalist, distorted the scene when he described it.'[8] Esterházy's stories about the implementation of the expropriations and confiscations are tragicomic too. In the invented dialogues he portrays the communist people's commissioners as foolish and fanatical, lacking any sense of tradition and history, without memory, no match at all for the Esterházys. Grandfather Móric was the first to encounter the new regime and Péter describes with pride how he behaved during those days of upheaval. He was the model aristocrat, noble to the core. 'It would have been difficult to look down on him from below.'[9]

But Book II of *Celestial Harmonies* is more than anything a monument to Mátyás Esterházy, Péter's real father among all those 'fathers'. After the war, Mátyás was initially allowed to settle in Budapest, where he and his wife Lily started a family. In 1951 he was deported to Hort, where the Esterházys, including Grandpa, were forced to lodge with a peasant family. Mátyás was put to work as a farm labourer, harvesting melons, and later as a roadmender.

Sometimes when he worked nearby, my brother and I would sneak a look (on the sly). We were awfully proud of him. Naked to the waist, he smoothed out the bitumen, while black streaks of dirt slithered down his body. From nearby someone would bellow at him now and then, *fuck it, Count, don't you fuck it up again!* Beads of sweat glistened on his back and around his waist and also his forehead. He wiped it off with his lower arm and fixed his glasses – a professor naked to the waist, smart and strong.[10]

Pride is the subtext of Péter's description of Mátyás. Working humble jobs such as assistant parquet layer, at the service of former subordinates, Mátyás retained his dignity. Péter regarded him as behaving in a way that demonstrated what spiritual nobility means. The children never heard him talk about the family's former wealth, even though for Péter Esterházy there was no escaping that past as he grew up. In primary school he was taught by political hardliners, whose grievances caused them to lash out against capitalism, exploitation, large-scale land ownership, feudal rulers and so forth. On a school trip the teacher pointed indignantly to one of the Esterházy castles: 'Another appalling example of feudalism'. And a little later: 'Whenever we reached yet another hunting lodge, the boys shrugged, that's yours, too, I bet, and I said you betcha, whose do you think it is.'[11] Along with his brother he jabbed his middle finger in the air once again. (That particular brother, Márton, was later to play 29 times for the Hungarian national soccer team. One is either an Esterházy or one is not.)

In the 1970s, the family's situation improved somewhat. Mátyás was given translation assignments, which must have suited him better than labouring on the land. He produced English and German translations of works including histories of the Benedictines in Hungary, Hungarian folk wisdom and superstition, and porcelain art. Péter recalls the long lonely days his father spent at the typewriter. Meanwhile the regime kept a close watch on the family. When grandfather Móric, who had left for Vienna, died in 1960, Mátyás was refused an exit visa to attend the funeral, on grounds of 'national interest'. Péter Esterházy also describes his father's darker side, his alcoholism and absences, but mainly he reveres him as a man who was not bowed or brought to his knees by his reversal of fortunes. One day Péter asked him whether they were in fact poor. His father looked around the room: 'Well . . . at this point in time I wouldn't call it rich'. He said that poor is not the opposite of rich, that a person who is not rich is not necessarily poor. Poor people are even lower down the scale, they are destitute; the poor are poorer than poor. 'No, son, we're not poor, we're just living in poverty'.[12]

Revised Edition

After the fall of the Berlin Wall in 1989 and the departure of the Soviet troops stationed in Hungary, eagerly waved off over the course of 1990, part of the archive of the Hungarian state security service was transferred to the Historical Institute in Budapest and made available for research. In the autumn of 1999, Péter Esterházy asked an acquaintance to find out whether there was any material about him. Perhaps he had been bugged or watched, or perhaps not, he writes, 'but I wanted to know objectively, and somehow or other I felt it was my democratic duty as a citizen as well – if not to clarify the past, then to pay attention to the past as it emerges from the examination of any relevant documents'.[13] Still busy finalising the manuscript of *Celestial Harmonies*, he did not visit the Institute until 28 January 2009. He arrived without any sense of disquiet. What did he have to fear? He was greeted with coffee. On the table lay three brown folders. So, apparently files had indeed been kept on him. The archivist did not seem entirely at ease.

> He kept touching the files briefly. He said there was something he had to tell me, but I mustn't be alarmed. I curved my mouth downwards reproachfully, but he said that he had a sense it was his duty to show me this and that, well . . . let's say that I would not be happy about it, and well . . . that he really didn't know, that perhaps it would be easiest if I looked inside them myself and then I'd see what it was, that is, what it was all about, and he slid the files towards me. Somehow or other, that little gesture contained something terrible. This was a work file, an agents' file – he heaved an incomprehensibly deep sigh, as if the existence of agents was a personal sorrow of his – one agent's reports.[14]

Péter Esterházy opened the top file – *and recognised his father's handwriting*.

The files make clear that shortly after the Hungarian Revolution of 1956, Mátyás Esterházy was recruited under the code name Csanádi. The first file was begun on 5 March 1957. Mátyás Esterházy, it turned out, had been an informant.

That first time, eye to eye with handwriting he had always so admired and that now proved his father had led a double life, Péter's hand began shaking so much that he had to lay it down on the table. Shortly after that, he rushed out of the Historical Institute in horror – 'No one must see my face now'.[15] But a few days later he came back and began the painful task of systematically working his way through the files. Then, over a period of 18 months, Péter Esterházy wrote another book, called *Revised Edition*. The above quotes are from the first few pages. Like *Celestial Harmonies*, the book is many different things at the same time. It includes excerpts from the reports Péter's father Mátyás wrote, to an important extent about his forebears and later about his immediate family, extracts from the diary Péter began keeping after his confrontation with the secret files, comments on those diary entries, historical notes about the show trials and executions in the time when his father served the regime as an informant, and thoughts about *Celestial Harmonies* in the light of his new knowledge about Mátyás Esterházy.

It is impossible to do justice to the feelings described by Péter Esterházy in *Revised Edition* by paraphrasing and quoting. There is shame, sorrow, anger, hatred and injured pride, but there is also pity for his father, pity for himself, disillusion, bewilderment that such a large part of his father's life took place completely outside his field of vision, and astonishment: Why? Why? Questions he cannot begin to answer, since his father died two years earlier. His bouts of weeping in the first few months, as he worked through the files, are eventually abbreviated in the text to a 't' for tears. The passages copied from the files are printed in red, the colour of shame.

Péter Esterházy's initial impression was that his father had written down only things that the secret services would already know, but it soon became clear that new and valuable information was included, such as 'It has come to my attention that residents of Csobánka called L.R., T. and Sz. took part in armed action in Budapest in October'.[16] Or: 'During the events of October, the red star was removed from the monument to heroes in Csobánka; I have heard that the culprit was the son-in-law of the sand and gravel merchant B.S., by the name of Sz'.[17] The hope that his father was quietly playing tricks on the secret services gave way to the certainty that he really did betray people. In the files, which cover the period up to March 1980, Mátyás Esterházy told his handlers which of his contacts were corresponding with foreigners, what he had heard from his old friends in the aristocracy, which of them sent him messages of condolence when relatives died and what kinds of activities were engaged in by relatives who were living outside Hungary. There were even stories that Péter, as a boy of 18, had told his father. What made reading the files unbearable was that so many of the names mentioned in them were up to that point simply uncles and aunts, friends of his parents, acquaintances who visited their home and perhaps, with hindsight, were invited purely so that they could be sounded out. In the way in which 'Csanádi' sought contact with his victims, Péter sees the charm at work that he so admired in his father when he was a child and now finds so repulsive.

Revised Edition is written in desperation. The thought that his father was working as an informant when prominent intellectuals, politicians, artists and members of the former aristocracy were being imprisoned or executed in the wake of the Hungarian Revolution causes shame that for Péter affects not just the past but the present – because meanwhile *Celestial Harmonies* has been published. The Hungarian novelist and former dissident György Konrád tells him in a birthday letter that Péter has written beautifully about his father. During signings, people say with tears in their eyes how moved they are by the affectionate portrait of Mátyás.

More than anything, the secret service documents are an assault on his memory. He opens the fourth file and reads:

I can report that Péter Esterházy (born in Budapest, 14 April 1950) is taking his leaving exams at the Piarist Grammar School and has up to now always been among the outstanding pupils. He has applied for the entrance exam to study mathematics at Loránd Eötvös University. I request that the interior ministry support his admission, assuming he achieves the required number of points in the entrance exam. Csanádi.[18]

The request was granted. A memo was sent to the Ministry of Internal Affairs, instructing that his application should be accepted. Péter had always assumed he was admitted purely on the basis of good marks at school. He has fond memories of attending football matches with his father, but now it turns out they were able to go only because the secret service arranged for them to have tickets. It was also the secret service that ensured Péter was given a passport for a trip to Vienna. Reading the files, he has to rethink all those incidents and events of his childhood. They now mean something else. His father is not the father he remembered, so Péter is no longer the son he remembered being. The revision of his memories leads to the long, depressing stream of 'revisions' that gives the book its title. What is he to do with his memories of his father's resilience, his pride in a man who had everything taken from him yet retained everything that mattered?

Without that pride he would have been unable to write his books and candid essays of the 1980s and 1990s, he says now, and it is precisely that pride that has been eroded. Perhaps the saddest 'revision' of all is this:

> My father has now, only now, become the Count of nothing. This has now gained (is going to gain) a weighty significance. Up to now it was more a nice and apt expression. A true expression but somehow also a triumphant one: those nobodies, those wretches are clearly not wretches, not nobodies, they are clearly all too rich (except that they pay less property tax than a hundred, three hundred, four hundred years ago). They are rich, because they have kept the most important thing: themselves.[19]

That sense of triumph has gone. The father's treachery is not an additional memory, it is a memory that changes everything and irreparably harms some of the most precious memories of all. With every file he opened, Péter Esterházy found himself robbed of more of his memories.

Archive and memory

In Esterházy's dealings with the Historical Institute where all this misery originated, the archive and the human memory seem to abide by the traditional division of roles. Péter's memories turn out to be capable of revision. They change in colour, feeling, taste and significance; they now refer to a different past from that which existed when the secret service documents were still stored unopened on the shelves. The files, by contrast, have remained what they always were: the written record of a long career as a secret agent. That is what they were when they lay on the table during Esterházy's first visit and that is how they were returned to the archive when he left. The differences between a file in an archive and a memory in a brain are so great, we might say, that the popularity among archivists of the comparison between archive and memory seems inexplicable.

In writing about documents, Péter Esterházy underlines once again their special status as reports of unchangeable facts that can never be revised. In his earlier work he simply checked sentences against other sentences, not against reality. But at the start of *Revised Edition* he writes:

> However quick a lie may be, the truth will catch up with it. Until now I have done what I liked with the facts, documents and manuscripts, whatever the text wanted me to do. Now that is no longer possible. I have to swallow everything. Until now I have pushed whatever I liked down readers' throats, I was lord and master, reality merely an imaginary servant.[20]

It is because of this new relationship that *Celestial Harmonies* is a novel and *Revised Edition* a work of non-fiction, a distinction between genres that places dossiers and documents on the side of the archive along with reality and truth.

But here we do not need to concur with Péter Esterházy. *Revised Edition* also allows itself to be read in a way that shows how vague the boundaries are between facts, memories and documents. For a start, what we read in the secret service documents is only partly determined by the text. A remarkable number of the people Mátyás was instructed to spy on turn out, according to his reports, to be no longer politically active. They 'reside in seclusion', 'keep themselves to themselves', 'have no interest in politics'. One man has gone to live in the countryside and found work in forestry, another is 'busy at home with his bees'. Of one of Péter's uncles, Mátyás writes: 'at the moment he is looking after canoes on the Római bank, on the Béke beach, where he lives, and politically he is completely passive'.[21] Such reports are meaningful only against the background of an interpretation that depends on the reader. Did Mátyás Esterházy want to spare these people? Did he secretly sabotage the work he was asked to do?

Had these particular contacts really withdrawn from politics? Not even Péter Esterházy can be sure in all cases, but he is at least in a position to consider various interpretations, each of which gives a different significance to the files. The same goes for a report from 1958. 'Csanádi' had been asked to record 'expressions of political opinion during everyday conversations'. His reports would serve 'above all to reflect the opinions of class-alien elements'. 'Csanádi' has little success to report. 'In the course of the conversation I kept bringing up the matter of the elections. In general I detected little interest, the reason for which may have been that in Csákvár the fair was in town, so it was hard to stick to that subject'.[22] Péter remembered that visit to the fair. His father and he, aged eight at the time, sat surrounded by their former servants:

> It's possible that we betray them intelligently. Nothing happens to anyone, no names are mentioned, but still, they sit there enjoying themselves at the fair together, drinking. They feel honoured, and they think very highly of themselves for daring to be seen in public with 'the landowner' (with his son), and anyhow they really like Daddy, they like him because he's nice; to your health Matyika, to yours Dodóka, t [tears], <nothing, they're all used up> then the agent goes home, his children hang on him like fruit on a tree; what has he brought back from the fair (presents), his wife sniffs at him a little suspiciously, seeking strange smells, then the agent goes to sit at his desk: be quiet, your father's working! And he begins to write: In the course of the conversation I kept bringing up the matter of the elections . . .[23]

Again, it is Péter's memories that determine the interpretation of the reports. Whether 'Csanádi' was assiduous or circumspect in his work, whether that remark about the elections is factual or ironical, depends on knowledge that cannot be found in the files and has to be brought into play by Péter. In fact everything mentioned in the files is surrounded by comments, memories, explanations, confirmations, denials, clarifications – in other words, it is because of the son's memories that the father's notes acquire a significance that makes it possible truly to read them, to understand what they say.

Nor is Péter Esterházy's reading the last word on the subject. He has privileged but not exclusive access to the meaning of his father's files.

After the publication of *Revised Edition,* several former dissidents joined the Hungarian debate about betrayal. Writer and former president Arpad Göncz said he knew only one person who truly became an informant of his own volition, the rest were forced, sometimes in response to threats, sometimes to protect their families. Férenc Köszeg expressed himself in similar terms: 'Mátyás Esterházy was arrested and repeatedly beaten; no one has the right to condemn him'.[24] Their readings of the 'Csanádi' files led to other interpretations again.

Here lies an essential similarity between documents and memories. The same may happen with the 'Csanádi' files as with Péter Esterházy's own memories, a revision so fundamental that it points to a different set of facts, a different past, a different reality. Documents do not just need human memories to interpret them, they change as those memories are brought into play. Archivists who call their archives 'memories' are therefore ultimately right, although the similarity goes rather deeper than the simple notion that both memories and archives have to do with the preservation of the past. Archives share the fluidity of the human memory. Archives too can forget.

Betrayal is perhaps the harshest way to make clear to someone that memories should not be seen as assets in the bank or valuables safely stored away. After the Stasi archives were opened several books appeared in Germany in which people describe how, without knowing it, they were spied on by close friends, family members, even their partners. Susanne Schädlich's favourite uncle turned out to have been a Stasi informant and she describes the dislocating effect that knowledge had on her memories of him.[25] It seemed as if those memories had lost all validity; each of them needed to be reconsidered and nothing of what the uncle did or said retained its previous meaning. All this gave her a different childhood from that which she remembered having.

Memories are not affected only by drastic political circumstances. Anyone discovering long-term betrayal by a friend, a loved one or a colleague will find themselves not just with a future that looks different but with a different past as well. All those memories of a dinner party are now accompanied by the knowledge that the betrayal was already going on. Memories have the capacity to change in hindsight. The tainted memory remains a memory, but no longer of what was originally remembered. It becomes a form of forgetting, too. It is both at once.

CHAPTER ELEVEN

The Mirror That Never Forgets

In 'The Oval Portrait', one of those remarkable stories by Edgar Allan Poe that seems to start somewhere in the middle, a man chances upon an abandoned castle in the Apennines. He takes up residence in a remote turret apartment for the night. The walls are hung with paintings from floor to ceiling and there is a small book that turns out to contain descriptions of them. He sits reading it for hours, looking up at the paintings from time to time. When he moves the candelabra, the light falls into a niche and suddenly the portrait of a young woman becomes visible, in an oval frame. The face staring at him out of the niche moves him deeply and he has to shut his eyes to calm himself. Then he looks at the painting fixedly for up to an hour to divine the secret of its effect. Its spell must lie, he realises, in 'an absolute life-likeness of expression, which, at first startling, finally confounded, subdued and appalled me'.[1] He moves the candelabra back to its former position and turns his attention to the book to find the story of the painting. It is a portrait of the painter's bride. Her husband asked her to pose and the radiant young woman spent many hours in the gloomy turret room he used as a studio. The painter, utterly absorbed in his work, failed to notice that his wife's health was suffering from the long days spent in the dismal light of that room. Slowly but surely she grew weaker. As the painting neared completion weeks later, he concentrated on it to the exclusion of all else. Eventually all it required was a few final touches to the mouth and eye. Then it was finished. 'For one moment, the painter stood entranced before the work which he had wrought,' the narrator reads in the book. 'But in the next, while he yet gazed he grew tremulous and very pallid, and aghast, and crying with a loud voice, "This is indeed *Life* itself!" turned suddenly to regard his beloved: – *She was dead!*'[2]

End of story. What did Poe imply by it? 'The Oval Portrait' was published in 1842. The daguerreotype had already taken America by storm and portraits were being made by travelling daguerreotypists or at studios in towns for a reasonably affordable sum. Was Poe referring to this development? Is his story a metaphor for the superiority of the painter who, unlike a photographer, can put real life and expression into a portrait? Was he trying to stress that a portrait, painted 'from the life', might sometimes not merely portray that life but seem to take it over, in the way that portraits, whether paintings or photographs, can displace memories?

As early as January 1840, just a few months after news of the invention of the daguerreotype first crossed the Atlantic, Poe wrote an article about the new technique.[3] He was mesmerised by it. He describes in detail how, in what he calls 'sun painting', a smooth copper plate is first covered with a polished layer of silver, then the surface is made sensitive by being held over iodine vapour. The plate is placed inside a camera obscura 'and the lens of this instrument directed to the object which it is required to paint. The action of the light does the rest.'[4] At first there is nothing to be seen on the plate, but after a brief treatment it displays 'the most miraculous beauty', of a kind that cannot be expressed in words. Only a reflection in a perfect mirror comes anywhere close, 'for, in truth, the Daguerreotyped plate is infinitely (we use the term advisedly) is *infinitely* more accurate in its representation than any painting by human hands'.[5] The new invention is an instrument of truth, of sublime perfection.

The astonishment Poe must have felt when he first laid eyes on a daguerreotype makes the meaning of 'The Oval Portrait' all the more of a puzzle. The story is not set at any particular time, so it may perhaps take place before the introduction of the daguerreotype, but the thoughts he attributes to his narrator about the 'absolute life-likeliness' of the painting and the painter's horrified exclamation – 'This is indeed *Life* itself!' – are responses found in their hundreds in those years, in diaries, newspaper articles and letters. It is as if he was connecting the enchantments of a new technique with a traditional genre as old as art. Did Poe feel disappointed, two years after his article about the invention, by the lifelike nature of the portraits that could already be seen everywhere? Had he concluded that 'infinitely more accurate' did not necessarily mean they expressed what life contributes to a face? Did he associate the recording of a face, frozen in time, with death? It is impossible to know. Poe never offered an explanation of 'The Oval Portrait'. Seven years later, in 1849, he posed for an oval portrait himself, a daguerreotype, and shortly afterwards, as if to illustrate his own story, he died in mysterious circumstances.

The questions Poe raised by writing his story and article are no less real today, a century and a half later – even, or perhaps especially, for a generation that has grown up in a time when photography is ubiquitous. Today, at least in the richer countries of the world, an intensive photographic documentation of our lives begins at birth, but the wishes and hopes that people had of the portrait in Poe's time are still with us, for example in many people's desire to own a drawing or painting of a loved one after their death rather than merely photographs. If none has been made in life, some people will take a photo to an artist and ask for a posthumous portrait. There is apparently something that photography, which has changed technically out of all recognition since 1839, cannot provide, perhaps that very thing that compelled Poe to make his central character a painter, rather than a daguerreotypist.

Eclipse

Even people with good memories for faces generally have poor memories for the history of faces. It is hard to recall what your neighbours or colleagues looked like five or ten years ago, even though you would probably have no difficulty recognising them from photographs taken at that time. Even when it comes to your own parents, children or partner, you would probably admit you have more chance of remembering a photo from 10 years ago than the face itself. It is as if a person's current appearance gets in the way of memories of what they used to look like.

Memories of our loved ones' faces are not safe even after they die. A friend told me that after his father's death he took a photograph to a painter to have a portrait made. The portrait was a success. A few small details aside, it was a good likeness, not just of the photograph but of the father as his son remembered him in the final years of his life. He had been in possession of the portrait for about five years when, on looking at it closely, he noticed that although he could recall which details he had found less than true to life, he could no longer actually see any discrepancy. The inaccuracies had disappeared, because there was no longer anything in his memory from which the portrait deviated.

It is hard to decide what had happened in those five years. Did the painted portrait slide in front of the memory, like a slow eclipse that refuses to clear? Or did the memory fade and eventually disappear, and would that have happened anyway, with or without the painting? Either way, the effect is the same. To my friend, the portrait, for all its faults, has become the face of his father.

It did not take the invention of photography to make people aware that portraits deployed to combat forgetting can themselves pose a threat to our memories. Nor is the effect limited to portraits. In his autobiography *La Vie de Henry Brulard*, Stendhal describes crossing a dangerous mountain pass as a 17-year-old boy. Thirty-six years later he still remembers vividly the fear he felt during the climb, but he can no longer call up any images. As for the descent, however: 'I can clearly picture the journey down. But I won't conceal the fact that five or six years later I saw an engraving of it which struck me as a very good likeness, and now I remember nothing but the engraving.'[6] He goes on to point out the risk of souvenirs:

> That's the danger of buying engravings of the fine pictures you see on your travels. Soon you remember only the engravings, and your real recollection is destroyed.
>
> That's what happened to me about the Sistine Madonna in Dresden. Müller's fine engraving has destroyed it for me, whereas I can perfectly well picture the bad pastels by Mengs in the same gallery in Dresden, of which I have never seen an engraving anywhere.[7]

Stendhal wrote this between 1835 and 1836, a couple of years before the invention of photography, but the disturbing internal tension he puts into words – that tension between wanting to have something that will help you remember and the worry that memories may be displaced by such a souvenir, or not even by the souvenir itself but by memories of the souvenir, memories that oddly prove more persistent – has probably never been so intensely felt as it was by the first generation of people ever to lay eyes on photographs.

The mirror with a memory

The American inventor and painter Samuel F.B. Morse became familiar with the daguerreotype process even before its official announcement on 19 August 1839. He was in Paris to patent his own invention, the telegraph, and he had heard rumours of a spectacular technique for conserving the images produced by a camera obscura. He offered to demonstrate the telegraph to Daguerre in return for an introduction to the daguerreotype. He was astonished by what he saw. The pictures were so sharp, he wrote to a New York newspaper in March 1839, that letters on a notice board illegible to the naked eye could be made out through the lens of a strong magnifying glass. The only problem, he was told by Daguerre, was the exposure time. It might be as long as half an hour, and anything that moved would end up blurred on the plate, or absent altogether. Daguerre said he doubted that his technique could ever be used for portraiture. He expected it to flourish in other traditional genres of painting, such as the still life, the townscape and the landscape.

Morse got to know the technical details of the procedure only after that official announcement. Back in New York, he immediately began experimenting. Within a few months he had managed to take a good picture of his daughter. On both sides of the Atlantic people worked feverishly to reduce the exposure time, but the Americans took the lead, so it was in America that the first daguerreotype portraits were made.[8] Within about 10 years the daguerreotype was mainly being used for portrait photography – with disastrous consequences for portrait painters, in both the Old World and the New. In 1850, of all the dozens of miniaturists in Marseille, only two were left who could live from their work.[9] They each painted some 50 portraits a year, whereas almost 50 people were making daguerreotypes, each turning out an average of 1,200 portraits a year for a tenth of the price of a miniature. There are comparable statistics for other cities and other countries. This rapid expansion was fuelled by the rise of a relatively prosperous middle class. The portrait, previously reserved for the aristocracy, was soon a favourite status symbol among the bourgeoisie and eventually, when it became cheaper still, a mass product for all social classes.

The newspaper articles that introduced the daguerreotype to a broad public were full of metaphors borrowed from painting. Morse described the pictures taken as 'Rembrandt perfected' and praised the attractive chiaroscuro. Poe explained that in 'sun-painting' the lens had to be pointed at 'the object which it is required to paint'. Professional practitioners made use of both the networks and the jargon of painters; they worked in 'studios', showed their work in 'salons' and asked their clients to 'pose'. At the same time they stressed that their procedure produced work superior to even the most successful painting.

The technique of the daguerreotype was presented as excluding any possibility of deception. It was the light itself that 'painted'. The human contribution was purely technical. No matter how naive the saying 'a photograph never lies' may seem in our own time, for its first 20 years the accurate – because direct – recording of people, objects and events was an ever-present element in the rhetoric of photography. In fact it was photography that mercilessly demonstrated how deceitful painters had always been in the past. In an article published in 1846, an anonymous author wrote that the flattery of painters was notorious: 'Everybody who pays, must look handsome, intellectual, or interesting at least – on canvas. These abuses of the brush the photographic art is happily designed to correct. Your sun is no parasite.'[10] In 1841, Ralph Waldo Emerson had praised the authenticity of the daguerreotype in his diary: 'No man quarrels with his shadow, nor will he with his miniature when the sun was the painter'.[11] Many photographers regarded the rapid decline of the miniature as the welcome end of a dubious sector. Their own moral superiority was derived from the automated nature of the daguerreotype. The camera was a truth-loving instrument.

In 1859, doctor and essayist Oliver Wendell Holmes warned his readers that photography had become so commonplace that there was a danger of forgetting what a miraculous invention it was. Previously the situation had been: 'The man beholdeth himself in the glass and goeth his way, and straightway both the mirror and the mirrored forget what manner of man he was.'[12] Photography, he wrote, is the 'invention of the mirror with a memory'.[13] That became a metaphor with which everyone could identify: photographers, because it underlined how truthful the new medium was, and portrait painters, because they did not actually regard the mirroring of reality as the purpose of their art.

In portraiture, the daguerreotypist interpreted the image seen in a mirror as 'true to life' or as 'life itself'. In 1849 an American practitioner wrote that not long ago an elderly lady had come to his studio and looked intently at the portraits on display there.

All at once she uttered a low exclamation, and then sunk, half fainting, upon a sofa. Water was brought to her, and after a little while she was restored to self-possession. She then stated that news of the death of her only daughter, a resident in the west, had been received by her a few days before. Remembering that a likeness had been taken a short time previous to her going to the west, the faint hope had crossed her mind that there might be a duplicate in the rooms of the Daguerreotypist. She had found it, and gazed once more into the almost speaking face of her child![14]

It was a recurring twist in memoirs and articles by photographers. As late as 1889, photographer Abraham Bogardus wrote of a woman who came to him with a portrait of her long deceased husband that was covered by a film of dirt. He went to the back room to clean it and when he held it out before her again he had to rush to her aid, as she fainted with shock. 'It was just as if her husband had been brought back from the grave for her to see.'[15] This was not merely photographers' rhetoric. Diaries and correspondence tell of the exaltation felt by those who saw the portrait of a loved one, even if the person depicted was still alive. In 1843 the poet Elizabeth Barrett (later to become Elizabeth Barrett Browning) wrote that she would love to have a daguerreotype of everyone dear to her, not just because of the likeness but for the 'sense of nearness'. 'I would rather have such a memorial of one I dearly loved, than the noblest Artist's work ever produced.'[16] In families that did have painted portraits, a daguerreotypist might be invited after a death to make several photographs of the painting that could be given out as keepsakes.[17] The reverse, having a portrait painted or drawn based on a photograph, as happens today, would have seemed an absurdity to Barrett and her contemporaries.

The viewing of a daguerreotype was an intimate matter. Like its 'truth-loving' character, this intimacy was inherent to the technique. Practically all daguerreotypes were 'sixth plates', measuring roughly seven by eight centimetres. The layer of silver recording the image was fragile and needed to be covered with a sheet of glass. The picture was presented in a protective case or holder that was often decorated with valuable materials such as leather, velvet and varnished wood. Portraits were not hung on walls, so they were not visible at all times. Viewing one involved seeking out a place where the light was good, opening the case, sliding the velvet aside and holding the surface in such a way that the picture was free of reflection. Looking was personal. It must indeed have given that 'sense of nearness' that Elizabeth Barrett wrote about. The observer was alone with the person in the portrait.

'That look, how came it there?'

The middle class that was so well served by portrait photography was expanding numerically even before Daguerre's invention, so the desire to mechanise portraiture as far as possible had been around for some time. In 1786, Frenchman Gilles-Louis Chrétien had invented a 'physionotrace', an ingenious device made of laths, cogs, hinges and pulleys with which the profiles of faces could be engraved on a copper plate.[18] In 1807, British physicist and chemist William Hyde Wollaston developed the *camera lucida*. The artist would look at an object through a prism and trace its outline on paper. The apparatus liberated the amateur, in the words of a travel writer who had worked with it himself, from 'the triple misery of Perspective, Proportion and Form'.[19] Then there were the 'pantograph' and the 'prosopograph'. Tracing devices of this kind became largely forgotten technology after the arrival of photography, but in the first few decades of the nineteenth century widespread use was made of them.

In the literature of the period, resistance can be felt here and there to all that tracing and mechanisation of portraiture. In fact the arena was already being created in which the battle over the relationship between painted and photographed portraits would be fought out after 1839. In 1837 Nathaniel Hawthorne wrote 'The Prophetic Pictures', a short story into which he wove themes that still dominate our thinking about portraits, their relationship to life, to time and to memory.[20]

Walter invites his fiancée Elinor to pose for a portrait. He intends to commission a painter who has recently arrived in Boston: 'They say that he paints not merely a man's features, but his mind and heart. He catches the secret sentiments and passions, and throws them upon the canvas, like sunshine – or perhaps, in the portraits of dark-souled men, like a gleam of infernal fire.'[21] His portraits inspire great respect, but also an ill-defined fear. Some people, daunted by 'the art which could raise phantoms, at will, and keep the form of the dead among the living, were inclined to consider the painter as a magician.'[22] Another rumour about him was doing the rounds. His gaze was said to be so penetrating that he could catch the future of his subject in a portrait. He painted a prophesy.

Hawthorne interrupts the story by musing as to why we want to have our portraits painted. After all, we can always look in a mirror. The reason must be that the image in the looking glass disappears when we walk away and a little later vanishes from our memories. 'It is the idea of duration – of earthly immortality – that gives such a mysterious interest to our own portraits.'[23] Walter is seeking earthly immortality for himself and his fiancée, portraits in which they would not grow old. But when they come to look at the completed portraits they are profoundly shocked. The longer they look at Elinor's picture, the more sad and anxious her expression seems.

'That look!' whispered she, and shuddered. 'How came it there?'

'Madam,' said the painter, sadly, taking her hand, and leading her apart, 'in both these pictures, I have painted what I saw. The artist – the true artist – must look beneath the exterior. It is his gift – his proudest, but often a melancholy one – to see the inmost soul, and, by a power indefinable even to himself, to make it glow or darken upon the canvas, in glances that express the thought and sentiment of years. Would that I might convince myself of error in the present instance!'[24]

There is no error. Over the course of her marriage, Elinor comes to look more and more like her portrait. It depresses her so much that she eventually hangs a silk curtain in front of it, supposedly to protect it from dust. Years later, the artist visits the couple to see the paintings, which have continued to haunt him. He has not only placed the past 'in that narrow strip of sunlight, which we call Now' but summoned the future to meet it there. He is truly a prophet.[25]

Hawthorne was himself fascinated by the mirror that never forgets. In 1851 he published the novel *The House of the Seven Gables*. The plot revolves around a portrait by a young daguerreotypist called Holgrave. 'I

make pictures out of sunshine,' he says modestly, but he adds that the
sunlight, far from merely depicting, 'actually brings out the secret character with a truth that no painter would ever venture upon, even could he
detect it'.[26] The portrait Holgrave has made is so extraordinarily sharp that
it betrays something about the man who posed for it, a feature invisible to
the naked eye that has to do with events that took place among his forebears. The novel suggests that the daguerreotypist can record not only a
person's present but his past, even the history of his family.

It is a remarkable reversal. In 1840, Poe wrote that the enchantment
and perfection of the daguerreotype are more sublime that those of any
painting, yet two years later he gave not a daguerreotypist but a painter
the power over life and death in his story. In 1837, Hawthorne made a
painter a character not bound by the ordinary laws of past, present and
future, yet in 1851 he transferred that mystery without further comment
to a daguerreotypist. The portrait painter and the photographer, it seems,
not only shared jargon and metaphors but derived their prestige from the
same magical ability to remove a face from the normal course of time and
life.

By about 1860, the most important arguments concerning the similarities and differences between painting and photographing a face had been
aired. In some artistic genres the battle had been well and truly lost. Some
painters of miniatures clung on bravely, on occasion appealing to precisely
those things for which they were reproached. When an apprehensive
Queen Victoria asked the renowned Swiss miniaturist Alfred Chalon
whether he did not feel threatened by photography, the polyglot answered:
'Ah, non Madame, photographie can't flattère.'[27] It would get him nowhere;
in the mid-1850s retouching was invented. That other perennial defence of
the painted miniature, concerning the loss of colours and halftones in the
hard black-and-white of the daguerreotype, would eventually become irrelevant, first because of colourisation, then with the invention of colour
photography.

The tension between the photograph and the painted portrait has
never been resolved, although in some ways the relationship between
them has changed over time. The two genres soon became interwoven,
professionally, technically and artistically. Many penniless miniaturists
took jobs with photographers, colouring and retouching their work, which
furnished them with a new way of applying their talent for pleasing the

subject. Sometimes portrait painters became photographers, often outstanding photographers, since a painter's eye was useful in matters of composition and lighting. Mixed techniques emerged. In 1863 a procedure was developed whereby photographs could be printed on a canvas, giving the portraitist a perfectly accurate underpainting.[28] It created a new genre, photo-painting, which according to a letter to a photography journal 'produces a work which has all the merit of photographic accuracy, and which at the same time [gives the painter] free scope for his talent'.[29] In 1860s America, the genre of the tintype or ferrotype became popular, a collodion negative on a lacquered iron plate whose black background created the impression that it was the positive of the photograph.[30] These tintypes were painted, again by former portrait painters. The result, once framed and mounted on a wall, fell somewhere between a photograph and a painting. Depending on which technique was dominant, the viewer saw either a photograph with paint added or a painting with a photograph underneath, but in either case this was a hybrid depiction of the person who had posed. It demonstrates just what people were expecting of it, a combination of the advantages of the two techniques, the realism of photography, a detailed record, with the interpretation and expressiveness of a painting. Unfortunately, in the case of tintypes the outcome was more or less the opposite. As a result of the underlying realism they make a surreal impression, while the thick layer of paint erases individuality and thereby actually gives them a more mechanistic feel.

Meanwhile, portrait painters were making increasing use of photographs as preparatory studies or as an alternative to posing. Their clients, now so familiar with photography, were less and less willing to sit for hours on end. With historic paintings in which many people needed to be recognisable, only the most important figures might pose, those at the centre of the composition, while those nearer the back were asked to provide a photographic portrait. Despite his aversion to photography, the celebrated British portrait painter William Powell Frith frankly admitted that in painting the marriage of the Prince of Wales in 1863 he had made use of photos, including one of Disraeli, without losing much by it, since his 'face on the canvas was certainly no larger than a shilling'.[31]

Opinions remained divided about one of the arguments for the superiority of either photography or portraiture. Antoine Claudet, Daguerre's licensee in London, wrote in 1865 that miniatures could be 'more or less accurate', but only photographs gave 'perfectly exact resemblances that at least please the heart and satisfy the memory'.[32] Lady Elizabeth Eastlake believed it was precisely in that accurate resemblance that a lack of selectivity lay. In an 1857 essay she wrote that photography ultimately betrayed its mechanistic nature by portraying the buttons of a coat with the same clarity as the features of a face. Photographic portraits, she felt, are in nine cases out of ten no more than 'facial maps'. They provide 'accurate landmarks and measurements for loving eyes and memories to deck with beauty and animate with expression.'[33]

Both Claudet and Lady Eastlake point to memory, but the contrast between them is telling. To Claudet the photograph seems to satisfy the memory because it records what someone really looked like, the face we would see if we stood next to the subject and looked in the mirror. Lady Eastlake believes the photograph does not perform a service for the memory, rather it is the memory that must serve the photograph. Without 'loving eyes and memories' there would be only the accurate but lifeless mirror image. The viewer turns it into the face of a loved one.

The portrait of Matilda

One of the largest collections of daguerreotypes in the Netherlands is held by the Enschedé family of Haarlem.[34] As printers and newspaper publishers, they were intensely interested in technological innovations and within a few weeks of the announcement of the invention of the daguerreotype, Johannes Enschedé ('Johannes III') recorded in his diary the purchase of a daguerreotype and not long afterwards a camera. The archive contains more than 80 daguerreotypes, mostly portraits, more than can be found in the archives of the Dutch royal family. In letters exchanged by family members, the excitement caused by the new technique is palpable, but they also wrote that through the new portraiture something could be expressed that had to do with remembering and forgetting, with the 'loving eyes and memories' to which Lady Eastlake had referred.

Johannes IV, son of Johannes III, had lost his heart to Matilda Lambert, a Parisian who occasionally stayed in Haarlem with mutual friends. Their wedding was planned for 29 November 1849. Matilda wrote from Paris on 26 October that she was very much looking forward to the portrait her future father-in-law had promised to have made of himself. A few days later, her fiancé was able to write that her wish had been fulfilled:

> My father has had his portrait made as a daguerreotype. See what an influence you are already having on us and especially on my father! He has never wanted to comply with our wish to have his portrait made, but he needs only to hear from you that you would like it and he immediately goes off to pose. The portrait is extraordinarily sharp, although his expression is rather fierce.[35]

Johannes IV promised to bring it with him when he came to Paris. Johannes III received a letter from Matilda by return post. 'How happy I was to hear that you have had your portrait done for me. I will treasure it greatly and keep it all my life as one of my most valuable memories.'[36] As so often happens, Matilda conflated photography and memory. She expressed her fondness for her future father-in-law by promising to cherish the picture as long as she lived. Unfortunately that was not long. She died within six years of her marriage.

Three years after Matilda's death, Johannes IV remarried. His new wife, Henriette Mirandolle, made a stylish entrance into the family. At some point in the months before the wedding she went to the Amsterdam painter Frederik Willem Zürcher and asked him, as it says on the receipt, 'for a painted portrait based on a daguerreotype'.[37] How this portrait was received by Johannes IV and his then seven-year-old son Jan (Johannes V) is described in a letter from Johannes IV to Matilda's mother, with whom he had kept in close contact:

> She has marked her entrance into her new family very magnanimously by sending Matilda's portrait, which is extremely successful. Jan immediately recognised his mother. The two girls who were here with me when I opened the crate that arrived from Amsterdam were moved to tears just as I was on seeing the features of she who is no longer in our midst. Naatje burst out sobbing. Jan Willem, who can generally be quite a harsh judge, admitted that he has hardly ever seen such a perfect likeness. I tell you, a woman who begins her new phase of life in such a way understands her task, as wife and mother and with a consciousness of her great responsibility.[38]

It is a gesture that has not lost its power to move. The portrait indicated that she had not come to replace Matilda or to succeed her, rather that she wanted to help to cherish the memories of the earlier love in her husband's life. It was a homage to Matilda's memory, but it was also a carefully considered departure from convention. In wealthy families of those years it was usually daguerreotypes of painted portraits that were made and distributed. Henriette did the opposite. Perhaps her gesture of 1858 helps us to understand why in our own time we still have portraits painted from photographs. The result is a single painting, as unique as the person portrayed in it.

The death portrait

In late 1839, Samuel Morse made a portrait of his daughter. Unfortunately it has since been lost, but it must have looked sinister. The plate had to be exposed for so long that blinking was inevitable, so Morse asked her to pose with her eyes closed. Six months later the exposure time had been reduced to such an extent that subjects could pose with their eyes open, but the absolute stillness necessary for a sharp portrait gave a deathly look to faces for a long time to come. The portrait that made time stand still required the avoidance of any movement, first by means of invisible supports to steady the head, later by the adoption of a practical pose with a hand under the chin, or with a couple of fingers held against the temple. The seriousness of all those early portraits was not merely the result of knowing that the daguerreotypist was on the point of taking a picture that would immortalise you forever; it also flowed from the requirement to adopt an expression you could sustain. A smile was not an option.

Many portraits were intended as mementos, often of a betrothal, a birthday or an anniversary. But sooner or later, as many people realised, the portrait would come to represent the subject long after his or her death. From that point of view, every portrait was a memento mori. The photographer borrowed from painting the methods of acknowledging this. A man or woman would pose with an open pocket watch, or with an hourglass on a nearby table, or a snapped flower in their lap. Not every symbol of mortality used by painters was appropriate for photography, but photographers kept intact the moralising connotations of posing. It was as if you had to pay a price for the vanity of having your portrait done. You were required to demonstrate profound awareness of the other meaning of the word vanity – futility or emptiness.

All too soon after the invention of the daguerreotype, a genre of portraiture emerged that needed no symbolism: the death portrait.[39] In the era of the daguerreotype this last portrait was often the first, especially when the subject was a child. A single photograph was both memento and memento mori. It would remind the parents for the rest of their lives of both the death of the child and the fleeting nature of life.

Type 'post-mortem photography' into Google Images and hundreds of examples of death portraits will appear on your screen.[40] Most are from the first half-century of photography. After that, post-mortem photography began to disappear, as a public genre at least. What were the parents, widows, widowers or children of the deceased expecting or hoping for? There are few sources to help us answer that question, but the 'poses' of the people portrayed give some indication.

In many portraits the deceased are recorded the way they are: dead. The body is laid out with eyes closed, in a shroud, hands together, clasping a cross or a rosary. Faces exude an atmosphere of peaceful surrender. Whatever may have preceded death – sickness, struggle, resistance – the deceased is now ready for the transition. This was what those left behind wanted to remember as a final image. It was a pose that fitted the notion of dying as passing on, with its metaphors of 'eternal peace' or 'falling asleep'. Clients wanted to see that peace portrayed in the final picture and photographers published advertisements that claimed they could comply with their wishes. Southworth & Hawes in Boston advertised in 1846 that they were able to photograph 'Deceased Persons' in such a way that they are 'so natural as to seem, even to Artists, in a quiet sleep'.[41] Their daguerreotypes of dead persons prove they had perfect command of the art. To the bereaved this was at the same time a portrait that would represent their loved one in a broader circle of family and friends. The means of communication and travel available at the time were such that not everyone could attend the funeral. A portrait gave them a chance to take a final look.

To the modern eye, unused to confronting the dead, these photographs have an eerie quality, but there is a far more shocking category of death portraits, in which the deceased poses *as if still alive*. Certain conventions and techniques were deployed in the production of this illusion. In the case of babies and young children, attempts were usually made to suggest that the child was asleep, but in a kind of sleep from which it might wake at any moment. The child would be laid in a parent's lap or on a divan, accompanied by a doll or a hobby horse so that on waking it could go on playing. With older children and adults, an entire arsenal of aids was deployed to make the body pose as if alive. The eyes were artificially fixed open or retouched to appear so. There are even examples of death portraits in which the subject looks straight at the lens, *standing up*. You can barely believe the boy is dead, until a caption points out that behind his shoes is the base of the heavy iron stand holding him upright, that the thickening around his waist, under his jacket, is a brace, and that the left arm resting on the back of a chair is held there by a wire. Only the swollen hand of the other arm, which hangs straight down, betrays the fact that the boy is dead.

It was a matter of professional pride to create a photograph in which no hint of death could be seen. An editor at the *Photographic and Fine*

Arts Journal wrote in 1858 that he had recently seen a daguerreotype of a deceased girl that was as animated as a portrait taken in life: 'It has all the freshness and vivacity of a picture from a living original – the sweet composure – the serene and happy look of childhood. Even the eyes, incredible as it may seem, are not expressionless, but so natural that no one would imagine it could be a post mortem execution.'[42] To make the eyes gleam, some photographers retouched their pictures with mica, while others put drops of glycerine into the eyes. In the case of the portrait of Sarah Lawrence, who died in about 1847, it was probably the

latter. A drum was placed at the girl's side as she lay on her back, drumsticks were put in her hands and the photographer must then have climbed a ladder above her and pointed his camera straight down. Perhaps his aim was slightly off; Sarah seems to be looking at a spot slightly to one side of the viewer.

In other death portraits the deceased have been lifted into a chair, in their everyday clothes, and surrounded by objects associated with them. There is a portrait from 1868 of a man in an easy chair in which the impression of sleep is reinforced by a newspaper lying in his lap as if having slipped out of his hands as he dozed off after a long day at work.[43] Who knows, perhaps that was a familiar sight to his family and was therefore how they wanted to remember him.

Most post-mortem photos in which the dead person is posing as if still alive are from America and Britain, but they were made in continental

Europe too, and the effect can be surreal. When an editor by the name of Reitmayer killed himself in 1864 by swallowing potassium cyanide, his body was taken to the studio of Viennese photographer Albin Mutterer.[44] A post-mortem portrait was made that with its natural expression, vague smile and cigarette between the fingers gives the impression that Mutterer really did have the power to bring a person back to life. In many death portraits the deceased is not alone. Babies and children are laid in someone's lap; older children are embraced. Family members stand next to the child as if he or she is still among them. In some the dead person is standing upright with an arm around a brother or sister. Although the eye is drawn to the dead rather than those accompanying them, these portraits also testify to the feelings of the parents and children posing with the deceased. They were displayed next to other photographs on dressers, on walls, or in the family album.

Post-mortem photographs were intended to 'keep the form of the dead among the living' as Hawthorne wrote of his mysterious portrait painter in 1837. But parents – and most of these portraits were of children – wanted the picture to be as animated as possible and were prepared to go to great lengths to achieve this. In some cases it meant the body had to be taken to the photographer's studio, although during epidemics of scarlet fever or diphtheria, for example, that practice was forbidden because of the danger of infection. When portraits were made at home, a considerable amount of equipment had to be brought in. Invoices often included the cost of renting a carriage.[45] Solutions had to be found for rigor mortis and discolouration of the skin. Post-mortem photography was a time-consuming, expensive and technically

advanced genre, so it amounts to proof of the intensity of the desire to keep the deceased alive in the memory.

Sometimes relatives were keen to do more than simply cherish their memories and portraits. They wanted a record of themselves commemorating the departed.[46] This led to the genre of the portrait within a portrait, in which people were photographed with a photograph of their loved one. Whether the photo in a photo was a post-mortem portrait (as often happened in the first 10 or 20 years of photography when no earlier picture had been taken) or a portrait made during life, it was always one that could be held, placed on the lap or clasped tight to the chest. The memento itself was at the heart of the composition. The loving way in which the portrait was clutched, whether turned towards the subject or towards the viewer, indicated the care with which their memory was cherished by the living.

Even the photo of a photo as a keepsake of a keepsake drew upon long-standing conventions of painting. Parents posed with their children, all of them, the dead included as portraits within the portrait. The bereaved have always used all available means to keep their deceased loved ones in their thoughts. The genre is still with us. Even now people sometimes pose with photos of the dead, although the photo within a photo is always one taken in life. The death portrait is no longer something to be put on public view. The decline set in a century ago, as soon as there was a fair chance that people had been photographed regularly when they were alive. This marked the end of that posthumous duty that seems so morbid to us when we first encounter the genre: to maintain the semblance of life long enough for a portrait to be made that will help those left behind recall what came before death.

Dead people are still photographed, although no longer by professional photographers.[47] Now it is the intimates of the dead who sometimes take a few final shots. Those pictures are not shown in public, not even in the family album, but kept hidden and looked at in the way daguerreotypes once were, at moments when the owner can be alone with them. If we no longer photograph the departed, then it is because we prefer to remember people when they were still living, and if we need photos for that, then they will already exist. They find their way into commemorative albums or even into PowerPoint presentations made for the funeral. It is now the corpse itself that has to look as much alive as possible. In those many cultures where mourners are invited to view the deceased, cosmetic techniques and other aids are used to cover up all traces of death, and they are at least as sophisticated as those of a nineteenth-century photographer. We still try to create an illusion of a dead person who seems to be asleep, as peaceful as those babies once looked in their death portraits.

'Rubbing one against the other'

After his wife Emma kills herself, Charles Bovary, grief-stricken, struggles to carry on with his life. He concentrates on honouring her memory, travelling twice to Rouen to choose a grave monument, studying some hundred designs, thinking about what he wants to have engraved on the tomb, racking his brains as to the most beautiful symbol, the best text. But in the middle of all this remembering and commemorating, he becomes aware of something disturbing: 'There was one strange thing, and that was that, though Bovary was always thinking about Emma, he began to forget her. And he was filled with despair as he felt her image fading from his memory, despite all the efforts he made to retain it.'[48]

Flaubert introduces his description with 'there was one strange thing,' but this experience is a well-known phenomenon among mourners. Sometimes a person who loses a loved one may realise with shock even after just a few days that their face cannot be called to mind. As in Charles Bovary's case, it causes profound despair: if I've already forgotten something as familiar as the face, what will be left of my memories in a few months or years from now? That forgetting of a face so soon after death is fortunately a transitory phase, part of the grief and dislocation that, remarkably enough, can also cause the opposite, namely a hallucination that suddenly makes the dead person present once more as an image or a voice.

In the slightly longer term, however, the memory of a face, an expression, a glance, or the way the face looked as it moved will indeed fade. In resisting this we often turn to photographs as the most obvious aid to the memory. In 1857, again in *Madame Bovary*, Flaubert described what can happen. One of Emma's lovers, Rodolphe, has a box of memorabilia, including letters, handkerchiefs and locks of hair. Among them is a miniature of her: 'From looking at this image and recalling the memory of its original, Emma's features little by little grew confused in his remembrance, as if the living and the painted face, rubbing one against the other, had effaced each other.'[49] Precisely the thing intended to support a memory actually puts it in peril. 'A photo preserves something,' Rudy Kousbroek wrote, 'but it is not always obvious that through that very process of preservation something is lost. A portrait photograph, especially of a dead person, dislodges the recollection of them; the photo pushes it away, replaces it, makes something fade in the memory.'[50] When you take a photograph you do not end up with both the memory and the picture. Right from the start your memories are mixed up with the photograph and after a while the photo becomes mixed up with your memories. The question is, for the psychologist at least, why do photos have this effect? Is it really because of the photograph that the memory disappears? Why can we not retain both? Lack of space perhaps?

Our memory for faces is part of the visual memory, the capacity of which is vast, as became clear in the early years of psychology. The classic experiments designed to discover just how capacious it is were carried out in the 1960s and 1970s and its limits were found to be a receding horizon. In an experiment in 1967, test participants were shown 612 pictures, each for six seconds. They then had to look at two pictures and say which of them had been included in the series of 612. They were correct in 98 per cent of cases. Another experiment used more than 2,500 colour slides, each shown for between five and ten seconds. A day and a half later the participants managed to recognise those slides among other slides with an accuracy of 90 per cent. This is a remarkable success rate, especially since there was nothing particularly striking to be seen in the slides: a tree, an aircraft, a dog. In a follow-up experiment, participants looked at 10,000 slides, so many that they had to be shown over a five-day period, 2,000 per day.[51] Those too were to a great degree correctly identified several days later. There is no way to determine the capacity of the visual memory, since anyone attempting to do so will run up against another limit first, that of human tolerance for boredom. Lack of space is not the problem.

But, you might say, what an experiment like that tests is recognition rather than memory. Saying you have seen a picture before is not the same as being able to call it to mind. This is an objection that points the way to an explanation for the fading of faces in our memories. Information in the visual memory allows itself to be updated, quite readily in fact. If on leaving the cinema you remembered all the places where you had ever parked your car or bicycle just as clearly as you remembered the last of them, then you would be thoroughly confused. You might have to wander the streets until you had checked every single one. The memory seems to dispense with outdated information, overwrite it or make it inaccessible. Whichever is the case, only the latest information is activated. It is easy to see the evolutionary advantage of this, but the same useful mechanism also removes our memories of what the faces of our parents, children, wives, husbands and friends used to look like. Memories of their faces are continually being revised and renewed, and in the process earlier versions are removed. What makes looking at photographs such a melancholy affair is that it reminds us of what we have forgotten.

This is not the only ambiguity in the relationship between photographs and memories. Photos, it is often said, have a permanency that a memory can never acquire. Our memories die with us and what we are in the memory of others dies with them. A photograph remains. But what exactly remains of a photograph?

In *Out of Mind* by J. Bernlef, dementia sufferer Maarten Klein and his wife Vera leaf through their photo album. Their family doctor felt it would be a good way to 'get Maarten's memories in order'. The photos of long ago bring back many memories: the war, the food of those days, the furniture, the outings, the holidays in boarding houses, the children when they were young. But photos of later years mean nothing to him. 'Maybe it's because of the photographs themselves,' Maarten muses:

A camera makes no distinction between important and unimportant, foreground and background. And at this moment I myself seem like a camera. I register, but nothing and nobody comes closer, jumps forward; no one touches me from the past with a gesture, a surprised expression, and these buildings, streets and squares exist in towns and cities where I have never been and shall never go. And the closer the photographs approach the present, as appears from the dates written underneath, the more impenetrable and enigmatic they seem to become.[52]

Here Bernlef creates a mirror effect. Things that have lost sharpness and significance in Maarten's memory disappear from the photographs too. They do so gradually and in accordance with what has been known since the late nineteenth century as Ribot's Law, after the French psychologist Théodule Ribot who discovered that memory loss in dementia begins with recent memories and then moves further back. This eliminates any prosthetic value photos might have. When the doctor comes round a few days later and asks how he got on looking at photos, Maarten says: 'Seeing photographs is quite different from looking at photographs. . . . Anyone can look at photographs, but seeing a photograph means being able to read it.' He goes on, 'You can't read that photo album on the table for the most part because you lack the necessary background information. You weren't there. In other words, you cannot form any further pictures about what is in there. . . . It isn't your past.'[53]

Dementia intensifies the ambiguities seen in the relationship between photos and memories even in ordinary, healthy lives. Personal photos sometimes turn time around in just the same way, even without memory loss, in the sense that as we age, older photos may call up more memories than recent ones. The fact that Maarten can say all kinds of things about photos of long ago but draws a blank with photos from the past 10 or so years is a grotesque manifestation of the mechanism that operates in every ageing memory. A photograph needs memories in order to mean anything.

At a flea market or when inspecting lots in advance of an auction, you may come upon a photograph album compiled in the late nineteenth century, so long ago that you can be certain that everyone in it is dead, even the youngest, that little girl on someone's lap. The people who once remembered them must be dead by now too. It is often unclear how such albums came to be among the rubbish, but there may have been no descendants left, or perhaps those who remained had no interest in pictures of unknown relatives. The photos are not their past. Like the eyepieces of a stereoscope, memories give depth to the photos you insert, creating a third dimension, drawing you in as if you are right inside the picture for a moment and involved with what you can see there. Without memories we lose any hint of perspective. We look at the pictures in a forgotten album the way Maarten looks at his recent photos, seeing nothing.

CHAPTER TWELVE

The Second Death

Between the summer of 1793 and the summer of 1794, Paris resembled one big prison. The new revolutionary regime, which had declared France a Republic in September 1792, requisitioned monasteries, churches and barracks and used them to hold people arrested on suspicion of counter-revolutionary activities. It was a time that has gone down in French history as the Terror.[1] Some 7000 suspects were brought before the Revolutionary Tribunal set up to try people for crimes against the Revolution. At the peak of the Terror, in June and July of 1794, more than 1,370 men and women were sentenced to death and executed by guillotine on the Place de la Révolution.

As for the crimes they had committed, the accusations varied widely. Sometimes the charges were treason, embezzlement or corruption. Others were suspected of maintaining dubious contacts or of having written something that could be interpreted as in conflict with the spirit of the Revolution. A house search might turn up a letter from abroad that had not been reported. Sometimes there was even less evidence. People might find themselves arrested purely and simply because they were 'suspected of being suspect'.[2] Financial offences – or presumed financial offences – were punished particularly harshly. The revolutionary regime had passed a series of decrees in quick succession designed to prevent the French state from being deprived of money or goods. From one day to the next, for example, a 'law on *émigrés*' declared possessions belonging to members of the former aristocracy who had fled abroad to be forfeit, making them the property of the Republic. Many dukes, counts and marquises rushed headlong back from Switzerland or Holland to ensure they were officially registered as resident in France. That meant they needed fake residence permits, and in many cases they were arrested as a result and saw their capital confiscated. The 40 temporary prisons in Paris filled up with aristocrats, as well as former judges and officers of the royal court, and priests who had refused to swear an oath of allegiance to the state. Legislation was arbitrary in the extreme, its enforcement cruel and repressive.

The public prosecutor of the Revolutionary Tribunal was called Antoine Quentin Fouquier-Tinville. On his appointment he was awarded an annual salary of an ominous 666 livres. He managed to secure the conviction of just about everyone brought before him. Once they had fallen into the hands of Fouquier-Tinville and his powerful judicial apparatus, most of those arrested had no illusions about their chances of getting out alive. Conviction meant certain death; there was no right of appeal. A stay of execution could be granted in one circumstance only: if the convict was pregnant, her beheading would be postponed until one day after childbirth, which meant that the first contractions announced not only the coming of a child but the approach of death.

Those about to be executed were given permission to write farewell letters, of which several hundred have been published.[3] Even two centuries later, one cannot fail to be moved by these letters, but they also prompt a sense of intrusion. They are not addressed to us but to loved ones, children, parents, husbands or wives, brothers and sisters, friends, or whoever the condemned person chose as the recipient of their final message, so we are violating the pact of intimacy that exists implicitly between a letter writer and the intended recipient. This feeling is compounded by the fact that we are reading them *instead* of the person addressed. None of the letters ever reached its destination. Each and every one was intercepted, scrutinised for information that might be of interest to the Revolutionary Tribunal and then stored away in the prison archives. None of the children, parents, husbands, wives or friends ever laid eyes on them. That is, incidentally, the reason we have them. Later, under a milder regime, valedictory letters were delivered to the next of kin and virtually all have been lost. It is an ironic reversal: bypassing the memories of those for whom they were intended, the letters ended up in the archives, where they continue to keep the memory of the Terror alive.

What all the letter writers have in common is the certainty that within 24 hours, often much sooner, they will be dead. They know they are writing the last words they will ever be able to say to their loved ones. They realise they will soon be alive only in the memories of family and friends. Now that the hour of death is at hand those memories loom large. In their darkest moments, they seek comfort in the prospect of being remembered. In our own day it has been referred to as 'the second death': you are only truly dead when you are gone from the memory of those you left behind. Their first death, on the scaffold, was inevitable and they had no choice but to resign themselves to it, but none wanted to accept a second death. They all tried to find their own way of expressing it, but essentially the message is the same in all cases: 'do not forget me'. Indeed that is the most common form of words.

They did not usually limit themselves to that simple plea. Practically every letter includes instructions on how their memory should be preserved. Sometimes it was a matter of how to treat mementos, more often how to deal with the memory itself. What could be done to keep forgetting at bay? What memories should those left behind cherish and what would they do well to forget? How should they treat children who were still too young to comprehend what had happened to the father or mother they remembered? And above all: how did the writer want to live on in memory? What kind of wife or husband, father or mother, son or daughter, lover or friend had they been? What did they wish to pass on to their loved ones? What, if you only had a couple of pages in which to express it, was the most essential thing about yourself that you wanted to commit to the memory of others? These questions had suddenly become urgent.

But before we start looking at the letters, let us take a few steps back. Why these in particular? There are several comparable collections. Letters written by members of the resistance under regimes of military occupation, for example, who knew they would be executed at dawn. Or by soldiers surrounded by an enemy they knew would take no prisoners. Or by Polar explorers who knew they were never going to make it back. Why a collection from the time of the Terror?

One reason is our sense of embarrassment. The discomfort of reading a letter not addressed to us is proportional to its proximity to our own time. It becomes insurmountable with regards to notes thrown from trains going to the concentration camps by people who were contemporaries of our parents or grandparents. A distance of 200 years does not eliminate all sense of intrusion, but the knowledge that we are seven or eight generations removed from the addressee makes it easier to set aside that feeling of impropriety.

The second reason is that we can identify with the content of those farewell letters, despite the distance in time, to an extent that really ought to amaze us. It struck me only after I had read 20 or 30 of them. There is very little in the way of prayer. The late eighteenth century was a time of faith and piety, yet no more than a handful of these letters allude to being reunited with loved ones in an afterlife. The comfort most of them seek is more secular and closer to home. Their life after this life is that which people who loved them preserve in their memories. What they hope for or desire precisely reflects what so often dominates today's death notices, letters of condolence and funeral orations: the promise to make sure the dead person lives on by cherishing good memories of them. This gives the letters an immediacy that cuts right across all those intervening generations. They are from long ago and yet also of our own day.

The comfort of a portrait

Many of the letters stretch across time in both directions. The condemned look back on lives that are about to come to an end and turn their minds to how those left behind will keep the memory of them in their hearts. The intensity of the desire to be remembered is clear from the efforts made by many to pass on something that could help sustain that memory. If circumstances allowed, they sent mementos: a ring, a portrait, a medallion. Several managed to have a miniaturist make a drawing of them, which they enclosed with the letter.

Fearful that the Terror would culminate in civil war, Charlotte Corday travelled by stagecoach from Caen to Paris on 9 July 1793 and took a room in a hotel. Nearby she bought a long kitchen knife. In her room she wrote a declaration to the people of France. The key figure in the horrors of the Terror was in her view Jean-Paul Marat, journalist and agitator, and at that point leader of the Jacobins. On the morning of 13 July she knocked on the door to his house and said she had a list of the names of Girondists who were planning a revolt. She was sent away. That evening she tried again and this time she was admitted and spoke to Marat who, because of

Charlotte Corday, after she had posed in her cell for the portrait that she wanted to leave her loved ones as a 'token of her memory'.

a skin disease, dealt with many of his affairs from the bath. While he was copying down the names of the conspirators she pulled out the knife and stabbed him to death.

Corday knew she would pay for the attack with her life. She made no attempt to flee. In prison she asked for a painter of miniatures, accompanying her request with arguments aimed at keeping her memory alive, even if it meant being remembered for a crime:

> Since I have only a few moments left to live, might I hope, citizens, that you will allow me to have my portrait painted. I would like to leave this token of my memory to my friends. Indeed, just as one cherishes the image of good citizens, curiosity sometimes seeks out those of great criminals, which serves to perpetuate horror at their crimes.[4]

At her trial she considered the portrait drawn by the court artist such a good likeness that she invited him to finish it in her cell. According to a newspaper article, she posed 'with unimaginable tranquillity and gaiety'.[5] On 17 July 1793 she was executed, four days after the murder of Marat and 10 days before her 25th birthday.

It says a great deal that someone who left a written political testimonial, expounded upon her motives during her trial and sent a valedictory letter also went to such trouble to leave a portrait of herself. The picture was intended as a 'token' that would preserve her in the thoughts of others. In her letter she said farewell to her father and sister, but it seems it was the portrait that she believed would do most to preserve her memory.

The hope of leaving at least a portrait is also expressed in the detailed instruction contained in an unsigned letter to Fouquier-Tinville:

I beg you, citizen public prosecutor, to be so kind as to send to my son, a child of ten, staying in the Rue de Berry, my portrait, which you will find on a portfolio in my red morocco writing-set, which must have been handed over to you. You are taking from him a mother whose picture, at least, must remain with him.[6]

One of the prisoners – who ultimately survived – later described how comforting it was to be able to leave a portrait behind. 'It was still a pleasure to have locks of our hair cut off, to stick them around medals, portraits and send them to our wives, our mothers, our children, to those dear persons that we would never see again.'[7] Conversely, the condemned prisoners often longed for a miniature of their loved ones. Lawyer Camille Desmoulins begged his wife Lucile to send him her likeness as quickly as possible. If necessary the painter should have her pose twice a day. 'In the horror of my imprisonment that day will be a treat for me, a day of entrancement and ecstasy, the day that I receive your portrait. Send me meanwhile a lock of your hair to press to my heart. My sweet Lucile!'[8] He was executed on 5 April 1794. Later that week his wife was also arrested. On 13 April she met the same fate as her husband.

The prisoners kept those little portraits with them as long as they could. Another of the letters is from a widow by the name of L'Herbette, who had heard that a miniature of her was found on her husband's corpse. 'Since I think my face can be of interest only to those who know me,' she wrote to Fouquier-Tinville, 'I dare to hope that you will not refuse to return it to me.'[9] She offered to reimburse the Republic for the cost of the gold frame. She must have found it unbearable to think that the last token of her held by her husband was now in the hands of those responsible for his death.

Some of the condemned tried to leave something behind that would find its way not into a personal memory but into the collective memory, into history. Decommissioned captain Millin de Labrosse, more of a hothead than was good for him, had allowed himself to be drawn into a quarrel with a provocateur and in his anger said the wrong thing. His case is perhaps not the most tragic of those times, but it might be described as the silliest. He wrote to Fouquier-Tinville that he had invented an 'aero-stat', a special kind of air balloon, of which there was a cardboard model in his cell. Eleven years earlier the first manned flight with a balloon had been made by the Montgolfier brothers; presumably Millin de Labrosse felt he had thought of a vital improvement. He offered to explain its construction to the revolutionary committee. That would take less than two hours, so he could still be executed within the 24 hours specified by the court. He wrote that his concern was not to secure any postponement. His final statement is a reference to the memory he hoped to leave: 'I am resigned. I shall die resigned. I am not trying uselessly to prolong my life, but I admit that I am still thinking of what might be done so that my name may be remembered, when the time of anger is past.'[10] He was not asking for a longer life but for a life in the memory that we call history. There is no indication that anyone took the trouble to come to his cell for a moment to look at his cardboard balloon. His letter disappeared into the archive with all the rest. The name Millin de Labrosse does not feature in the history of the air balloon, but ironically his letter ensured he would be remembered as the man who wanted to be remembered.

Most of the prisoners had all their possessions taken from them and they will have had no illusions about the return of their valuables. Department administrator Pierre-Jean Sourdille-Lavalette swallowed his wedding ring before he was executed. But in a letter it was possible to designate objects outside the prison as keepsakes and to allocate them to specific individuals. The Marquis de Gouy d'Arsy, 41 and convicted of conspiracy, wrote to his wife:

> To my eldest son I send the key to my little case; I have wrapped it in paper, which contains a few important words for him and his brothers; you will give to all the others some other object that belonged to me and which may prove to them that I love them all equally. Let them copy out this letter and you, my dear, keep the original, for it concerns you.[11]

That last point, that the letter itself is intended as a memento, seems so obvious that it might escape our notice, but many of the farewell letters include instructions as to what should be done with it. With the insouci-ance of a 20-year-old, Étienne-Pierre Gorneau had spoken disparagingly of the republican institutions and was convicted after anonymous tip-offs.

At the end of a long letter to his father and the other members of his family he wrote: 'I take my sincere farewell of all my friends and relations: I embrace them for the last time. I want my father to keep this letter for his descendants, to remind them that I existed and perished on the scaffold, a victim of my opinions.'[12] For the Marquise de Charras, too, a letter was all she could leave. To her husband and three children she wrote, 'As long as I live, my heart is yours. I am close to the fateful moment. Never forget me. I ask my poor children to keep this last note from me for ever. Farewell, I send you my last breath.'[13]

Sometimes the letter served as a chance to say something to the children that they would not yet understand or might all too quickly forget. Etienne François Maulnoir, a former magistrate, wrote to his wife: 'Talk often of me, especially to the young ones who will scarcely remember seeing me. Keep this letter and read it to them that they may see that all my wishes were for their happiness and to give them an upbringing that may enable them to earn a living, since I leave them no fortune.'[14] Such passages are not uncommon; the letter would need to bridge a gap of 10 or 15 years to reach a time when the final words could truly be taken to heart.

'My children, here is my hair'

A miniature and the letter itself – what else could be left? An earlier letter had been confiscated from Jeanne-Charlotte de Rutant, aged 23, that told of the day-to-day concerns of the aristocratic family of which she was part. The seemingly blank reverse side, on which she had written in ink that became visible only when the letter was held over a candle flame, carried information about emigrants, enemy troop movements and a secret manifesto. She was arrested and condemned to death. Three hours before her execution she wrote a farewell letter to her brother. All she could add to the letter was her hair. 'I hope they will allow you to have my hair, which will not have been touched by the executioner. . . . Share my hair between you, my beloved, and do not forget me though your hearts ache when you remember me, farewell!'[15] It was not only women who sent locks of hair. Philippe Rigaud, 36, sentenced to death for supplying uniforms of inferior quality, added a lock of hair to the little he was able to dispatch. 'I am sending you, my dear wife, the only thing that still belongs to me; you will receive it in my letter, it is a tuft of my hair. When you look at it, think sometimes of someone who loved you well.'[16] But of all the condemned prisoners who sent hair, none made such efforts to get that bequest into the hands of relatives as the princess of Monaco.

Françoise-Thérèse Choiseul-Stainville, French by birth, was married at 15 to Prince Joseph, of the Grimaldi family. As princess of Monaco she was entirely uninvolved with French affairs at first, but that changed when the principality was annexed by France in 1793. From one day to the next she became a French citizen again, and to avoid being subject to the 'law on émigrés' she hurried to Paris. At first she was at liberty there, but after her husband sided with rebels she became subject to new legislation, rapidly passed, called the 'law on suspects', and her arrest was ordered. Fouquier-Tinville showed no mercy. Françoise-Thérèse was sentenced to be guillotined. She had two daughters, Honorine aged 10 and Athénaïs who was eight. She herself was 27.

Once in detention she had hardly any tangible possessions to leave, but she dealt with what remained with steadfast determination. She reported to the prison authorities that she was expecting a child. She needed a delay of only one day to carry out her plan. She plaited her hair and cut it off with a shard of glass she had managed to obtain. Then she wrote a short note to Fouquier-Tinville to impress upon him that he must ensure the plait reached her daughters. She admitted she had lied about her pregnancy:

Françoise-Thérèse Choiseul-Stainville, princess of Monaco (1767–94).

I did not soil my mouth with this lie out of fear of death, nor to avoid it, but to give me one day more, so that I might cut my own hair, and not have it done at the hands of the executioner. It is the only legacy that I can leave to my children; at least it must be pure.[17]

She was clearly concerned that this lie would detract from her memory, since in a letter to her children's governess she asks that her aunt Louise, the duchesse de Choiseul, 'know the reason why I postponed my death, that she may not suspect me of weakness'.[18] Lastly she wrote a letter to her daughters, to accompany the plait of hair. It included detailed instructions on how to treat her bequest.

> My children, here is my hair. I have postponed my death one day, not out of fear, but because I wanted myself to cut off these sad remains of me that you might have them: I did not want it to be left to the hands of the executioner and these were my only means. I have spent one more day in this agony, but I [words crossed out] do not complain.
>
> I ask that my hair be placed under glass, covered with black crêpe, put away for most of the year and brought out only three or four times a year in your bedchamber so that you may have before you the remains of your unfortunate mother who died loving you and who regrets her life only because she can no longer be useful to you.
>
> I commend you to your grandfather: if you see him, tell him that my thoughts are with him and that he stands in place of everything for you, and you, my children, take care of him in his old age and make him forget his misfortunes.[19]

Françoise-Thérèse's marriage made her part of the Grimaldi family, which had ruled Monaco for five centuries. She must have had experience at caring for and conserving memorabilia left by earlier generations. Could that be where she got the idea of a bell-jar and mourning veil? The bell-jar may have been intended to preserve the scent, the black crêpe to prevent the hair from fading, but odour and colour would have been better preserved in a casket. Might she not instead have been trying to find a way to preserve its vitality as a keepsake? With her instructions about lifting the veil only once a year and moving the hair into the children's room no more than three or four times a year, Françoise-Thérèse seems to have been concerned less about conserving the plait than about the arrangements for remembering her. What she wanted to avoid at all costs was the overfamiliarity of any memento permanently on view, which eventually makes it cease to function as a memento at all.

The princess met her end in a city where Proust more than a century later would wonder why the madeleine cake he had tasted revived old memories, whereas he had often seen those same madeleines at the baker's shop without any associations being sparked by them. Proust mused that the continual repetition of the visual experience had robbed the madeleines of their associative power. All those different associations had gradually erased each other, so that 'nothing now survived, everything was scattered'.[20] Strict rules on how to deal with the hair were the best guarantee against precisely this loss.

On the morning of the execution, 26 July 1794, a witness saw that the princess had her hair and the letters with her when she was led to the cart. He heard her call to a guard: 'Swear to me, in the presence of these honest men, whom the same fate awaits, that you will carry out for me this last service, which I expect of a human being.'[21] Whether or not he made that promise is unknown; the plait and the letters were unceremoniously consigned to the prison archives.

There is a cruel irony in the way history treated the princess of Monaco. While the cart was on its way to the place of execution, edging slowly through a jeering crowd, Paris was already abuzz with rumours that a revolt against Robespierre had begun. Some tried to block the convoy in order to prevent the executions, but soldiers of the Republican Guard came up to them at a brisk trot, cleared a path and ordered the cart to be driven faster. Twenty minutes later, Françoise-Thérèse was executed. On the day following her death, Robespierre was toppled and the day after that he too was guillotined. It was the beginning of the end of the Terror. Many death sentences were commuted or revoked. If the princess had kept up the 'deception' of her pregnancy for longer than the single day that so weighed upon her conscience, she would probably have returned to her daughters. Even in calmer times, the letter never reached the girls. The plait of hair was deployed as a memento only once, in 1934, in a Paris museum, to commemorate not Françoise-Thérèse but the French Revolution.

Without debts or guilt

A portrait in miniature, a lock of hair, a plait or the letter itself were material means of reinforcing the memory. Everything else needed to come from the content of the letter. It is no surprise to find a wide variety of themes, but most striking are the things they have in common.

Practically every letter gives precise instructions on how to deal with financial matters. Sometimes there are outstanding loans. Friends and family are instructed to seek out people said to owe money. A man called Bottagne writes that Descharmes owes him 600 livres and adds some practical advice: 'Ask him for them on my behalf before he learns of my death.'[22] Far more common are instructions to settle debts. A lady's maid is still owed two years' wages, a gardener should be given 70 livres, a bill for eight livres from a wigmaker must be paid. However small the debt – an unpaid bill for a meal, a kitchen maid's wages – it is impressed upon relatives that everything must be settled, sometimes to the last sou. Poiré, convicted of having royalist sympathies, ends his letter to his wife with the bill presented to him for food received in prison – 'Six pounds of meat at fifteen sols, making the sum of four livres, four sols' – and then closes with 'Farewell, farewell'.[23] Sometimes the letter had already ended with the final embrace and fond kisses when a postscript was added with the instruction to pay some particular servant, maid or gardener what was due to them.

As well as outstanding bills, there were often items that needed to be returned to their rightful owners. Jean-Jacques Barbot, a teacher who had been careless enough to express in a letter his nostalgia for the time before the Revolution, had all kinds of things at home that had been lent to him by parents of his pupils. In the rather naive expectation that Fouquier-Tinville would put his affairs in order for him, he spelled it all out:

> Those objects are firedogs, shovel and tongs, a clock that is on the mantelpiece, three red armchairs and a print that is over the chest-of-drawers, presenting: Clairon d'ange Amédée. There is also a chair belonging to Citizen Lemercier, with a collection of the newspaper, *Le Moniteur*, part of which is bound, and the rest in sheets. This is to be found in a cupboard beside the chimney: it seems to me only just that these various objects should be returned to Citizen Lemercier, to whom they belong.[24]

The care with which such instructions were noted down, even in hasty scribbles on the way to the gallows – in such and such cabinet are a dozen handkerchiefs marked SS that must be returned to Sophie – underlines the fact that no one wanted to die in the knowledge that there were still outstanding debts.

The same went for debts in the figurative sense of the word. They are a central motif in almost all the letters: guilt and innocence, forgiveness and reckoning. First of all there was the writer's own innocence. Every letter entreats loved ones to give no credence to the accusations that have led to conviction. This is sometimes repeated three or four times in one letter. Georges Vincent, an estate agent who was sentenced to death on suspicion of being in contact with conspirators in Brittany, asks his wife to embrace the children for him and to tell them their father died with a clear conscience. A couple of lines further on he writes that they 'can be proud of the death of their father, who left his head on the scaffold an innocent victim of the Revolution'. Another few lines later he explains that people allow themselves to be blinded by error and passion and that as a result the blameless are often punished instead of the guilty. He closes with a tender kiss and farewell: 'Pray heaven you will be happier than your unhappy father, who dies innocent and has nothing with which to reproach himself.'[25] Similar statements can be found in all the letters, written by people who want to live on in memory as having acted in good faith, who will have departed this life with a clear conscience and have the right to be remembered as fathers or mothers, sons or daughters who died innocent deaths.

A different kind of accounting again can be found in some of the letters. Occasionally matters of guilt and innocence need to be settled and the letter or memento itself serves as a form of retribution. Catherine Laviolette called for a miniaturist and asked to be portrayed with her hand resting on a skull. The memento was intended for her husband, who had run off with a mistress. She held him responsible for her arrest. In a few cases people are identified by name as those who betrayed the writer of the letter and therefore as having his or her death on their conscience. But such letters can be counted on the fingers of one hand. Far more often they concern a willingness to forgive or a request for forgiveness. Gueau de Reverseaux sent one of his last letters to a man from Rouen who had betrayed him. 'I write to you, citizen, at the point of death, to assure you that I shall take with me into the grave no resentment against you or against any of those who – I believe unwittingly – have brought me to where I am . . . I forgive with all my heart those who may have been my enemies.'[26] Claude-François Berger, sentenced for monarchist sympathies, wrote to one of his daughters:

I would solicit your prayers and those of all our friends whom I shall
not see again until Eternity. I shall appear there in a few hours, may
God be pleased to show me mercy and forgive my innumerable sins as
I forgive with all my heart my judges, who are clearly in error in
declaring me convicted of a crime for which I never gave a thought.
Similarly, I forgive my enemies who are the cause of my arrest and
death.[27]

Such a turn of phrase, expressing forgiveness with reference to the
prospect of divine mercy, is remarkably rare in these letters, but even
without any mention of the judgement of a higher being, the person to be
preserved in memory must be one who died with a clear conscience, who
had set matters straight with his loved ones, had left no debts, had given
everybody what belonged to them and in those final moments had shown
a willingness to forgive.

Sacrifice

Each letter was many things at once. Often the writers had to face the fact
that the letter itself would bring the news of their execution. The farewell
letter was therefore also a death notice. How to find the words to tell your
loved ones that you are dead? Some addressed the letter to a friend or
family member who was instructed to soften the shock of the news.
Others did their best to introduce a few sentences at the start about an
adverse turn taken by the court case. More telling are traces of tears, or
shaky handwriting, even when the prisoner writes about facing up to fate
with calm and dignity.

As well as a death notice, the letter was often a last will and testament.
Dated and signed, it stated how affairs were to be settled. The instructions, with all those lists and sums of money, contrast oddly with the lines
in which leave is taken. 'I end. My tears water my letter. Dry your own.
Send me about fifteen francs.'[28]

But the letter was something else, too. The death had been announced,
affairs had been put in order – and now? Now the letter that caused so
much sorrow also had to bring comfort. Towards the end it becomes a
message of condolence. Once again the subject is remembering and forgetting, but this time the writer's aim is not to seek comfort but to offer it.

By his mid-twenties, Antoine de Lavoisier had established a reputation as an astronomer, chemist and mathematician. When he was in his late twenties he married Marie-Anne Pierrette Paulze, who was approaching 14. She became his most dedicated assistant. She learned English so she could translate the work of Joseph Priestley for him and took drawing lessons in order to illustrate his books. Lavoisier made his name by weighing gases, substances that until then were thought impossible to weigh. He split water into hydrogen and oxygen and identified elements by their weights. Privately wealthy but politically progressive, he served the new revolutionary regime with plans for tax reform and the introduction of the metric system, but he fell under suspicion as a result of having been an administrator of the Ferme Générale, which collected duties on behalf of the king, and despite his services to the national government he found himself in difficulties as the owner of extensive estates when the 'law against rent' was suddenly introduced. His reputation could not save him. The letter he wrote to his wife on the eve of his execution reads like a message of condolence. To comfort her he again had to weigh the unweighable: the imponderable advantages and disadvantages of dying at the age of 50. He writes:

I have had quite a long career and, above all, a happy one and I believe my memory will be accompanied with some glory. What more could I wish for? The events in which I find myself caught up will probably spare me the inconveniences of old age. I shall die in perfect health, that is one advantage that I must count among the many that I have enjoyed.[29]

Others tried to make their loved ones think of the time after their initial acute sorrow. Gueau de Reverseaux told his family they could take comfort from the thought that memories which now brought such unhappiness would eventually have a salutary effect: 'The first moments are painful but then the memory of those who have been dear to us leaves a sweet sensation in the soul that is not unpleasurable. I hope my dear wife and children will soon find themselves in that situation.'[30]

All these elements – the recognition of sadness, one final piece of good advice, the encouragement to resume life, the assurance that time will do its healing work – occur time and again in the letters, as they do in messages of condolence today, but here condolence is offered by the very person whose death was about to be mourned. This gave the writers the opportunity to go one step further, a step only they could take, that would be inappropriate in any other letter of condolence. In their attempts to bring comfort, some urged their loved ones not to remember them but to forget. This often came in the final lines. Antoine-Pierre-Léon Dufresne, a doctor from Normandy, wrote to his wife: 'I have no counsels to give you. You follow those that you have to follow, but believe me when I say that you should forget your husband.'[31] Public notary Jean-François Dufouleur de Courneuve, sentenced to death for falsifying legal documents, wrote to his wife: 'Farewell, I embrace you a thousand times. Remember sometimes your unhappy husband, what am I saying, on the contrary, do everything you can to efface him from your memory, if that is possible.'[32]

It seems Dufouleur does not quite know what to request. How could it be otherwise? The comfort he hopes for lies in the desire to be remembered. The comfort he tries to offer lies in his sacrifice of exactly that. For the sake of the happiness of his loved ones he was prepared to relinquish his place in their memories and die the second death.

The last letter

One of the farewell letters bears a remarkable signature, that of the public prosecutor himself, Antoine Quentin Fouquier-Tinville. Ever the dedicated bureaucrat, in the years of the Terror he had worked through great stacks of paperwork in his office above the prison: reports from informants, anonymous tip-offs, charge sheets, police files and those final documents in a series of short and inexorable legal proceedings, the verdicts. Every day he had issued arrest warrants, interrogated suspects, heard supplications, rejected pleas for mercy. After the fall of Robespierre he was arrested and imprisoned. He spent a year in a windowless cell, without candles.[33] When he was finally brought to court, the charge turned out to be just as vague as those on the basis of which he had managed to have hundreds convicted: suspicion of serious irregularities and arbitrary acts. Fouquier-Tinville, a married man of 49, was sentenced to death. He was treated in the same way as all the others. His possessions were declared forfeit. He too was allowed to write a farewell letter.

On the eve of his execution, he wrote to his wife that he was innocent and would die with a clear conscience and clean hands. Like all the condemned, he tried to find comfort in the memories of his loved ones:

Through all these disastrous events, there has remained to me one ray of satisfaction, or rather of consolation, and that is the knowledge that you are convinced of my innocence; that knowledge at least gives me hope that you will not fail to repeat to our children that their father died wretched, but innocent, that he always enjoyed your trust and esteem; I beg you not to abandon yourself to grief and to preserve your health for your own sake and for that of our poor children.[34]

He ends by writing:

With an aching heart and tears in my eyes, I take my leave of you, your aunt and my poor children. I embrace you a thousand times. Alas! what sweet satisfaction it would give me to see you again and hold you in my arms! But, my good friend, it is all over with me, we must not think on it further![35]

Fouquier-Tinville, seated at a chest full of 'prosecution evidence'.

Two years earlier, a condemned man had written in a farewell letter: 'Sooner or later, the scythe of time crops all heads, levels all.'[36] Fouquier-Tinville is almost certain to have seen that letter. In his own farewell letter, death indeed seems the great leveller. Below his signature he adds, 'The only token of my friendship that it is in my power to give you is a lock of my hair, which I beg you to keep safe.'[37] Like the plait left by the princess of Monaco, it got no further than the archive that on his orders was so meticulously preserved.

'Children forget quickly'

What is French about these letters? What is eighteenth-century about them? A great deal, without doubt. The fear of dying while staff or suppliers still had money owing to them is bound up with the way people thought about honour in those days, especially in the social stratum to which many of the writers belonged, that of the aristocracy or wealthy bourgeoisie. To determine what exactly was or was not specific to social relations as they then stood, in the France of Revolution and Terror, would require comparison with collections of farewell letters from other times and other cultures, and I have not done that here. But a fleeting glance at one of those other collections is sufficient to show that farewell letters from a different century, a different country, written in quite different circumstances, are striking for their similarities to those in the French collection, rather than for their differences.

In the winter of 1942–43, part of the German army found itself surrounded at Stalingrad. When it became clear they could expect no relief, the men were given permission to write letters that would be loaded onto the last plane to leave the city. Most soldiers knew this would be their last letter home. Seven postbags were taken off the plane in Germany and held. Delivering them to the families, the army leadership decided, would damage morale on the home front. The letters ended up in the archives.[38] The soldiers express their bitterness and disillusion regarding the high command, but the subjects they touch upon in writing to their families are the same as in the letters written during the Terror: the comfort a portrait can bring and the attempt to send one more photograph; concern about the grief the letter will cause parents, wives or children; instructions regarding their final wishes; the assurance that the writer of the letter will die an honourable death; requests for forgiveness for mistakes or disagreements in the past. But above all there is that same tension between the desire to live on in the memories of loved ones and the awareness that the happiness of those loved ones depends upon them not allowing their lives to be stymied by memories. One voice speaks for many, that of a nameless soldier to his wife:

> In January you will be twenty-eight. That is still very young for such a good looking woman ... You will miss me very much, but even so don't withdraw from other people. Let a few months pass, but no more. Gertrud and Claus need a father. Don't forget that you must live for the children and don't make too much fuss about their father. Children forget quickly, especially at that age.[39]

Suicide notes

Farewell letters like these have a sinister counterpart: suicide notes. They too have been collected, by psychologists and psychiatrists hoping to learn something about what motivated the people who wrote them. Again these are letters written under pressure of time, if in a sense self-imposed, and they generally originate from a moment even closer to death. The decision may sometimes have been made long ago, but the act itself is often carried out in an atmosphere of sudden haste, which shows through in the things people write. These are truly notes written at the last minute, in a hurry, and they are often confused, set down on any scrap of paper that happened to be to hand, such as the back of an envelope or a page from a diary. They also share with farewell letters the inclusion of those last few things a person is able to say. These writers too know that soon they will live only in memory. Nevertheless, the contrasts are more striking than the similarities.

Prisoners condemned to death during the Terror, soldiers surrounded at Stalingrad and all those others facing an inevitable death made every effort to send one final message to their loved ones. This is precisely what people ending their own lives generally decline to do.[40] Statistics have been collected assiduously for a century and a half concerning the proportion of people committing suicide who leave a written message, and they reveal a curious uniformity.[41] Women leave a note just as often as men, older people as younger, married as single. Parents write to their children just as often as children to their parents. There is no apparent link to socio-economic status or ethnic background, nor to factors such as previous suicide attempts or psychiatric problems.[42] Yet this 'just as often' is misleading, since the biggest surprise of all to anyone looking at the figures for the first time is that only one in every four or five leaves any kind of note at all. Even that figure is an overestimate, since in the case of lone deaths, such as drownings, the absence of a suicide note means that there is a good chance the death will be recorded as accidental. Of the few letters and notes that are written, many are unaddressed or addressed to no one in particular, such as whoever happens along, or the police. Only just over half are intended for someone close, such as a husband or wife, parent, child, brother or sister.[43] One might wish that this fact was more widely known. For every person who receives a personal note, very many are left with empty hands.

There are all kinds of reasons for this distressing absence of any message to close family members or friends. People who have survived suicide attempts tell of the narrowing down of thought and action, the haste, the desire to get it over with and to avoid being stopped at the last moment by any further act or reflection. It is a narrowing that is perhaps necessary at that moment and deliberately preserved; it does not allow for the distraction of writing a note.

But might we not seek at least part of the explanation in those farewell letters written by people who did *not* choose to die? Consider: if a person about to end their own life wants to live on in the memory of loved ones, how can they find the words to request being spared a second death if they themselves have chosen the first? How can you ask not to be forgotten if you could have stayed? How can you write about how you would like to be remembered when you know that you will only be burdening your loved ones with the memory of what you are about to do? How can you find the words to comfort someone when you are the cause of their grief? All those phrases that flow so naturally from the writers of farewell letters are impossible here. Perhaps we should see the absence of a suicide note as a measure not just of despair and confusion but of the realisation that what is impossible to express is impossible to convey to your loved ones in writing. The suicide note that remains unwritten is an indication that something cannot, with sincerity, be written down.

Incantation

The farewell letters that emerged from Fouquier-Tinville's archives contain everything from a tear-stained cry from the heart to a five-page document of final instructions almost worthy of a public notary. Folded into the letters were locks of hair, rings and medallions, handkerchiefs, buckles and brooches. None of those items were delivered to the families. Would it have made any difference? Was anyone forgotten because the plea not to forget never reached its intended recipient? Did the lack of a tangible memento make it harder to hold on to the memory of a lost loved one? Were any of these people remembered less affectionately because the letter describing how they wanted to be remembered never arrived?

After a moment's thought, the answer becomes clear. Anyone forced to say goodbye hopes to live on in good memories and anyone who loses someone solemnly promises themselves they will cherish those memories. But what one person hopes and another promises can never be more than an incantation. Both know that memory accepts no commands, that it goes its own way, even concerning those we loved best. All those locks of hair and medallions – do they not actually demonstrate our impotence in the face of our own memories? If our most precious recollections could be stored away safely and impregnably, we would need no mementos. What counts, when it comes to cherishing memories, is not the result but the love and devotion expressed by the attempt.

CHAPTER THIRTEEN

The Art of Forgetting

For over 40 years, the philosopher Immanuel Kant was supported in his bachelor existence by a faithful manservant called Martin Lampe, a former soldier in the Prussian army who was blessed with a sense of punctuality that Kant valued highly. Unfortunately, in 1802, when Kant was 78 years old, a dispute arose between the two men. Three biographers, contemporaries of Kant, declined to say what was at issue, although there are hints of alcoholism and theft. For whatever reason, Kant asked Lampe to leave. He was replaced by another former soldier, with a loud voice that Kant never did get used to in the two years that remained to him.

Kant had shared half a lifetime with Lampe. Lampe meant a knock on the bedroom door at five in the morning ('Time to get up!'). Lampe meant being told that the midday meal was ready ('Lunch is on the table').[1] Lampe meant a hand holding out the umbrella, polishing the silver buckles, powdering the wig, sharpening the quills.

Getting Lampe out of his house proved far easier for Kant than getting Lampe out of his memory. He certainly tried, with all his might in fact, as is clear from a note that was found in his study shortly after his death. It read, 'The name Lampe must now be completely forgotten'.[2]

Many writers, poets and philosophers have attempted to express our impotence with regard to memory, but never more touchingly than Kant did with that command. To tell yourself to stop thinking about something is one thing, to remind yourself in writing of what you need to forget is one powerless step further.

Kant was well versed in the literature of mnemonics. In the classic *ars memoriae*, developed in about 500 BC by the Greek poet Simonides, an orator takes a walk through an imaginary house, leaving in every room a symbolic representation of what he needs to remember. While making his speech, he mentally walks through the house and finds in their designated places all the things he intends to touch upon. Kant did not use this method. He thought the procedure too laborious. Apart from anything else, it required you to have an excellent memory to start with. What he must have longed for in those first weeks after Lampe left was an art of forgetting. There is no such thing. In fact it is impossible even to imagine what it might be. The reverse of mnemonics? Paying attention to what you want to forget simply tends to remind you of it. This is the paradoxical effect that the note about Lampe must surely have had on Kant's memory.

Even in the time of Simonides, when a good memory was an essential and highly respected instrument in art and public life, there were those who bemoaned the absence of an art of forgetting. Several treatises on rhetoric mention the story that when Simonides offered to introduce politician and general Themistocles to his *ars memoriae*, the general brushed the suggestion aside: Simonides would do better to teach him how to forget things he wanted to forget. What Themistocles needed was an *ars oblivionis*.[3]

Simonides was unable to help him. Even in our own time the art of forgetting exists only as a thought experiment. What if we were able to have certain memories removed? What would the consequences be? Would we be wise to make use of such a technique? In 1976 the Dutch cartoonist Marten Toonder asked himself that question in 'The Little Book of Forgetting', one of his many stories featuring a bear named Oliver B. Bumble.[4] It contains a brief philosophy of forgetting.

Toonder wrote the story when he was in his mid-sixties. In philosophising about memory and forgetting, age is not without significance.

Hocus's Little Book of Forgetting

The story starts with a number of problems that arise because of Bumble's forgetfulness. He forgets names, appointments and promises. He has completely forgotten that he promised his loyal servant Joost a pay rise, and the next day at breakfast he stares in bewilderment at a knot in his handkerchief: what on earth was it he must not forget? His other measures against forgetting fail too. He carefully notes in red ink, 'Don't forget Miss Doddle's birthday', but he finds the note a day too late. This cannot go on. He has hurt several people deeply by his forgetfulness. While dusting, Joost thinks: 'Mr Oliver has now raised my salary, just as he promised, but I had to urge him again and again. The worst thing of all is that he'd forgotten. Something beautiful inside is broken, if I can put it like that. I wish I could forget it. . . .'[5] Miss Doddle feels insulted too, as she tells Bumble's friend Tom Puss: 'He forgot about me! I don't want to hear a word about him! I hate him! I . . . I want to forget him. Completely forget him.'[6]

By chance, Hocus P. Pas, master of the black arts and self-styled 'physician', has discovered something that can free people from oppressive memories. In his practice he has a notebook, the Little Book of Forgetting, in which anyone can write down anything they want to forget. Hocus scatters a canister of fine sand over it and hey presto, the memory is gone. Among his first clients is Joost, who goes to him in the hope of forgetting that Bumble forgot about him, but when he comes to think about it there are other things he wants to forget, such as that embarrassing time when Mr Oliver caught him pouring a simple local wine into a bottle with an old label. Miss Doddle writes in the Little Book of Forgetting that Bumble forgot about her. Little by little, many of the residents of Rommeldam come round to write down memories in the book. Only the civil servant Dorknoper refuses to write anything in it – after all, 'the government never forgets'. He prefers to write in his own notebook: 'I have here a little book of remembering, if I may make a little joke'.[7]

The technique seems simple. Write something down and cover it with sand. But the effect is powerful. Bumble speaks to Miss Doddle as she is on her way back from visiting Hocus. She fails to recognise him. Along with the memory of that one insult, she has forgotten everything to do with Bumble. Joost has become so confused that he forgets not only what he wanted to forget but that he ever visited Hocus. Tom Puss is extremely worried and Bumble, with his finely tuned intuition, senses that no good can come of all this. He seeks help from highly placed townsfolk in the Little Club. 'How will it end, if everyone can have a bit of their memory snipped out?' But he finds himself in a minority of one. The mayor thinks he is too much of a pessimist. 'You'd do better to forget it. There are some things that are best forgotten. Otherwise people would be unable to sleep.'[8] And the Marquis de Canteclaer adds that forgetting is sometimes necessary between gentlemen.

Bumble is not content with this. Along with Tom Puss he goes to see Hocus P. Pas. While Bumble keeps him talking, Tom Puss goes up to the attic and discovers that Hocus has carefully kept all the sand he threw over the memories. There is a cupboard in which each forgotten memory is preserved in its own little bag. Later it turns out he was planning to empty all the sand onto the shifting Walmzander Dunes, where all that hatred, all those lies, threats and insults would go on blowing about for eternity. After many twists and turns, during which the river of forgetting overflows its banks and washes across the Walmzander Dunes, Bumble and Tom Puss bring everything to a satisfying conclusion. Bumble explains to Miss Doddle exactly what has happened and although there is a lot she does not understand – 'maybe because I've got a hole somewhere in my memory' – she is happy to accept the invitation to a celebratory dinner at Bumblestein.[9] In his kitchen Joost, cheery as ever, is pouring cheap wine into Burgundy bottles again.

The tone of 'The Little Book of Forgetting' is playful, mild and ironic. The need for a technique of forgetting arises from Bumble's forgetfulness. In 1976 Marten Toonder was 64. Did he notice that on reaching such an age you not only begin to forget names but can sometimes insult people unwittingly by your forgetfulness? Anyone who has ever been completely forgotten by someone – you cooked a great dinner, everything was ready in anticipation of a wonderful evening, but your guest forgot to come – knows what an indelible experience it is. Being forgotten is certainly memorable. Much of our forgetting in daily life is the result of inattention, of nonchalance, which creates an assumption that can work against you when you become more forgetful, as Bumble discovers. His forgetting is interpreted as a sign of an uncaring attitude, almost as a character fault. 'The Little Book of Forgetting' is an invitation to see such things with a more forgiving frame of mind. Joost and Miss Doddle need not have taken Bumble's forgetfulness so personally.

Reading between the lines, perhaps Toonder is also saying that the forgetting in 'to forgive and forget' is not real forgetting, either in the story or in the reality of human memory. Hocus invites people to write in his 'Little Book of Forgetting' and generously tells them that all is forgotten, but then he pours the sand carefully into a bag and secretly keeps it. Is that not a powerful image of how our memories deal with those things we promise to forgive and forget? If the offence is repeated, it invariably becomes clear that we did not do a great job of forgetting, in fact almost the opposite, since what was supposed to be forgotten turns out to have been written down in something that resembles a criminal record rather than a book of forgetting. In each person's brain, a master of the dark arts records precisely what we 'forgive and forget'.

There is no real darkness in the story, however. Nothing comes of Hocus's evil plans and eventually the waters of oblivion wash over all the ugliness written down in the 'Little Book of Forgetting'. A few blank patches are left in memories here and there, but they do not do very much harm. The mayor puts it all down to getting older. Other guests fail to notice any gaps. During a meal at the end of the story, everyone cheerfully discusses the follies of memory.

'Rarely do memories bring any comfort'

'The name Lampe must now be completely forgotten,' Kant impressed upon himself. Classicist Harald Weinrich wonders whether this note, at first sight an exhortation to forget Lampe, might be open to a rather different interpretation.[10] In the final years of his life, Kant's memory deteriorated rapidly. His symptoms suggest Alzheimer's disease; by the end he no longer recognised even his closest friends. Kant had a reputation to maintain as a contagiously witty conversationalist and the last thing he will have wanted was to bore his friends by repeating himself. He seems to have noted down what he and his friends had talked about. Repeating yourself and thereby betraying the fact that you have forgotten what you said yesterday is the fear of every Alzheimer's sufferer.

Might it not be the case, Weinrich asks himself, that the note about Lampe was written by Kant to remind himself not to start telling people yet again about the need to forget Lampe? That would not make the note any less touching, in fact almost the opposite, since according to this reading it was less an instruction than an injunction of the more desperate kind, and one that would soon no longer be needed.

Within a short time, Lampe would indeed be forgotten, along with everything else.

The Kant whose memory let him down must have been a terrible sight to behold. In the space of less than two years, the disease extinguished one of the brightest minds of the Enlightenment. His sister, who had never understood a word of *Critique of Pure Reason,* now had to finish his sentences for him. Set beside the difficulty of remembering the simplest, most everyday things, all that philosophising about an *ars memoriae* or an *ars oblivionis* was of no significance at all. Kant's personal life had been marked by punctuality and discipline, characteristics that are the first to be undermined by forgetfulness. The notes he wrote to himself were little more than visible evidence of the trouble Kant must have taken to maintain his grip. He kept to himself the growing unease familiar to all dementia sufferers, and later the fear of losing his memory altogether. His friends must have felt deeply sad that the evaporation of his memories meant Kant could no longer look back on a long and well-spent life.

Marten Toonder reached an age attained by only the toughest of men and was lucid to the last. But he cared little about the former and the latter was a mixed blessing. After more than 50 years of married life, his wife Phiny Dick died. He found a new love in Tera de Marez Oyens, but she died less than a year after their wedding. He had survived three of his four children. His contemporaries had fallen by the wayside one by one. From 1996 onwards he lived in a retirement home for artists in Laren, lonely and sombre. As far as he was concerned, death would have been welcome years before. He sat out his time and it seemed a long wait. In the summer of 2005 he died in his sleep, at the age of 93.

In the final four or five years of his life he gave a number of interviews and wrote several articles. Everyone has an inner age that remains the same throughout life, he explained. He was still 20, even though he was now 92.[11] That 20-year-old was poorly housed in an ailing body: 'The carcass doesn't fit any more. A harsh fate, you know. I don't care for it at all. I don't see the point, either. I hate it.'[12] But even more than by his physical decline, he was tormented by his memory. He repeatedly referred to the way it was starting to let him down and some memories that he would expect to comfort him had started to oppress him. His reflections, here and there no more than catchphrases, rendered up a new philosophy of forgetting, but this time that of someone who knows he is entering the final years of his life and has reached the bitter conclusion that his own memory has turned against him. In these contemplations, all playfulness has evaporated. Bumble's forgetfulness, still funny in 'The Little Book of Forgetting', has become a curse. 'I'm bad at remembering names. It's one of the types of forgetfulness that come first. And that's terrible, you know. Terrible. Sometimes I can't even remember my grandchild's name.'[13] Other memories are unpleasantly vivid. 'Sometimes you think the dead have become vague shadows. But one day there they are in front of you, full of life. When you least expect it.'[14] His memory was no longer under control. Doors would open abruptly without any action on his part. 'All of a sudden you see faded figures right there in front of your nose.'[15] In old age the memory is increasingly like Dorknoper's little book of remembering. This was a far cry from the mild and nuanced view of memory that he held in his mid-sixties. He could no longer see it from the necessary distance. His own memory had begun to mutiny.

Reading those interviews it becomes clear that for Toonder memories were more than personal, inner possessions. He was the kind of man who enjoys beautiful experiences only if he can share them with loved ones. What he went through on his own left him unmoved and easily slipped out of his memory again. Often it was those closest to him who pointed out how delightful a particular experience was. It almost seemed as if only then could it become a memory. Many of his best memories, Toonder wrote in a contribution to a book on beauty and consolation, were significant to him only because of Phiny. He recalled a summer's afternoon with her in an Irish bay:

> The tide was coming in and the water was making babbling noises along the beach as the sun scattered it with sparkling points of light.
>
> 'Diamonds,' she said, and because of that, the image sank deep into my memory. Without memories there is no beauty. If I've seen something enchanting, I need someone to tell me how beautiful it is. And if I can find the words, I want to be able to say them to someone. The happiness derived from that shared emotion gives rise to the memory. But when the other person is no longer there, the emotion is missing, and that in turn creates a feeling of sadness, because it means the entrance to beauty is locked.[16]

He brings up the subject time and again. The most beautiful memories are shared memories, and it is precisely those memories that feel like a burden because the person he shared them with is no longer there. They now point to what is missing. When he looks back in his autobiography to the darkest period in his life, the time immediately after Phiny died, he recalls a line from a letter he received from a good friend: 'You had such a long and rich life together. Count the gold beads in the necklace of your memory and you'll never be alone.' It is a sentence of the kind that can be found in many different forms in conventional letters of condolence, but Toonder feels all the more lonely because of those good memories. 'I laid that comfort aside with a sense of bitterness then, because my good memories were precisely the hardest to deal with.'[17]

His contribution to that book on beauty and consolation ends with a desolate sentence: 'Rarely do memories bring any comfort, because they remind us of what will never again be the way it was.'[18] Memories once cherished with care and love now cause pain. Toonder must have felt betrayed by his own memory. Finding yourself alone, there are times when you would like to write your fondest memories in a book of forgetting.

Questions About Forgetting

Has anyone ever offended you by forgetting something about you?

Do you recall having offended anyone by forgetting something about them?

Have you ever been embarrassed by what you *did* turn out to have remembered? A single example is enough.

Do you feel uncomfortable when reminded in public of something you had forgotten?

How convincing do you find the notion of unconscious plagiarism? Do you think it could happen to you?

Do you have photographs that show you in situations of which you have no memory at all? If so, do they tend to be old or recent?

Which shortcomings of your memory do you find particularly irksome?

In which situations have you regretted not having total recall?

Repression

Are you prone to repression? What leads you to that conclusion?

Are there any shortcomings of your memory for which you consider yourself fortunate?

If there was a technique for forgetting, would you make use of it?

Have you ever wished you could make someone forget a memory of you?

Have you ever resisted hearing something in order to protect a precious memory?

Revision

Do you have a good memory for memories? In other words, are you good at remembering the *history* of your memories?

Do you recall events in a way that you know is different from how you used to remember them?

Have you ever noticed or experienced something that forced you to revise your past? Have there ever been new memories that changed something in earlier memories?

Do you have memories that you have never told anyone about because you are worried their reaction would spoil those memories?

Do memories of a good friend change if you fall out with them?

Has anyone ever robbed you of a fond memory? Have you ever robbed someone of a fond memory?

Shared memories

Do you and your partner have shared memories? What leads you to believe you do?

Does something change in shared memories when the person you share them with is no longer alive?

If your partner was asked to describe to you three fond memories of you, do you think you would already know one of them? Two? All three?

Does your partner know what your most precious memories of him or her are?

First and last memories

How often have you told someone your earliest memory?

Has it ever troubled you that your children will have forgotten almost everything they experience in their first few years of life? If so, did it trouble you at the time or later?

Do you have less faith in your memories the older they become?

Do you take care of your memory?

Do you take care of your memories?

Do you take special care of your memories of loved ones who have died? If so, how? If not, why not?

Do you derive comfort from the prospect of being remembered after your death?

Is that comfort limited to the memories of your loved ones?

Notes

Forgetting: An Introduction

1. D. Draaisma, *Metaphors of Memory* (trans. Paul Vincent), Cambridge 2000. (Originally published as *De metaforenmachine. Een geschiedenis van het geheugen*, Groningen 1995).
2. G. Sperling, 'The information available in brief visual presentations', *Psychological Monographs: General and Applied*, 74 (1960), 11, 1–29.
3. H. Weinrich, *Lethe. Kunst und Kritik des Vergessens*, Munich 2000, 11.
4. E. Tulving, 'Are there 256 different kinds of memory?', J.S. Nairne (ed.), *The Foundations of Remembering. Essays in honor of Henry L. Roediger, III*, New York / Hove 2007, 39–52.
5. The questions originally appeared in *Tagebuch 1966–1971* but were later published separately as M. Frisch, *Fragebogen*, Frankfurt am Main 1992.

1 First Memories: Islands in the Stream of Forgetting

1. P. Lejeune, *Le pacte autobiographique*, Paris 1975 (rev. edn. 1996), 362.
2. E. Canetti, *The Tongue Set Free. Remembrance of a European Childhood* (trans. Joachim Neugroschel), London 1979, 3. (Originally published as *Die gerettete Zunge: Geschichte einer Jugend*, Munich 1977.)
3. Canetti, *The Tongue Set Free*, 3.
4. M.J. Eacott and R.A. Crawley, "The offset of childhood amnesia', *Journal of Experimental Psychology: General*, 127 (1998), 22–33.
5. N. Scheepmaker, *De eerste herinnering*, Amsterdam 1988.
6. Scheepmaker, *Herinnering*, 50.
7. Scheepmaker, *Herinnering*, 129.
8. Scheepmaker, *Herinnering*, 15, 134.
9. Scheepmaker, *Herinnering*, 127.
10. Scheepmaker, *Herinnering*, 66.
11. Scheepmaker, *Herinnering*, 97.
12. Scheepmaker, *Herinnering*, 49.
13. Scheepmaker, *Herinnering*, 37.

14. P. Blonsky, 'Das Problem der ersten Kindheitserinnerung und seine Bedeutung', *Archiv für die gesamte Psychologie*, 71 (1929), 369–90.
15. C. Verhoeven, *De glans van oud ijzer: herinneringen, 1928–1982*, Baarn 1996, 9.
16. D. Draaisma, *Why Life Speeds Up as You Get Older* (trans. Arnold Pomerans and Erica Pomerans), Cambridge 2004, 15–30. (Originally published as *Waarom het leven sneller gaat als je ouder wordt*, Groningen 2001.)
17. K. Nelson and R. Fivush, 'The emergence of autobiographical memory: a social cultural developmental theory', *Psychological Review*, 111 (2004), 486–511.
18. Scheepmaker, *Herinnering*, 51.
19. D. Kohnstamm, *Ik ben ik. De ontdekking van het zelf*, Amsterdam 2002.
20. C.G. Jung, *Memories, Dreams, Reflections* (trans. Richard and Clara Winston), New York 1962 (rev. ed. New York 1989). (Originally published as *Erinnerungen, Träume, Gedanken*, 1962.)
21. Kohnstamm, *Ik ben ik*, 37–8.
22. F. Fivush, 'The stories we tell. How language shapes autobiography', *Applied Cognitive Psychology*, 12 (1998), 483–7.
23. Scheepmaker, *Herinnering*, 124–5.
24. G. Simcock and H. Hayne, 'Breaking the barrier? Children fail to translate their preverbal memories into language', *Psychological Science*, 13 (2002), 3, 225–31.
25. Simcock and Hayne, 'Breaking the barrier?', 229.
26. R. Fivush and K. Nelson, 'Parent-child reminiscing locates the self in the past', *British Journal of Developmental Psychology*, 24 (2006), 235–51.
27. Cited in K. Sabbagh, *Remembering Our Childhood. How Memory Betrays Us*, Oxford 2009, 11.
28. J.A. Usher and U. Neisser, 'Childhood amnesia and the beginnings of memory for four early life events', *Journal of Experimental Psychology: General*, 122 (1993), 155–65.
29. Eacott and Crawley, 'The offset of childhood amnesia', 22–33.
30. Scheepmaker, *Herinnering*, 22.

2 Why We Forget Dreams

1. M. Jagger and K. Richards, 'Ruby Tuesday', 1967.
2. H. Havelock Ellis, *The World of Dreams*, London 1911.
3. M.W. Calkins, 'Statistics of dreams', *American Journal of Psychology*, 5 (1893), 312
4. Calkins, 'Statistics of dreams', 312.
5. L. Strümpel, *Die Natur und Entstehung der Träume*, Leipzig 1874.
6. S. Freud, *The Interpretation of Dreams* (trans. A.A. Brill), London 1913, 10 ff. (Originally published as *Die Traumdeutung*, Leipzig/Vienna 1900.)
7. J. Delboeuf, *Le sommeil et les rêves*, Paris 1885.
8. Havelock Ellis, *World of Dreams*, 229–30.
9. Havelock Ellis, *World of Dreams*, 218.
10. J.J.F. de Lalande, *Voyage d'un François en Italie*, Venice 1769, 294.
11. M. Jouvet, *Slapen en dromen* (trans. W. Hünd), Amsterdam/Antwerp 1994, 60. (Originally published as *Le sommeil et le rêve*, Paris 2000.)
12. Jouvet, *Slapen en dromen*.
13. F. Crick and G. Mitchison, 'The function of dream sleep', *Nature*, 304 (14 July 1983), 111–14.
14. J. Winson, *Brain and Psyche. The Biology of the Unconscious*, New York 1985.
15. The film can be found by searching on YouTube using the keywords 'histoire' and 'crime'.

16. L. Wright, *Clockwork Man*, New York 1992.
17. Havelock Ellis, *World of Dreams*, 214.
18. L.F.A. Maury, *Le sommeil et les rêves*, Paris 1861, 4th edn, 1878, 161–2.
19. Havelock Ellis, *World of Dreams*, 7.
20. W. Dement and E.A. Wolpert, 'The relation of eye movements, bodily motility and external stimuli to dream content', *Journal of Experimental Psychology*, 55 (1958), 543–53.
21. Dement and Wolpert, 'The relation of eye movements', 550.
22. J. Nelson, 'A study of dreams', *American Journal of Psychology*, 3 (1888), 367–401.
23. Nelson, 'Study of dreams', 384.
24. M. Jouvet, *De dromenweger* (trans. E. Gratama & J. Noorman), Amsterdam 1994. (Originally published as *Le château des songes*, Paris 1992.)
25. Cited in Jouvet, *De dromenweger*, 289.
26. E. Aserinsky and N. Kleitman, 'Regularly occurring periods of eye motility, and concomitant phenomena, during sleep', *Science*, 118 (1953), 273–4.
27. J. Antrobus, 'Cortical hemisphere asymmetry and sleep mentation', *Psychological Review*, 94 (1987), 3, 359–68.
28. J.A. Hobson and R.W. McCarley, 'The brain as a dream state generator: an activation-synthesis hypothesis of the dream process', *American Journal of Psychiatry*, 134 (1977), 1335–48.
29. D. Foulkes, *Dreaming. A Cognitive-Psychological Analysis*, Hillsdale, NJ 1985.
30. Foulkes, *Dreaming*, 165.
31. D. Dennett, *Consciousness Explained*, London 1991, 10–13.
32. The Book of Daniel 2.
33. See I. Hacking, 'Dreams in place', *The Journal of Aesthetics and Art Criticism*, 59 (2001) 3, 245–60.
34. The 1545 German translation by Martin Luther has '*Es ist mir entfallen*'. The King James Bible (1611) renders it as 'The thing is gone from me' (Daniel 2: 5). Some translations omit the phrase altogether.
35. Dement and Wolpert, 'The relation of eye movements', 544.

3 In Memory of Henry M.

1. D. Washburn, 'Waiting for H.M.', http://voiceofsandiego.org/2008/12/23/waiting-for-h-m/ (accessed 24 September 2014).
2. J. Annese et al., 'Postmortem examination of patient H.M.'s brain based on histological sectioning and digital 3D reconstruction', *Nature Communications* 5: 3122 (doi: 10.1038/ncomms4122).
3. W.B. Scoville and B. Milner, 'Loss of recent memory after bilateral hippocampal lesions', *Journal of Neurology, Neurosurgery and Psychiatry*, 20 (1957), 11–21.
4. D.H. Salat et al., 'Neuroimaging H.M.: A 10-year follow-up examination', *Hippocampus*, 16 (2006), 936–45.
5. G. Watts, 'Henry Gustav Molaison, H.M.', *The Lancet*, 373 (7 February 2009), 456.
6. P. J. Hilts, *Memory's Ghost. The Nature of Memory and the Strange Tale of Mr. M.*, New York 1995.
7. E.S. Valenstein, *Great and Desperate Cures. The Rise and Decline of Psychosurgery and Other Radical Treatments for Mental Illness*, New York 1986.
8. Valenstein, *Great and Desperate Cures*, 78.
9. J. El-Hai, *The Lobotomist. A Maverick Medical Genius and his Tragic Quest to Rid the World of Mental Illness*, Hoboken, NJ 2005.

10. Valenstein, *Great and Desperate Cures*, 142.
11. W.B. Scoville, 'Selective undercutting as a means of modifying and studying frontal lobe function in man', *Journal of Neurosurgery*, 6 (1949), 65–73.
12. Hilts, *Memory's Ghost*, 92
13. W.B. Scoville, 'The limbic lobe in man', *Journal of Neurosurgery*, 11 (1954), 64–6.
14. Hilts, *Memory's Ghost*, 96.
15. D. Draaisma, 'Losing the past', *Nature*, 497 (2013), 313–4.
16. Scoville, 'The limbic lobe', 66.
17. Hilts, *Memory's Ghost*, 100.
18. B. Skotko, D. Rubin and L. Tupler, 'H.M.'s personal crossword puzzles: understanding memory and language', *Memory*, 16 (2008), 2, 89–96.
19. K. Danziger, *Marking the Mind. A History of Memory*, Cambridge 2008, 176–82.
20. S. Corkin, 'Lasting consequences of bilateral medial temporal lobectomy: clinical course and experimental findings in case H.M.', *Seminars in Neurology*, 4 (1984), 249–59.
21. S. Corkin, 'Acquisition of motor skill after bilateral medial temporal lobe excision', *Neuropsychologia*, 6 (1968), 255–65.
22. Hilts, *Memory's Ghost*, 114.
23. B. Milner, S. Corkin and H.-L Teuber, 'Further analyses of the hippocampal amnesic syndrome: 14-year follow-up study of H.M.', *Neuropsychologia*, 6 (1968), 215–34.
24. Hilts, *Memory's Ghost*, 122.
25. W.B. Scoville, 'Amnesia after bilateral mesial temporal-lobe excision: introduction to case H.M.', *Neuropsychologia*, 6 (1968), 211–23.
26. A. Bereznak, 'The memory remains', *The Guardian*, 9 March 2009.
27. Washburn, 'Waiting for H.M.', 1.
28. S. Corkin, 'What's new with the amnesic patient H.M.?', *Nature Reviews / Neuroscience*, 3 (2002), 153–60.
29. Washburn, 'Waiting for H.M.', 2.
30. Washburn, 'Waiting for H.M.', 3.
31. As stated, the website has been changed since this book was originally written. For the current page on H.M. see http://thebrainobservatory.ucsd.edu/hm, or follow the link at the observatory's home page (thebrainobservatory.org).
32. Corkin, 'What's new?', 159.
33. S. Corkin, *Permanent Present Tense: The Unforgettable Life of the Amnesic Patient, H.M.*, New York 2013.

4 The Man Who Forgot Faces

1. J. Bodamer, 'Die Prosop-Agnosie', *Archiv für Psychiatrie und Nervenkrankheiten*, 179 (1947), 6–53.
2. Bodamer, 'Prosop-Agnosie', 11.
3. Bodamer, 'Prosop-Agnosie', 16. Cited from the partial translation by Hadyn D. Ellis and Melanie Florence, 'Bodamer's (1947) paper on prosopagnosia', *Cognitive Neuropsychology*, 7 (1990), 2, 81.
4. Bodamer, 'Prosop-Agnosie', 18.
5. Bodamer, 'Prosop-Agnosie', 35.
6. O. Sacks, *The Man Who Mistook His Wife for a Hat*, London 1985.
7. Sacks, *The Man Who Mistook*, 10, cited from the 1986 edition.
8. A.J. Larner, 'Lewis Carroll's Humpty Dumpty. An early report of prosopagnosia?', *Journal of Neurology, Neurosurgery, and Psychiatry*, 75 (2004), 1063.

9. T. Kress and I. Daum, 'Developmental prosopagnosia: a review', *Behavioural Neurology*, 14 (2003), 109–121.

10. I. Kennerknecht, T. Grüter, B. Welling, S. Wentzek, J. Horst, S. Edwards and M. Grüter, 'First report of prevalence of non-syndromic hereditary prosopagnosia', *American Journal of Medical Genetics*, 140 (2006), 1617–22.

11. D.J. Grelotti, I. Gauthier and R.T. Schultz, 'Social interest and the development of cortical face specialization. What autism teaches us about face processing', *Developmental Psychobiology*, 40 (2002), 213–25.

12. L. Yardley, L. McDermott, S. Pikarski, B. Duchaine and K. Nakayama, 'Psychosocial consequences of developmental prosopagnosia. A problem of recognition', *Journal of Psychosomatic Research*, 65 (2008), 5, 445–51.

13. A.L. Wigan, *A New View of Insanity. The Duality of the Mind, Proved by the Structure, Functions, and Diseases of the Brain, and by the Phenomena of Mental Derangement, and Shown to be Essential to Moral Responsibility*, London 1844. See also Chapter 7.

5 A Slope, Followed By an Abyss

1. For example, K. Maurer and U. Maurer, *Alzheimer. The Life of a Physician and Career of a Disease*, New York 2003.

2. For the life of Korsakoff and the syndrome named after him, see D. Draaisma, *Disturbances of the Mind* (trans. Barbara Fasting), Cambridge 2009, 147–68. (Originally published as *Ontregelde geesten*, Groningen 2006.)

3. S. Korsakow, 'Eine psychische Störung, combiniert mit multipler Neuritis (Psychosis polyneuritica seu Cerebropathia psychica toxaemica)', *Allgemeine Zeitschrift für Psychiatrie und psychisch-gerichtliche Medicin*, 46 (1890), 475–85. Cited from the translation by Maurice Victor and Paul I. Yakovlev, 'S.S. Korsakoff's Psychic Disorder in Conjunction with Peripheral Neuritis', *Neurology* V (1955), 397.

4. S. Korsakow, 'Erinnerungstäuschungen (Pseudoreminiscenzen) bei polyneuritischer Psychose', *Allgemeine Zeitschrift für Psychiatrie*, 47 (1891), 390–410.

5. M.S. Albert, N. Butters and J. Levin, 'Temporal gradients in the retrograde amnesia of patients with alcoholic Korsakoff's disease', *Archives of Neurology*, 36 (1979), 211–16.

6. N.J. Cohen and L.R. Squire, 'Retrograde amnesia and remote memory impairment', *Neuropsychologica*, 19 (1981), 337–56.

7. N. Butters and L.S. Cermak, 'A case study of the forgetting of autobiographical knowledge. Implications for the study of retrograde amnesia', in D.C. Rubin (ed.), *Autobiographical Memory*, Cambridge 1986, 253–72.

8. É. Claparède, 'Récognition et moïté', *Archives de Psychologie*, 11 (1911), 79–90.

9. Claparède, 'Récognition', 85.

10. P. Graf and D.L. Schacter, 'Implicit and explicit memory for new associations in normal and amnesic subjects', *Journal of Experimental Psychology: Learning, Memory, and Cognition*, 11 (1985), 501–18.

11. R.A. McCarthy and E.K. Warrington, 'Actors but not scripts: the dissociation of people and events in retrograde amnesia', *Neuropsychologia*, 30 (1992), 7, 633–44.

12. McCarthy and Warrington, 'Actors', 634.

6 Your Colleague Has a Brilliant Idea – Yours

1. J. Verne, *From the Earth to the Moon* (trans. Lewis Mercier and Eleanor E. King), London 1873. (Originally published as *De la terre à la lune*, Paris 1865.)

2. When asked, Rudy Kousbroek said he did not recall having used this metaphor in his own work. Even after the publication of a shortened version of this chapter in the science supplement of *NRC Handelsblad* (9 January 2010) no one claimed to be its rightful owner.

3. R. P. Gruber, 'Minds that think alike or cryptomnesia?', *Journal of the American Society of Plastic Surgeons*, 119 (2007), 6, 1945–6.

4. A.-C. Defeldre, 'Inadvertent plagiarism in everyday life', *Applied Cognitive Psychology*, 19 (2005), 1033–40.

5. R. Dannay, *Current Developments in Copyright Law*, New York 1980, 681.

6. T. Flournoy, *From India to the Planet Mars*, New York 1963. (Originally published as *Des Indes à la planète Mars. Étude sur un cas de somnambulisme avec glossolalie*, Paris 1900.)

7. Flournoy, *From India to the Planet Mars*, 405.

8. Flournoy, *From India to the Planet Mars*, 405.

9. F.W.H. Myers, *Human Personality and its Survival of Bodily Death*, vol. 1, London 1903, XVI.

10. H. Freeborn, 'Temporary reminiscence of a long-forgotten language during the delirium of broncho-pneumonia', *The Lancet*, 80 (1902), 1685–6.

11. S. Freud, *The Psychopathology of Everyday Life* in *The Standard Edition of the Complete Psychological Works of Sigmund Freud* (trans. James Strachey), Vol. VI. London 1956–70, 144. (Originally published as *Zur Psychopathologie des Alltagslebens*, Berlin 1904.)

12. Freud, *Psychopathology*, 144.

13. H.C. Warren, *Dictionary of Psychology*, Boston 1934.

14. A.S. Brown and D.R. Murphy, 'Cryptomnesia: delineating inadvertent plagiarism', *Journal of Experimental Psychology: Learning, Memory and Cognition*, 15 (1989), 3, 432–42.

15. L.-J. Stark, T.J. Perfect and S.E. Newstead, 'When elaboration leads to appropriation: unconscious plagiarism in a creative task', *Memory*, 13 (2005), 6, 561–73.

16. L.-J. Stark and T.J. Perfect, 'Whose idea was that? Source monitoring for idea ownership following elaboration', *Memory*, 15 (2007), 7, 776–83.

17. Vai's account can be found on the DVD *Live at the Astoria, London* (2003) and can be heard by selecting 'Bangkok' in the audio commentary.

7 The Galileo of Neurology

1. A.L. Wigan, *A New View of Insanity. The Duality of the Mind, Proved by the Structure, Functions, and Diseases of the Brain, and by the Phenomena of Mental Derangement, and Shown to be Essential to Moral Responsibility*, London 1844.

2. In 1985 a reissue appeared, which is now also out of print: A.L. Wigan, *The Duality of the Mind* (ed. J. Bogen), Malibu 1985. There is now a 2014 paperback facsimile version from Nabu Press available and the whole text is also available free online at https://archive.org/stream/39002086347094.med.yale.edu#page/n3/mode/2up

3. J. Bogen, 'The other side of the brain II. An appositional mind', *Bulletin of the Los Angeles Neurological Society*, 34 (1969), 135–62.

4. For a brief biography and a bibliography, see B. Clarke, 'Arthur Wigan and *The Duality of the Mind*', *Psychological Medicine*, Monograph Supplement, 11 (1987), 1–52.

5. Wigan, *Duality*, 326–29.

6. Cited in Clarke, 'Arthur Wigan', 18.

7. Anonymous, 'Notices of books', *American Journal of Insanity*, 2 (1845), 375–81.
8. Wigan, *Duality*, 39.
9. Cited in Clarke, 'Arthur Wigan', 21–2.
10. Wigan, *Duality*, 49.
11. Wigan, *Duality*, 39–40.
12. Wigan, *Duality*, 141.
13. Wigan, *Duality*, 142.
14. Wigan, *Duality*, 124–5.
15. Wigan, *Duality*, 178–80.
16. Wigan, *Duality*, 180.
17. Wigan, *Duality*, 83.
18. Wigan, *Duality*, 72.
19. Wigan, *Duality*, 73–4.
20. See the chapter devoted to Charles Bonnet syndrome in D. Draaisma, *Disturbances of the Mind*, Cambridge 2009, 11–39.
21. Wigan, *Duality*, 170.
22. J. Bodamer, 'Die Prosop-Agnosie', *Archiv für Psychiatrie und Nervenkrankheiten*, 179 (1947), 6–53.
23. H. Holland, *Medical Notes and Reflections*, London 1839.
24. Wigan, *Duality*, 102.
25. Wigan, *Duality*, 144.
26. Wigan, *Duality*, 392.
27. F.B. Winslow, 'The unpublished mss of the late Alfred Wigan, M.D., author of *The Duality of the Mind*', *Journal of Psychological Medicine* II: Appendix, 1849.
28. S.P. Springer and G. Deutsch, *Left Brain, Right Brain*, New York 1981 (edn 1993), 31.
29. Wigan, *Duality*, 418.
30. Draaisma, *Disturbances of the Mind*, 139.
31. Wigan, *Duality*, 57.
32. Wigan, *Duality*, 58–64.
33. Wigan, *Duality*, 60.
34. Wigan, *Duality*, 412 The poem is called 'Address to the unco guid, or the rigidly righteous'. Wigan seems to have quoted from memory. The lines actually go: 'What's done we partly may compute / But know not what's resisted'.
35. Wigan, *Duality*, 80.
36. Wigan, *Duality*, 63–4.

8 On Repression

1. S. Freud, *Fragment of an Analysis of a Case of Hysteria*, in *The Standard Edition of the Complete Psychological Works of Sigmund Freud* (trans. James Strachey), Vol. VII, London 1956–70, 3, 7–122. (Originally published in 1905 as 'Bruchstück einer Hysterie-Analyse'. Original text to be found in *Monatsschrift für Psychiatrie und Neurologie*, 18 (1995), 285–310, 408–67.)
2. Freud, *Fragment*, 12.
3. Freud, *Fragment*, 26.
4. Freud, *Fragment*, 23.
5. H.S. Decker, *Freud, Dora, and Vienna 1900*, New York 1991, 119.
6. Freud, *Fragment*, 15.
7. Freud, *Fragment*, 64.
8. Freud, *Fragment*, 69.

9. Freud, *Fragment*, 70.
10. Freud, *Fragment*, 78.
11. Freud, *Fragment*, 29–30.
12. Freud, *Fragment*, 29.
13. Freud, *Fragment*, 3.
14. Dora's father was 47, Freud 44.
15. Freud, *Fragment*, 121.
16. He published his memories of this consultation 35 years later, in F. Deutsch, 'A footnote to Freud's *Fragment of an Analysis of a Case of Hysteria*', *Psychoanalytic Quarterly*, 26 (1957), 161–3.
17. P. Mahoney, *Freud's Dora*, New Haven, CT 1996.
18. H. Cixous, *Portrait de Dora*, Paris 1976.
19. Freud, *Fragment*, 17.
20. Freud, *Fragment*, 6–7.
21. Freud, *Fragment*, 58.
22. E. Jones, *The Life and Work of Sigmund Freud. The Formative Years and the Great Discoveries, 1856–1900*, New York 1953, 374–5.
23. S. Freud, 'Repression', in *The Standard Edition of the Complete Psychological Works of Sigmund Freud, Vol. XIV*, London 1956–70, 141–58. (Originally published as 'Die Verdrängung' (1915). The original text can be found in S. Freud, *Studienausgabe*, Band III: *Psychologie des Unbewußten*, Frankfurt am Main 1975, 113–18.)
24. M.H. Erdelyi, 'Repression, reconstruction, and defense: history and integration of the psychoanalytical and experimental frameworks', in J.L. Singer (ed.), *Repression and Dissociation*, Chicago 1990, 1–31.
25. H.F.M. Crombag and P.J. van Koppen, 'Verdringen als sociaal verschijnsel', *De Psycholoog*, 29 (1994), 11, 409–15.
26. W.I. Thomas and D.S. Thomas, *The Child in America*, New York 1928, 571–2.
27. H. Merckelbach and I. Wessel, 'Recovered memories', *De Psycholoog*, 29 (1994), 3, 84–90.
28. B. Ensink, 'Reactie op "Recovered memories"', *De Psycholoog*, 29 (1994), 4, 148–9.
29. Crombag and Van Koppen, 'Verdringen', 410.
30. H. Merckelbach and I. Wessel, 'Assumptions of students and psychotherapists about memory', *Psychological Reports*, 82 (1998), 763–70.
31. W.A. Wagenaar, 'The logical status of case histories', in J.D. Read and D.S. Lindsay (eds.), *Recollections of Trauma. Scientific Evidence and Clinical Practice*, New York 1997, 109–26.
32. Crombag and Van Koppen, 'Verdringen', 409.
33. www.valseherinnering.eigenstart.nl (accessed 4 November 2014).
34. M. Pendergrast, *Victims of Memory. Incest Accusations and Shattered Lives*, London 1996, 361–6.
35. K. Pezdek and W.P. Banks (eds.), *The Recovered Memory / False Memory Debate*, San Diego 1996. M.A. Conway (ed.), *Recovered Memories and False Memories*, Oxford 1997.
36. E. Bass and L. Davis, *The Courage to Heal. A Guide for Women Survivors of Child Sexual Abuse*, New York 1988.
37. E. Showalter, *Hystories. Hysterical Epidemics and Modern Culture*, New York 1997.
38. E. Showalter, *The Female Malady. Women, Madness, and English Culture, 1830–1980*, New York 1985.
39. D.S. Holmes, 'The evidence for repression: an examination of sixty years of research', in Singer, *Repression and Dissociation*, 85–102.
40. Holmes, 'Evidence', 87.

41. Holmes, 'Evidence', 95–6.
42. S. Christianson and L. Nilsson, 'Functional amnesia as induced by a psychological trauma', *Memory and Cognition*, 12 (1984), 142–55.
43. Ensink, 'Reactie', 149.
44. O. van der Hart, 'Totale amnesie voor traumatische herinneringen. Een reactie op Merckelbach en Wessel', *De Psycholoog*, 29 (1994), 6, 240–5.
45. Van der Hart, 'Totale amnesie', 240.
46. J.M. Rivard, P.E. Dietz, D. Martell and M. Widawski, 'Acute dissociative responses in law enforcement officers involved in critical shooting incidents: the clinical and forensic implications', *Journal of Forensic Sciences*, 47 (2002), 1–8.
47. L. Schelach and I. Nachson, 'Memory of Auschwitz survivors', *Applied Cognitive Psychology*, 15 (2001), 119–32.
48. C.P. Malmquist, 'Children who witness parental murder: posttraumatic aspects', *Journal of the American Academy of Child Psychiatry*, 25 (1986), 320–5.
49. R. S. Pynoos and K. Nader, 'Children who witness the sexual assaults of their mothers', *Journal of the American Academy of Child and Adolescent Psychiatry*, 27 (1988), 567–72.
50. Comparable studies can be found in a special issue on the theme of trauma and autobiographical memory, *Applied Cognitive Psychology*, 15 (2001) and in R.J. McNally, *Remembering Trauma*, Cambridge, MA 2003.
51. S. Berendsen, 'Alarmbellen gaan te laat rinkelen. Een brandweervrouw met jarenlange klachten na een noodlottige brand', in H. Hornsveld and S. Berendsen (eds.), *Casusboek EMDR*, Houten 2009, 57–65.
52. Hornsveld and Berendsen, *Casusboek*, 60–1.
53. F. Shapiro, 'Efficacy of the eye movement desensitization procedure in the treatment of traumatic memories', *Journal of Traumatic Stress*, 2 (1989), 199–223.
54. F. Shapiro, *Eye Movement Desensitization and Reprocessing. Basic Principles, Protocols, and Procedures*, New York 1995.
55. R. Stickgold, 'EMDR: a putative neurobiological mechanism of action', *Journal of Clinical Psychology*, 58 (2002), 1, 61–75.
56. Hornsveld and Berendsen, *Casusboek*, 48.
57. H. Hornsveld and S. Berendsen, 'EMDR werkt! Maar hoe?' in Hornsveld and Berendsen, *Casusboek*, 41–52.
58. R.W. Günther and G.E. Bodner, 'How eye movements affect unpleasant memories: support for a working memory account', *Behaviour Research and Therapy*, 46 (2008), 913–31.
59. M.A. van den Hout and I.M. Engelhard, 'How does EMDR work?', *Journal of Experimental Psychopathology*, 3 (2012), 5, 724–38.
60. Hornsveld and Berendsen, *Casusboek*, 51.
61. C. DeBell and R.D. Jones, 'As good as it seems? A review of EMDR experimental research', *Professional Psychology: Research and Practice*, 28 (1997), 2, 153–63.
62. M.L. van Etten and S. Taylor, 'Comparative efficacy of treatments for posttraumatic stress disorder: a meta-analysis', *Clinical Psychology and Psychotherapy*, 5 (1998), 126–44.
63. J.I. Bisson, A. Ehlers, R. Matthews, S. Pilling, D. Richards and S. Turner, 'Psychological treatment for chronic post-traumatic stress disorder. Systematic review and meta-analysis', *British Journal of Psychiatry*, 190 (2007), 97–104.
64. Hornsveld and Berendsen, *Casusboek*, 157.
65. A. Struik, 'Getraumatiseerd door een eigen misdrijf. Behandeling van een 15-jarig meisje dat vrijkomt uit de jeugdgevangenis', Hornsveld and Berendsen, *Casusboek*, 259–64.

66. Struik, 'Getraumatiseerd', 261.
67. C.X. Alvarez and S.W. Brown, 'What people believe about memory despite the research evidence', *The General Psychologist*, 37 (2002), 1–6.

9 The Myth of Total Recall

1. For the various archaeological metaphors in the work of Freud, see the chapter 'Gradiva: psychoanalysis as archaeology' in L. Møller, *The Freudian Reading. Analytical and Fictional Constructions*, Philadelphia 1991, 31–55.
2. S. Freud, *The Interpretation of Dreams*, in *The Standard Edition of the Complete Psychological Works of Sigmund Freud, Vol. IV* (trans. James Strachey), London 1956–70, 20. (Originally published as *Die Traumdeutung*, Leipzig / Vienna 1900.)
3. J.W. Draper, *Human Physiology*, London 1956 (edn 1868), 269.
4. J.W. Draper, *History of the Conflict Between Religion and Science*, London 1878, 136. For photography as a favourite metaphor for permanent traces in the memory see D. Draaisma, *Metaphors of Memory*, Cambridge 2000, 119–25. (Originally published as *De metaforenmachine*, Groningen 1995.)
5. S. Korsakow, 'Erinnerungstäuschungen (Pseudoreminiscenzen) bei polyneuritischer Psychose', *Allgemeine Zeitschrift für Psychiatrie*, 47 (1891), 390–410.
6. S. Freud, *Interpretation of Dreams*, 20.
7. E.F. Loftus and G.R. Loftus, 'On the permanence of stored information in the human brain', *American Psychologist*, 35 (1980), 5, 409–20.
8. www.histori.ca/minutes/minute.do?id=10211 (accessed 5 November 2014).
9. The only biography of Penfield yet published was written by his grandson: J. Lewis, *Something Hidden. A Biography of Wilder Penfield*, Toronto 1981. See also the obituary by J. Eccles and W. Feindel, 'Wilder Graves Penfield', *Biographical Memoirs of Fellows of the Royal Society*, 24 (1978), 473–513.
10. Between 1909 and 1935, Penfield wrote a letter to his mother every week. She kept them carefully and towards the end of his life Penfield used them as the basis for his autobiography, which covers the period up to and including the opening of the Montreal Neurological Institute: W. Penfield, *No Man Alone. A Neurosurgeon's Life*, Boston/Toronto 1977.
11. W. Penfield and T. Rasmussen, *The Cerebral Cortex of Man*, New York 1951; W. Penfield and H. Jasper, *Epilepsy and the Functional Anatomy of the Human Brain*, Boston 1954.
12. W. Penfield, *The Excitable Cortex in Conscious Man*, Liverpool 1958.
13. Penfield, *The Excitable Cortex*, 28.
14. Penfield, *The Excitable Cortex*, 29.
15. W. Penfield, 'The interpretive cortex. The stream of consciousness in the human brain can be electrically reactivated', *Science*, 129 (1959), 3365, 1719–25.
16. W. Penfield, 'Engrams in the human brain. Mechanisms of memory', *Proceedings of the Royal Society of Medicine*, 61 (1968), 8, 831–40.
17. W. Penfield and P. Perot, 'The brain's record of auditory and visual experience. A final summary and discussion', *Brain*, 86 (1963), 4, 595–696.
18. Penfield, 'Engrams'.
19. W. Penfield, 'The electrode, the brain and the mind', *Zeitschrift für Neurologie*, 201 (1972), 297–309.
20. W. Penfield, *The Mystery of the Mind*, Princeton, NJ 1975.
21. E. Hadley, 'Movie film in brain: Penfield reveals amazing discovery', *Montreal Star*, 14 February 1957.

22. Anon., 'The brain as tape recorder', *Time*, 23 December 1957. Quoted from A. Winter, *Memory. Fragments of a Modern History*, Chicago/London 2012, 96.

23. W. Penfield, 'Memory mechanisms', *Archives of Neurology and Psychiatry*, 67 (1952), 178–98.

24. Penfield, 'Memory mechanisms', 192.

25. Penfield, 'Memory mechanisms', 192.

26. Penfield, 'Memory mechanisms', 193.

27. Penfield, 'Memory mechanisms', 194.

28. L.S. Kubie, 'Some implications for psychoanalysis of modern concepts of the organization of the brain', *Psychoanalytic Quarterly*, 22 (1953), 21–52.

29. V.W. Pratt, *Canadian Portraits. Famous Doctors: Osler, Banting, Penfield*, Toronto/Vancouver 1956 (ed. 1971), 141.

30. G.A. Ojemann, 'Brain mechanisms for consciousness and conscious experience', *Canadian Psychology/Psychologie Canadienne*, 27 (1986), 2, 158–68.

31. W.H. Calvin and G.A. Ojemann, *Conversations With Neil's Brain: The Neural Nature of Thought and Language*, Reading, MA, 1994.

32. L.R. Squire, *Memory and Brain*, Oxford 1987, 75–84.

33. Penfield, *The Excitable Cortex*, 29.

34. Penfield, 'Brain's record', 650.

35. Penfield, *Mystery of the Mind*, 25.

36. P. Gloor, A. Olivier, L.F. Quesney, F. Andermann and S. Horowitz, 'The role of the limbic system in experiential phenomena of the temporal lobe', *Annals of Neurology*, 12 (1982), 129–44.

37. Gloor et al., 'The role of the limbic system', 137.

38. Penfield, 'Memory mechanisms', 193.

39. *Total Recall* (1990). Directed by Paul Verhoeven, script by Ronald Shusett, based on the story 'We Can Remember it for You Wholesale' by Philip K. Dick.

40. H.F. Ellenberger, *The Discovery of the Unconscious*, New York 1970.

41. C.X. Alvarez and S.W. Brown, 'What people believe about memory despite the research evidence', The *General Psychologist*, 37 (2002), 1–6.

42. M.D. Yapko, 'Suggestibility and repressed memories of abuse: a survey of psychotherapists' beliefs', *American Journal of Clinical Hypnosis*, 36 (1994), 163–71.

10 The Memory of the Esterházys

1. H. Mulisch, *Mijn getijdenboek*, Amsterdam 1975, 64.

2. P. Esterházy, *Celestial Harmonies* (trans. J. Sollosy), New York 2004. (Originally published as *Harmonia Caelestis*, Budapest 2000.)

3. L. Starink, 'Er is een eenvoudige woord voor: verraad', interview with Peter Esterházy, *NRC Magazine*, 8 September 2004, 10.

4. Esterházy, *Celestial Harmonies*, 7.

5. L. Kósa (ed.), *A Cultural History of Hungary. From the Beginnings to the Eighteenth Century*, Budapest 1999.

6. R. Gates-Coon, *The Landed Estates of the Esterházy Princes. Hungary During the Reforms of Maria Theresia and Joseph II*, Baltimore/London 1994.

7. Esterházy, *Celestial Harmonies*, 594.

8. Esterházy, *Celestial Harmonies*, 595

9. Esterházy, *Celestial Harmonies*, 436.

10. Esterházy, *Celestial Harmonies*, 761.

11. Esterházy, *Celestial Harmonies*, 437

12. Esterházy, *Celestial Harmonies*, 632.

13. P. Esterházy, *Revised Edition*, as yet unpublished in English. Citations are translated from the Dutch edition: *Verbeterde editie* (trans. R. Kellermann), Amsterdam 2003, 7.
14. Esterházy, *Verbeterde editie*, 14.
15. Esterházy, *Verbeterde editie*, 15.
16. Esterházy, *Verbeterde editie*, 49.
17. Esterházy, *Verbeterde editie*, 49.
18. Esterházy, *Verbeterde editie*, 15.
19. Esterházy, *Verbeterde editie*, 42.
20. Esterházy, *Verbeterde editie*, 27.
21. Esterházy, *Verbeterde editie*, 62.
22. Esterházy, *Verbeterde editie*, 81.
23. Esterházy, *Verbeterde editie*, 81–2.
24. F. la Bruyère, 'Le fils blessé', Radio France Internationale, 6 June 2002, www.rfi.fr (1 August 2010).
25. S. Schädlich, *Immer wieder Dezember: Der Westen, die Stasi, der Onkel und ich*, Munich 2009.

11 The Mirror That Never Forgets

1. E.A. Poe, 'The Oval Portrait', in *Tales of Mystery and Imagination*, London 1910, 189.
2. Poe, 'Oval Portrait', 190.
3. E.A. Poe, 'The Daguerreotype', *Alexander's Weekly Messenger*, 15 January 1840, 2. Citations are from the reprint in A. Trachtenberg (ed.), *Classic Essays on Photography*, New Haven, CT 1980, 37–8.
4. Poe, 'Daguerreotype', 38.
5. Poe, 'Daguerreotype', 38.
6. Stendhal, *The Life of Henry Brulard* (trans. L. Davis), New York 2001. (Originally published as *La vie de Henry Brulard*, Paris 1890.)
7. Stendhal, *The Life of Henry Brulard*, 383.
8. J. Wood, 'The American portrait', in J. Wood (ed.), *America and the Daguerreotype*, Iowa City 1991, 1–26.
9. G. Freund, *Photography and Society*, London 1980, 11.
10. Anon. 'Daguerreotypes', *Littell's Living Age*, 9 (1846), 551–2. Cited in B. Mattison, *The Social Construction of the American Daguerreotype Portrait*, thesis 1995, published at www.americandaguerreotypes.com (accessed 7 November 2014).
11. E.W. Emerson and W.E. Forbes (eds), *Journals of Ralph Waldo Emerson*, New York 1911, 87.
12. O. Wendell Holmes, 'The stereoscope and the stereograph', in Trachtenberg, *Classic Essays*, 71–82.
13. Wendell Holmes, 'Stereoscope', 74.
14. T.S. Arthur, 'American characteristics; No. V – The daguerreotypist', *Godey's Lady's Book*, 38 (1849), 352–5.
15. A. Bogardus, 'Trials and tribulations of a photographer', *British Journal of Photography*, 36 (1889), 183–4.
16. Cited in D.E. Stannard, 'Sex, death, and daguerreotypes. Toward an understanding of image as elegy', in Wood, *America and the Daguerreotype*, 73–108.
17. Stannard, 'Sex', 96.
18. R. Rudisill, *Mirror Image. The Influence of the Daguerreotype on American Society*, Albuquerque 1971, 25.

NOTES to pp. 200–216   261

19. Cited in Rudisill, *Mirror Image*, 26.
20. N. Hawthorne, 'The Prophetic Pictures', in N. Hawthorne, *Twice-Told Tales*, 1837 (ed. Ohio 1974), 166–82.
21. Hawthorne, 'Prophetic Pictures', 167.
22. Hawthorne, 'Prophetic Pictures', 169.
23. Hawthorne, 'Prophetic Pictures', 173.
24. Hawthorne, 'Prophetic Pictures', 175.
25. Hawthorne, 'Prophetic Pictures', 179.
26. N. Hawthorne, *The House of the Seven Gables*, 1851 (ed. Oxford 1991), 91.
27. Cited in A. Scharf, *Art and Photography*, London 1968, 45.
28. Scharf, *Art*, 56.
29. Scharf, *Art*, 57.
30. G. Batchen, *Forget Me Not. Photography and Remembrance*, Amsterdam/New York 2004, 16–17.
31. Scharf, *Art*, 55.
32. Scharf, *Art*, 46.
33. E. Eastlake, 'Photography', in Trachtenberg, *Classic Essays*, 39–68.
34. J. de Zoete, '*In het volle zonlicht*'. *De daguerreotypieën van het Museum Enschedé*, Haarlem 2009.
35. De Zoete, '*Zonlicht*', 45.
36. De Zoete, '*Zonlicht*', 45.
37. De Zoete, '*Zonlicht*', 51. Antonie Frederik Zürcher was regarded as one of the best portrait painters in the Netherlands. For the portrait of Matilda he charged 90 guilders.
38. De Zoete, '*Zonlicht*', 50.
39. J. Ruby, *Secure the Shadow. Death and Photography in America*, Cambridge/London 1995.
40. The historian of photography Stanley Burns selected more than 70 death portraits from his own collection for his standard work on post-mortem photography: S.B. Burns, *Sleeping Beauty. Memorial Photography in America*, Altadena, CA 1990.
41. Burns, *Sleeping Beauty*, caption 11.
42. Cited in K. Sykora, *Die Tode der Fotografie, 1. Totenfotografie und ihr sozialer Gebrauch*, Munich 2009, 105. Cited in English in Burns, *Sleeping Beauty*.
43. Burns, *Sleeping Beauty*, caption 42.
44. Sykora, *Tode*, 113–14.
45. Ruby, *Secure the Shadow*, 71.
46. Batchen, *Forget Me Not*, 10–15.
47. A. Krabben, 'Onveranderlijk de eeuwigheid in', in B.C. Sliggers (ed.), *Naar het lijk. Het Nederlandse doodsportret 1500-heden*. Zutphen 1998, 148–76.
48. G. Flaubert, *Madame Bovary: Provincial Manners*, London 1886 (trans. Eleanor Marx-Aveling). (Originally published as *Madame Bovary. Moeurs de province*, Paris 1857.)
49. Flaubert, *Bovary*.
50. R. Kousbroek, 'Een parallelle natuurkunde', *NRC Handelsblad*, Cultureel Supplement 26 March 2004, 17.
51. L. Standing, 'Learning 10,000 pictures', *Quarterly Journal of Experimental Psychology*, 25 (1973), 207–22.
52. J. Bernlef, *Out of Mind* (trans. A. Dixon), London 1988, 48. (Originally published as *Hersenschimmen*, Amsterdam 1984.)
53. Bernlef, *Out of Mind*, 52–3.

12 The Second Death

1. G. Fife, *The Terror. The Shadow of the Guillotine: France 1792–1794*, New York 2004.
2. O. Blanc, *Last Letters. Prisons and Prisoners of the French Revolution 1793–1794* (trans. A. Sheridan), London 1987. (Originally published as *La Dernière Lettre: Prisons et condamnés de la Révolution 1793–1794*, Paris 1984.) See also C. Michael, *Abschied. Briefe und Aufzeichnungen von Epikur bis in unsere Tage*, Zürich 1944.
3. Blanc, *Last Letters*.
4. Blanc, *Last Letters*, 11–12.
5. Blanc, *Last Letters*, 12.
6. Blanc, *Last Letters*, 88–9.
7. Blanc, *Last Letters*, 50.
8. Michael, *Abschied*, 68.
9. Blanc, *Last Letters*, 6.
10. Blanc, *Last Letters*, 173.
11. Blanc, *Last Letters*, 206–7.
12. Blanc, *Last Letters*, 141.
13. Blanc, *Last Letters*, 158.
14. Blanc, *Last Letters*, 166.
15. Blanc, *Last Letters*, 117–18.
16. Blanc, *Last Letters*, 147.
17. Blanc, *Last Letters*, 69.
18. Blanc, *Last Letters*, 71.
19. Blanc, *Last Letters*, 70–1.
20. M. Proust, *Remembrance of Things Past* (trans. C.K. Scott Moncrieff), London 1983, 50. (Originally published as *À la recherche du temps perdu: Du côté de chez Swann*, Paris 1913.)
21. Blanc, *Last Letters*, 71.
22. Blanc, *Last Letters*, 89.
23. Blanc, *Last Letters*, 186.
24. Blanc, *Last Letters*, 123.
25. Blanc, *Last Letters*, 104.
26. Blanc, *Last Letters*, 89.
27. Blanc, *Last Letters*, 114.
28. Blanc, *Last Letters*, 143.
29. Blanc, *Last Letters*, 191.
30. Blanc, *Last Letters*, 89.
31. Blanc, *Last Letters*, 143.
32. Blanc, *Last Letters*, 202.
33. Fife, *Terror*, 336–40.
34. Blanc, *Last Letters*, 210.
35. Blanc, *Last Letters*, 210.
36. Blanc, *Last Letters*, 102.
37. Blanc, *Last Letters*, 210.
38. H. Schröter, *Stalingrad. The Cruellest Battle of World War II* (trans. C. Fitzgibbon), London 1960. (Originally published as *Stalingrad ... bis zur letzten Patrone*, Lengerich 1958.)
39. F. Schneider and C. B. Gullans, *Last Letters from Stalingrad* (intro. S.L.A. Marshall), New York 1962, 74.
40. I. O'Donnell, R. Farmer and J. Catalan, 'Suicide notes', *British Journal of Psychiatry*, 163 (1993), 45–8.

41. E.S. Shneidman and N.L. Farberow (eds.), *Clues to Suicide*, New York 1957.
42. B. Eisenwort, A. Berzlanovich, U. Willinger, G. Eisenwort, S. Lindorfer and G. Sonneck, 'Abschiedsbriefe und ihre Bedeutung innerhalb der Suizidologie', *Nervenarzt*, 11 (2006), 1355–62.
43. E.S. Shneidman, 'Suicide notes reconsidered', *Psychiatry*, 36 (1973), 379–94.

13 The Art of Forgetting

1. H. Weinrich, *Lethe. Kunst und Kritik des Vergessens*, Munich 1997, 92. (English translation *Lethe: The Art and Critique of Forgetting* (trans. S. Rendall), Ithaca, NY 2004.)
2. Weinrich, *Lethe*, 94.
3. Weinrich, *Lethe*, 24.
4. Published in book form as 'Het vergeetboekje', in *M. Toonder, Daar zit iets achter*, Amsterdam 1980.
5. Toonder, 'Vergeetboekje', 104.
6. Toonder, 'Vergeetboekje', 124.
7. Toonder, 'Vergeetboekje', 142.
8. Toonder, 'Vergeetboekje', 134.
9. Toonder, 'Vergeetboekje', 185.
10. Weinrich, *Lethe*, 103.
11. J. Vullings, 'Ik wacht op mijn tijd'. Interview with Marten Toonder, *Vrij Nederland*, 2 October 2004, 26–30.
12. Vullings, 'Wacht', 26.
13. Vullings, 'Wacht', 26.
14. Vullings, 'Wacht', 26.
15. Vullings, 'Wacht', 26.
16. M. Toonder, 'Herinneringen zonder troost', in W. Kayzer, *Het boek van de schoonheid en de troost*, Amsterdam 2000, 249.
17. M. Toonder, *Autobiografie*, Amsterdam 2010, 11.
18. Toonder, 'Herinneringen', 250.

Illustrations

Index